Global Transfer Pricing Principles and Practice

Fourth Edition

Global Transfer Pricing: Principles and Practice

Fourth Edition

John Henshall and Roy Donegan
Deloitte LLP

Bloomsbury Professional
LONDON · DUBLIN · EDINBURGH · NEW YORK · NEW DELHI · SYDNEY

BLOOMSBURY PROFESSIONAL
Bloomsbury Publishing Plc
41–43 Boltro Road, Haywards Heath, RH16 1BJ, UK

BLOOMSBURY and the Diana logo are trademarks of Bloomsbury Publishing Plc

Copyright © Bloomsbury Professional Ltd 2019

Reprinted 2022

OECD (2018), Revised Guidance on the Application of the Transactional Profit Split
Method: Inclusive Framework on BEPS: Action 10, OECD/G20 Base Erosion and Profit
Shifting Project, OECD Paris. https://www.oecd.org/tax/transfer-pricing/revised-guidance-
on-the-application-of-the-transactional-profit-split-method-beps-action-10.pdf

OECD (2018), Additional Guidance on the Attribution of Profits to Permanent Establishments,
BEPS Action 7. OECD Publishing. http://www.oecd.org/tax/transfer-pricing/additional-
guidance-attribution-of-profits-to-permanent-establishments-BEPS-action-7.pdf

OECD (2017), OECD Transfer Pricing Guidelines for Multinational Enterprises and Tax
Administrations 2017, OECD Publishing. http://dx.doi.org/10.1787/tpg-2017-en

OECD (2013), Action Plan on Base Erosion and Profit Shifting, OECD Publishing.
http://dx.doi.org/10.1787/9789264202719-en

OECD (2012), Model Convention on Income and on Capital 2010 (updated 2010),
OECD Publishing. http://dx.doi.org/10.1787/978926417517-en

OECD (2010), Commentaries on the Articles of the Model Tax Convention,
OECD Publishing. http://www.oecd.org/berlin/publikationen/43324465.pdf

OECD (2010), 2010 Report on the Attribution of Profits to Permanent Establishments,
OECD Publishing. http://www.oecd.org/ctp/transfer-pricing/45689524.pdf

OECD (1979) Transfer Pricing and Multinational Enterprises.
OECD Publishing. http://www.oecd-ilibrary.org/finance-and-investment/
transfer-pricing-and-multinational-enterprises_9789264167773-en

British Library Cataloguing-in-Publication Data

A catalogue record for this book is available from the British Library.

ISBN: PB: 978 1 52651 121 8

Typeset by Compuscript Ltd, Shannon
Printed and bound by CPI Group (UK) Ltd, Croydon, CR0 4YY

To find out more about our authors and books visit
www.bloomsburyprofessional.com. Here you will find extracts, author information,
details of forthcoming events and the option to sign up for our newsletters

Preface

WHY ANOTHER BOOK ON TRANSFER PRICING?

The origin of this book lies back in 2003, when our then colleagues Chris Adams and Richard Coombes wrote the first edition. Since then, transfer pricing has grown from a 'minor compliance nuisance' to the single most talked-about tax issue of the early twenty-first century.

Ten years later, I (John Henshall) wrote and edited the second edition to update the book for developments in legislation and tax audit approach. Yet the pace of change in both legislation and practice has increased so much that, just six years later, two further revisions have been required with this most recent version published in 2019, co-authored by Roy Donegan.

In response to the G20 call for action against Base Erosion and Profit Shifting (BEPS), the OECD[1] has managed a series of projects intended to bring international tax law and inter-government cooperation 'up to date'. Though not the only matter to be considered, a significant proportion of the output from this activity affects transfer pricing, specifically:

- the identification and valuation of transactions concerning intangibles (OECD BEPS Action 8);

- issues relating to risk and capital (OECD BEPS Action 9);

- transfer pricing of high-risk transactions (OECD BEPS Action 10);

- guidance for transfer pricing of financial transactions (OECD BEPS Action 4);

- documentation and Country-by-Country reporting (OECD BEPS Action 13); and

- the Mutual Agreement Procedure.

Transfer-pricing planning has become a key feature of tax management for multinationals and tax authorities alike. Attitudinal shifts are never easy, as they lead to significant changes in technique and approach; transfer pricing is no different. Transfer-pricing professionals now look at a very different landscape:

- Tax authorities continue to become more sophisticated in their selection of transfer-pricing audit cases and in the arguments that they employ.

---

1   Organisation for Economic Cooperation and Development; a forum where the member governments of 34 democracies with market economies work with each other, as well as with more than 70 non-member economies, to promote economic growth, prosperity and sustainable development.

The arm's-length *behaviour* of the companies involved is as much the focus as the arm's-length *pricing* of individual transactions.

- The expansion of transfer-pricing legislation, and penalties for non-compliance, and the exchange of information – by multinationals in their Country-by-Country reporting and their Master File, and by tax authorities under exchange of information protocols – continue to change the compliance landscape. More countries now specify minimum documentation requirements to evidence compliance with the arm's-length standard, and some countries also specify the date by which that material must be available, or how quickly the material must be provided to the tax auditor during audit. 'Transparency' is the new mantra.

- The guidance to tax authorities and to multinational groups on the application of the arm's-length principle is now much more detailed and, I believe, in the most part more useful. The OECD (through Working Party 6 which was set up to address problems in taxation and transfer pricing) has spent many years reviewing and overhauling both the Transfer Pricing Guidelines[2] (the Guidelines) and the Report on the Attribution of Profits to Permanent Establishments.[3] Work on the Guidelines is almost certainly never complete. In 2017, the OECD released a new version of the Guidelines which contained substantially revised and rewritten Chapters V (documentation) and VI (Intangibles), and the OECD have since began work on a new chapter which will deal with Financial Services. It will be a continuing effort by the OECD to make sure that its transfer-pricing guidance remains relevant as a global standard, and workable for developing as well as developed countries, particularly in terms of helping tax authorities to administer transfer-pricing principles in an effective and resource-efficient manner.

- Finally, firms like Deloitte and our competitors have helped businesses to implement transfer-pricing processes that deal with the business models that have evolved in today's increasingly competitive landscape.

This book is aimed at readers who understand business and finance, and perhaps tax also, and who are interested in transfer pricing, rather than being expert transfer-pricing advisers. If that describes you, then you should read on to gain an overall understanding of transfer pricing as it is practised today.

John Henshall

Partner, Deloitte

2019

---

2   OECD Transfer Pricing Guidelines for Multinational Enterprises and Tax Administrations.
3   OECD 2010 Report on the Attribution of Profits to Permanent Establishments.

Acknowledgements

The views expressed in this book are those of the authors, not necessarily those of Deloitte member firms. Any ideas put forward are illustrative and general; they are not a substitute for professional advice given in particular circumstances and in the light of particular facts.

Contributions to the text of this book were very gratefully received from the following members of Deloitte, with specific thanks to my co-author, Roy Donegan, and Danny Pilath who oversaw this rewrite project:

Roy Donegan

Danny Pilath

Sophie Brown

Mohit Malhotra

Giles Hillman

Eddie Morris

Clive Tietjen

Aengus Barry

Brenden Burgess

Greg Smith

Iain Whittles

Rafal Golaj

Contents

Contents

Table of Cases

Table of Statutes

Table of Other Guidance

About the Authors

John Henshall has been a tax professional for 30 years at the time of writing this book. Training initially with the UK tax authority, he became a Partner at Deloitte in 2001. John is currently global co-lead of the Business Model Optimisation service line and he has a particular interest in the transfer pricing of intangibles. Advising some of the largest multinationals, John's work often leads to Advance Pricing Agreements, tax audit defence work or Competent Authority claims. John has been consulted by governments concerning the modernisation of their approach to international taxation. He has often participated as a delegate to the open meetings of OECD Working Parties 1 and 6, considering the update of Chapter 1 of the OECD Model Tax Convention and Chapter VI of the OECD Guidelines for Multinational Enterprises and Tax Administrations. As a result, he has closely followed and provided input to the Base Erosion and Profit Shifting project which is administered by the OECD at the request of the G20. John lectures extensively and he is regularly published.

Roy Donegan has been a tax professional with Deloitte for 16 years at the time of writing this book. During that time, Roy has worked extensively with John on a wide range of transfer pricing matters. Roy now leads a sub-group in Deloitte that advises privately owned groups on transfer pricing matters.

Deloitte is one of the world's largest providers of transfer pricing services, with more than 2000 transfer pricing specialists around the world. Deloitte's professionals combine strong international tax and economic expertise with former tax authority experience; they work together in a global practice exclusively dedicated to transfer pricing solutions and the resolution of transfer pricing disputes. In addition to its strong international tax and economics base, Deloitte has extensive experience in Advance Pricing Agreement negotiations and Competent Authority claims.

Chapter 1

Transfer pricing: what is it?

WHAT IS TRANSFER PRICING?

1.1   The term 'transfer pricing' is now embedded in our vocabulary but what does it really mean? As a transfer pricing professional, with over 30 years of experience in international taxation, the author considers Winston Churchill's famous statement 'It has been said that democracy is the worst form of government except all the others that have been tried' could be adapted for transfer pricing and the arm's-length principle. Whilst this is not particularly helpful as a definition, it does ensure the right mind-set to learn about transfer pricing; our process and practices may not be perfect, they may have their faults, but the other alternatives would be at least as challenging and potentially more difficult for governments to implement.

1.2   Setting aside the attempts at a definition of transfer pricing currently popular in the western media, or popular internet-based reference sites, put simply, transfer pricing relates to a valuation standard imposed on multinationals by governments to ensure that the amount charged between related parties, when they transact, is fair. One way to understand transfer pricing is to think of an organisation's global business profits as a pie which, for taxation purposes, needs to be divided up between different countries whose residents have contributed to its making. That division should be undertaken in a principled and justifiable manner, and the total of all the portions should not be more, or less, than the whole pie. This exercise is necessary because taxation of business profits continues to be based on the national laws of each country, based on the profit earned by activity and assets in that country, whilst business becomes increasingly global in nature. Though the internal objectives of the globalised business might be best served by minimising the importance of corporate and national boundaries, tax law is based on the clear recognition of those same boundaries. Transfer pricing might, therefore, be considered to be the 'oil' that lubricates the coexistence of these opposing ideologies.

1.3   To begin, though, it is necessary to review some history.

WHERE DID TRANSFER PRICING COME FROM? THE GROWTH OF WORLD TRADE

1.4   Economic historians cite the fifteenth and sixteenth centuries as the origins of the multinational enterprise (MNE). This period saw the emergence of large companies predominantly based in what were then the superpower countries, trading large amounts of commodities in the colonies of their home countries. Yet it was not until early in the twentieth century that the manufacturing concepts of one country came to be exported to subsidiaries abroad. This growing interest in production accelerated markedly after the Second World War as developed countries began to invest heavily in the rebuilding of their economies. Many historians maintain that it was this period that laid the foundations for the current shape of the global economy.

1.5   The MNE established itself as a driver of global production and trade in the post-war years but the process has accelerated in more recent years. The most significant growth in the number of enterprises conducting business in more than one country has been seen in the closing years of the twentieth century, years in which the growth in world exports has consistently been greater than the growth in world Gross Domestic Product. Even though the early years of the twenty-first century were affected by a financial crisis and global slowdown, the importance to business of trading in more than one country has not diminished. There is limited data on trade transactions between related parties (despite growing attention from policymakers), but available evidence suggests that intra-firm trade represents a significant share of world trade.[1] The striking business development of the early twenty-first century is the velocity and scale of innovation-led change as computing power increases, communication difficulties decrease, and information asymmetry disappear; the undeniable power of Big Data and Artificial Intelligence will surely add to that trend[2].

1.6   There are numerous reasons for the increased growth in world trade over time, ranging from the desire of MNEs to access cheaper labour costs for production, to the increased demands from developing nations for a wider range of goods and services. Now we have a new phenomenon, in that many innovators and entrepreneurs no longer need to reside in a country driven by the location of physical assets, such as a factory; they are freed to live where they choose. Yet even at the start of the twentieth century there was little perceived need for the concept of transfer pricing. The reason for this was simply that differences, or potential for differences, between the territorial nature of taxing legislation and the actual behaviour of multinational enterprises remained small. At the turn of the twentieth century, 'international trade' still meant loading things onto a train, wagon or ship to export. As MNEs began to expand their manufacturing abroad they did so by a 'replication' process whereby an individual or management team was identified to run a business overseas which was a standalone copy of the parent's business but which operated in its local market. In this business model, related-party transactions were few in number and low in value, so the potential for local business profits to be affected by on-going related-party transactions was small.

---

1   See R. Lanz and S. Miroudot (2011), 'Intra-Firm Trade: Patterns, Determinants and Policy Implications', *OECD Trade Policy Papers*, No 114, OECD Publishing. Available at: http://dx.doi.org/10.1787/5kg9p39lrwnn-en.
2   See Disruptive Forces Blow Up 21st Century Business Models; Forbes, 28 Nov 2016.

1.7 What changed? In short, the revolution in communications and logistics allowed businesses to become more efficient and consequently more profitable. Reducing the cost of manufacturing, speeding the entry of new products to market, cutting the value of stock held in warehouses and taking a single product to several markets are all steps that increase profitability. Improvements in logistics and information systems led to a breakdown of the classic 'battery manufacturing' approach (adopted initially by the Ford corporation in USA to create a production line), allowed product manufacturing to consolidate around single factories, and improved communication allowed management to consolidate around a single location. These step-changes in business efficiency drove up the number and the value of related-party transactions and distanced the reality of modern (globalised) business further and further from mirroring (territorial) taxing legislation. This separation increased the risk that related-party transactions could have a substantial impact on the amount of profit on which an entity was subject to tax in each territory of operation, with a real or perceived preference from the business' point of view to have the larger share of the profits taxed in the territories with the lowest tax rate. As this risk increased, so did the awareness within tax authorities of their need to regulate their potential exposure to a loss of tax.

1.8 More recently the digitisation and hence 'dematerialisation' of products into services (think of the production and sale of records becoming the streaming of a music service) has created a new problem; it is now very easy to make sales into a country without having any physical presence or activity there, and that drives-down business tax receipts for the sales-country. Although some have proposed solutions to restore sales-country taxes – a move to unitary taxation and profit apportionment for MNEs, or to 'recognising' in transfer pricing value provision by the sales-country that is simply not seen between unrelated parties – no consensus has currently been reached by the governments of the world. (Significant effort has been put into this question by many countries under the G20/OECD Framework commonly referred to as BEPS, and likely that effort will continue).

WHERE DID TRANSFER PRICING COME FROM?
THE GROWTH OF TRANSFER PRICING RULES

1.9 If you ask the question 'Which country first introduced transfer pricing rules?' you will most often be given an incorrect answer, typically 'the United States of America'.

1.10 In fact, transfer pricing rules were first tried (unsuccessfully) in the United Kingdom in 1915. The UK tax authority lost a court case, *Stanley v The Gramophone and Typewriter Ltd* [1908] 2 KB 89 CA, and had to accept that not all of the profits made by a UK-based group could be taxed in the UK. For the first time the UK tax authority began to fear that cross-border tax opportunities were emerging. In those days, many UK companies with overseas operations acted through branches and, where local subsidiaries were established, the subsidiary would often be managed and controlled by a UK board, so were tax resident in the UK. In this business model there was little tax risk for the UK tax authority from incorrect transfer pricing. However, there was concern that non-UK resident companies might set up subsidiaries in the UK to do their selling for them, and these UK companies might be charged inflated prices, hence reducing their overall exposure to UK taxation.

1.11 This fear led to legislation in *Finance Act 1915, s 31(3)* which effectively said that, if it appeared that the conduct of the business had been arranged to leave the UK resident company with less than the ordinary profit which might have been expected to arise from that business, the non-resident would be chargeable to tax in the name of the resident (what we now know as an agency permanent establishment). It is also interesting to note that this pragmatic approach was confined to cases of abuse, not self-assessed, a subject to which we will return shortly. In the event, *Finance Act 1915, s 31(3)* was of little value. Later court decisions also cast doubt on the suitability of what was a 'machinery provision' (in the way that UK tax legislation works, legislation can give rise to a charge – a charging provision – or deal with how that charge is administered – a machinery provision) as a way to impose a charge to tax. The rule was abandoned and it was not until the 1950s that there was sufficient concern about the potential loss of tax from transfer pricing for legislation to return.

1.12 Departing historical fact for a moment, though returning to consider the history of global legislation again at **1.23** to reveal that the answer to the follow-up question 'who was next to legislate on transfer pricing?' is still not the United States of America, we now turn to define the issue of transfer pricing.

DEFINING THE ISSUE

1.13 When two (or more) related companies trade with one another, the price agreed between them is typically referred to as a 'transfer price'. When two unrelated parties transact with each other they are both interested in maximising the return that they make and so the price they ultimately agree is, in essence, fair to both. There is a concern amongst governments that, due to the special relationship between related parties, the transfer price which they agree might be affected by other interests and so be different from the price that would have been agreed between two unrelated parties. Whilst the overall pre-tax profit realised by the MNE on a global basis remains unchanged, the use, by accident or design, of non-arm's-length pricing could lead to different profit being recognised in each country than would have happened if the parties were not related to each other.

1.14 Why might this matter? Put simply, it matters because there is no single global tax system. It is often said that different tax rates and rules between states provide a perceived incentive for MNEs to manipulate their transfer prices. Recognising lower profits in one jurisdiction (the one with the higher tax rate) will reduce the total tax burden on the MNE, as compared to the position between unrelated parties, which means that the MNE will have more resources available to compete, or to return to its shareholders. In the absence of a rule, there is little or no incentive for businesses to focus attention on their inter-company prices beyond what they need to run their business. All tax authorities are concerned with the protection of their tax receipts, within the laws that are enacted in their country, so transfer pricing has been developed by governments as the means by which a tax authority can both require and check that a fair amount of profit is declared for taxation in their country, commensurate with the activities undertaken and assets owned by a business in that country.

1.15 It is fair to say that there was a time when the countries with transfer pricing rules were few in number and these rules were based on anti-avoidance measures rather than self-assessment. However, times have changed.

1.16 In the mid- to late twentieth century, many MNEs appeared to be relatively indifferent about the legal entity or country in which they recognised profit. Whilst there have been some examples of deliberate manipulation, the matter of profit location generally received genuine inattention. MNEs were managed by their board on the basis of what would now be called the profit-before-tax line of the accounts on a global basis and not by reference to earnings per share (which includes the effect of taxes paid) or by reference to individual entity profitability. The legal entity in which profit before tax arose was of little (or no) consequence to the commercial team; the key question was whether a particular product or product line was both profitable and contributing to the group's overall level of profitability at the 'Profit Before Interest and Tax' (PBIT) line of the accounts.

1.17 Tax authorities, however, take a very different view as they want to see the global profits split by country on a fair basis; as a result, transfer pricing rules the world over apply to individual legal entities rather than to the Group. The rules are applied to ensure that, where there is profit-generating activity in a territory, an appropriate return on that activity is subject to tax.

1.18 By the end of the twentieth century, management focus had moved on and businesses were managed by reference to earnings per share; what the business returned to its shareholders. Taxation took a place at the boardroom table and in business planning discussions. MNEs began to manage themselves by looking at the after-tax return and differing corporate tax rates around the world concentrated the attention of management on the question of where to locate activities, risks and assets. Businesses change constantly, and locating value-generating functions and risks in a higher tax rate jurisdiction will mean that the associated profit is both recognised and taxed at a higher rate. This reduces earnings per share, which in turn may have negative consequences for a MNE's share price, or its ability to compete. Locating those same functions and risks in a lower-tax rate jurisdiction will have the opposite effect. MNEs may be in a position to consider carefully where to locate functions, assets and risks and choose (all other factors such as local costs, skills, language, legal protection etc. being equal) to locate in lower-tax rate jurisdictions. This can lead to an outflow of functions and risks from high tax rate countries and into low tax rate countries together with the associated jobs, personal taxation, etc.

Governments know this and many use business taxes competitively to attract investment. Collectively governments have determined that such tax competition can be 'fair' provided that certain 'standards' are maintained.

THE ARM'S-LENGTH STANDARD – WHAT AND WHY?

1.19   The governments of the world defend their right to set business tax rates and so there continues to be a difference to the after-tax return that a MNE can achieve depending on where profits are earned and taxed. Tax authorities remain concerned that the price of transactions between related parties might be incorrectly reported to their disadvantage and many have reached the conclusion that legislation is required to protect against the potential loss of tax. The generally adopted solution is to require MNEs to calculate their taxable profits based on the transactions and prices that would have been entered into and agreed between unrelated parties. The underlying economic assumption is that all independent parties to a business transaction seek to maximise their own profit and, through this process, a deal is struck.

1.20   In this way the intention is that a 'fair' profit is achieved by each party, commensurate with the functions they perform, the assets they employ and the risks that they assume. This is the basis of the need, in transfer pricing work, to review the functions, assets and risks in a related-party transaction and to ensure that the reward earned by each party is similar to that which would have been achieved by unrelated parties. The outcome of this process is therefore referred to as 'arm's-length pricing'.

1.21   The need to understand functions, assets, capital and risks is fundamental to the theory and practice of transfer pricing and requires a 'functional analysis' to be performed for the entities involved in a related party transaction. This enables the MNE to understand the role that each entity plays and use this understanding to determine a fair pricing. Economic theory suggests that companies should receive a basic return on their assets at the very least, or they would not enter into transactions in the longer term, but this does not always imply that companies making losses or lower than basic returns are not pricing on an arm's length basis. Also, as the arm's-length principle is applied on an entity-by-entity basis, this does not necessarily mean that if a group is profitable overall then each entity should be profitable, or vice versa.

1.22   If a MNE is operating in a country or industry that is in recession, or if micro-economic pressures result in the company making a loss, then such a situation may still accord with the arm's-length principle. However, the company will need to evaluate its position and determine that unfavourable economic conditions are driving the loss, rather than losing money through non-arm's-length transfer pricing. Any such determination should include evidence of expected recovery and a recovery plan. Most tax authorities will, quite appropriately, not accept a situation where companies in their jurisdiction are persistently only breaking even (or making a loss) without justification.

A SPREADING FIRE – TRANSFER PRICING LEGISLATION AROUND THE WORLD

1.23 In **1.11**, it was noted that the first attempts at transfer pricing legislation by the United Kingdom, were ineffective and that the level of transactions within MNEs were not sufficient to drive the development of effective legislation. As the importance of MNEs grew, so did the consciousness of governments of the potential for loss of tax. When tax authorities returned to the legislative process, their first response was to invoke powers to stop abusive transactions (ie to regulate transactions with tax havens). The United Kingdom again was first to move, enacting short and simple legislation in the form of *s 37* of the *Finance Act 1951*, which survived until 1999 (due to consolidation of UK tax law) as *s 770* of the *Income and Corporation Taxes Act 1988*, when the UK and other jurisdictions starting taking this area much more seriously following a significant development in the United States in 1994.

1.24 The US government first introduced legislation in the late 1960s to combat the perceived erosion of the US tax base through transfer pricing manipulation. It was not dissimilar to the UK legislation enacted in 1951, being in the nature of an anti-abuse rule. However, in the mid-1980s, transfer pricing became a hot topic for the US Internal Revenue Service (IRS) and tax audits revealed that many companies could not justify their inter-company prices, let alone provide documentation to support them; remember, there was no law requiring them to do so at that time. The IRS reached the conclusion that a number of MNEs had formulated their transfer pricing strategies to minimise their US tax burden.

1.25 As a result, in 1994, the US government updated its transfer pricing legislation and became the first country to impose a greater compliance burden on MNEs. The new US rules required MNEs to produce contemporaneous documentation demonstrating that their transfer pricing policies satisfied the arm's-length principle and introduced penalties for non-compliance. The new legislation meant that the financial reporting of MNEs with foreign operations came under increasing scrutiny: transfer pricing, as we know it today, was born.

1.26 Running parallel to these developments, international cooperation at the Organisation for Economic Co-operation and Development (OECD) resulted in the creation and continual updating of their 'Transfer Pricing Guidelines for Multinational Enterprises and Tax Administrations' (the OECD Guidelines). The first comprehensive version of the OECD Guidelines was published in 1979, but the developments mentioned above helped to create the pressure for an updated version to be issued in 1995. The OECD has continued to update, and add to, the OECD Guidelines ever since, with Chapter IX (Business Restructurings) being added in 2010. In 2017 the current (at time of writing) Guidelines contain a significant amount of updating to Chapters I–III, Chapter V (Documentation), a completely new Chapter VI (Intangible Property). There is ongoing work to create a new chapter to deal with financing transactions. The OECD Guidelines were and remain pivotal in standardising the approach of tax authorities in many countries. As each country either introduced or updated its transfer pricing legislation, the impact of the comprehensive US rules was also a factor to take into account. There was a fear that transfer pricing compliance could cause MNE profits to be skewed in favour of countries with costly penalties – just to be safe. The development of legislation became commonplace as country after country adopted legislation requiring the self-adjustment of transfer pricing. Many of those countries also introduced penalties for non-compliance.

1.27 Today, MNEs are faced with the challenge of ensuring that their inter-company prices are consistent with the arm's-length principle such that they are reporting appropriate levels of taxable profit in each entity and country. MNEs know that they will be subject to scrutiny from tax authorities globally, as can be seen in Figure 1.1, which highlights the proliferation of transfer pricing legislation.

MODERN BUSINESS MODELS

1.28 The previous section focused on the extent to which transfer pricing rules and regulations have been introduced in numerous countries with increasing pace. This has significantly increased the attention MNEs must give to transfer pricing documentation and compliance. When the first edition of this book was published, it was said that transfer pricing was an issue for tax professionals who appreciate economics and for economists who understand the international tax context in which businesses operate. Today, transfer pricing must be viewed in the context of modern business models as well as understanding international tax and economics. Without considering the commercial realities of MNE trading, transfer pricing compliance is difficult. Tax authorities, too, have understood this fundamental change because transfer pricing can work:

- by setting the functions, risks and assets of the entities within a MNE and adopting the arm's- length pricing of transactions that follows, a particular tax burden will arise; or

- by taking into account the transfer pricing consequences and tax result, of locating functions, risks and assets in the process of deciding business strategy, management is actively controlling the MNE right down to the earnings per share line.

1.29 To return to the question of where transfer pricing is going, the development and increasing maturity of transfer pricing legislation and practice does not mean that it is going to stop being a burden in terms of corporate self-assessment, compliance, documentation and, potentially, penalties. Businesses can expect to see more of the same, from more countries. It also will mean more tax authority audits (with many leading to proposed adjustments) and more potential double taxation, with dispute resolution processes coming under increasing strain (see Chapter 11). In an effort to avoid this complexity and to minimise the risk of double taxation and mutual agreement procedure claims (see **11.47** onwards), we are already seeing significant growth in the

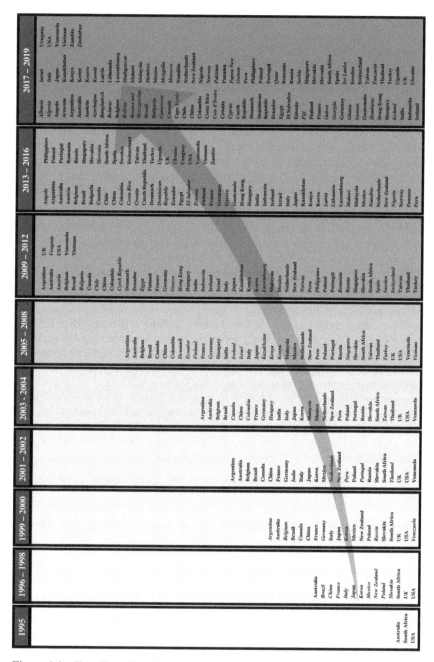

Figure 1.1 – Transfer pricing legislation

number of bilateral advance pricing agreements. Increased activity in the field of transfer pricing will also mean that transfer pricing analysis will become more sophisticated.

1.30   As part of their tax compliance process, MNEs are required to define, describe, justify, price and implement arm's-length transfer pricing. Definition and description incorporate legal aspects, such as ensuring that the allocation of functions and risk and the economic ownership of assets are established clearly in formal agreements. Justification in this context means establishing the credibility of a transaction as being of a type that third parties might enter into in similar circumstances. This requires a rigorous description and analysis of the business framework within which the transaction takes place. It also requires identification of third-party trading strategies and models that show similar approaches to functions and risks.

1.31   As well as self-assessment of a business's compliance with arm's-length pricing, it is also important that evidence of the third-party nature of related-party transactions is retained, as during tax audits, tax authorities will seek to understand the commercial purpose of business transactions.

1.32   Transfer pricing professionals (in tax authorities, private practice and in businesses) will note another developing trend; the increasing determination of transfer pricing disputes by National courts. So long as there has been transfer pricing legislation there has been the capacity for disagreement between tax authorities and taxpayers about the correct application of that law. However, where both tax authority and the taxpayer took reasonable positions as to the arm's-length price any dispute would commonly be settled by agreement leaving only access to the Mutual Agreement Procedure to remove double taxation. Increasingly it seems that agreement cannot be reached and the dispute is settled by a court and so transfer pricing professionals have access to an increasing body of case law around the world to aid their consideration of a particular case.

1.33   Few of those cases are limited to the application of local country transfer pricing law (one such example is the US *Altera*[3] case, the principle point of which (inclusion of stock option value in cost-sharing) was also considered by the Israeli Supreme Court in *Kontera*,[4] where the opposite conclusion was reached under Israeli law). Whilst cases concerning local transfer pricing law are of importance to that single country, other cases have greater potential geographic scope, and therefore value to the transfer pricing and tax professionals' community. Cases that consider the application of OECD-based concepts and principles, or which look at the detailed application of one or more methods to measure an arm's-length price or value in particular business transactions, can be of wider application. Decisions of a court in one country will not be binding on the tax authorities or courts elsewhere.

---

3   *Altera Corp. & Subsidiaries v Commissioner of Internal Revenue*, No 16-70496 (9th Cir. 2018).
4   *Kontera Technologies Ltd v Tel-Aviv 3 Assessing Office* 943/16.

They will however be informative (see the examples cited below), as each court is interpreting law based on international treaty – Article 9 of the OECD Model Tax Convention – and where possible, consistency in interpretation of the Treaty between countries is preferred. As cases are finalised, clearer direction regarding uncertain positions will result. With the frequency of TP cases showing no signs of abating, we should anticipate that for a few years we will see a growing wealth of guidance material regarding the application of TP laws and practices which have their foundation in the arms-length principle.

Chapter 2

OECD

BACKGROUND TO ARTICLE 9 AND THE TRANSFER PRICING GUIDELINES

2.1   Chapter 1 introduced the arm's-length standard – or arm's-length principle – as a fundamental of transfer pricing. Economic theory postulates that unrelated parties dealing at arm's length with each other will seek to maximise their own profit and hence achieve a 'fair' price. When dealing with a related party it is possible that other considerations might influence behaviour and disrupt the economic balance between them. Noting this, the OECD has adopted the arm's-length principle as the basis for pricing related-party transactions undertaken by multinational enterprises.

2.2   This idea first took shape in 1963. The first paragraph of Article 9 of the OECD Model Convention on Income and Capital (otherwise known as the OECD Model Treaty) reads:

> '[When] conditions are made or imposed between ... two [associated] enterprises in their commercial or financial relations which differ from those which would be made between independent enterprises, then any profits which would, but for those conditions, have accrued to one of the enterprises, but by reason of those conditions, have not so accrued, may be included in the profits of that enterprise and taxed accordingly.'

2.3   The commentary on this paragraph notes:

> 'This Article deals with associated enterprises (parent and subsidiary companies and companies under common control) and its paragraph 1 provides that in such cases the taxation authorities of a Contracting State may for the purpose of calculating tax liabilities re-write the accounts of the enterprises if as a result of the special relations between the enterprises the accounts do not show the true taxable profits arising in that State. It is evidently appropriate that adjustment should be sanctioned in such circumstances, and this paragraph seems to call for very little comment.'

The basic concept is straightforward, but there are significant difficulties when it comes to applying the idea in practice: first ascertaining whether or not the level of taxable profits has been influenced by the 'special relations' of the parties and second, if so, how to recalculate those profits to regain the proper balance.

13

2.4   The importance of testing inter-company pricing has grown steadily until, at the time of writing, it is one of the most relevant tax questions on the minds of finance directors responsible for multinational companies. For many years the OECD has been the key organisation to comment on the question of how to assess arm's-length pricing, publishing their 'Transfer Pricing Guidelines for Multinational Enterprises and Tax Administrations'. Over the years, this has been subject to update, expansion and revision; at the time of writing, tax authorities have recently completed an overhaul of Chapters I–III, V and VI the work for which took place under the G20/OECD Framework known as 'BEPS' (the Base Erosion and Profit Shifting initiative). Therefore we are using the versions published in 2009 and 2010 for some tax audit work but we are using the 2017 version for new transfer pricing compliance work. Consideration of, and revisions to, the OECD Transfer Pricing Guidelines has not stopped, and at the time of writing work on a new chapter to give enhanced guidance for financial transactions is ongoing. The 2017 revised Guidelines incorporate the reports delivered as BEPS Actions 8–10, which claimed to be 'interpreting' the OECD's view on the arm's-length principle. Page 10 of the report on Actions 8–10 says:

> 'This Report contains revised guidance which responds to these issues and ensures that the transfer pricing rules secure outcomes that see operational profits allocated to the economic activities which generate them. It represents an agreement of the countries participating in the OECD/G20 BEPS Project. For countries that formally subscribe to the Transfer Pricing Guidelines, the guidance in this Report takes the form of amendments to the Transfer Pricing Guidelines. Therefore this Report also reflects how the changes will be incorporated in those Guidelines.'

Throughout this book we refer to the current 2017 Guidelines simply as 'the OECD Guidelines', 'the Transfer pricing Guidelines' or just 'the Guidelines'. The Guidelines have been adopted as a guide by many countries, and incorporated into the domestic legislation of some, including the United Kingdom, to provide the definitive standard by which multinational enterprises (MNEs) should benchmark their inter-company prices. Other countries follow OECD guidance in transfer pricing matters even if it has not been specifically brought into their law.

2.5   The 2017 Guidelines consist in part of new material (eg Chapter VI) and in part of a revision and expansion of the guidance in an earlier OECD report, the 2010 'Transfer Pricing Guidelines for Multinational Enterprises and Tax Administrations', which in turn updated the 1995 and the 1979 publications. They also capture, but do not completely replace, material contained in two other OECD reports, namely 'Three Taxation Issues' (1984) and 'Thin Capitalisation' (1986). As mentioned, there is currently an effort to produce revised guidance for financial transactions; no doubt there will be future additions and updates, and this constant review process does raise an interesting question: by which version of the Guidelines should one be guided?

WHICH VERSION OF THE GUIDELINES?

2.6   The OECD has improved, updated and revised its Transfer pricing Guidelines on several occasions and will continue to do so in the future. That poses the question: which version of the Guidelines should be used when considering the arm's-length nature of a particular transaction? Unfortunately, the answer is not as simple as the question if one takes a strict and statutory approach. However, as we will see, in practical situations – including cases that have proceeded to a court hearing – save in particular cases there is often less confusion in the matter.

2.7   To understand the statutory position, the first point to consider is whether you are complying with local legislation or with the associated enterprises article of a double tax treaty based on the OECD Model Treaty. This is because the status of the Guidelines as an aid to interpretation can be different. For example, UK transfer pricing law requires the interpretation of UK rules in a way that 'best secures consistency' with 'the effect which, in accordance with the transfer pricing guidelines, is to be given, in cases where double taxation arrangements incorporate the whole or any part of the OECD model, to so much of the arrangements as does so' (see *Taxation (International and Other Provisions) Act 2010 (TIOPA 2010), s 164(1)(b)*). For the purposes of UK legislation, the Transfer pricing Guidelines are defined (see *TIOPA 2010, s 164(4)*) as set out below:

> '(a)   the version of the Transfer Pricing Guidelines for Multinational Enterprises and Tax Administrations approved by the Organisation for Economic Co-operation and Development (OECD) on 22 July 2010 as revised by the report, Aligning Transfer Pricing Outcomes with Value Creation, Actions 8–10 – 2015 Final Reports, published by the OECD on 5 October 2015, or
>
> (b)   such other document approved and published by the OECD in place of that (or a later) version or in place of those Guidelines as is designated for the time being by order made by the Treasury,
>
> including, in either case, such material published by the OECD as part of (or by way of update or supplement to) the version or other document concerned as may be so designated.'

The words 'as revised by the report, Aligning Transfer Pricing Outcomes with Value Creation, Actions 8–10 – 2015 Final Reports, published by the OECD on 5 October 2015' were inserted by *Finance Act 2016 (FA 2016), s 75(1)(a)*, with effect (in relation to provision made or imposed at any time) for corporation tax purposes, in relation to accounting periods beginning on or after 1 April 2016, and for income tax purposes, in relation to the tax year 2016–17 and subsequent tax years. Therefore, for corporation tax accounting periods beginning before 1 April 2016, UK tax law does not use the G20/OECD BEPS papers as an aid to interpretation of UK transfer pricing law, and thereafter it does. In turn, as the use of 2010 OECD material was actually brought into UK law only in 2011 (see *Finance Act 2011, s 58(1)*) it applies only to accounting periods for corporation tax beginning on or after 1 April 2011. Prior to that, OECD material up to 1 May 1998 (including the 1995 version of the Guidelines) was the reference point for interpreting UK legislation. Interestingly, the UK never did adopt the 2009 OECD Guidelines, and so this edition of the Guidelines cannot be cited as a precedent for interpreting UK transfer pricing law.

2.8   Therefore, when considering a transfer pricing question under UK domestic law, one would consult the Guidelines which were specified in relation to the tax accounting period under consideration, as UK 'transactional based' legislation looks to the payment or receipt that arises in a tax year. In other countries the Guidelines may have more, or less, force.

2.9   When considering the question of arm's-length pricing under an OECD-based tax treaty the interpretive value of the Guidelines is less clear. In some territories the Guidelines are indicative of what might have been in the minds of the parties when the treaty was negotiated. In that case the most recently published version of the Guidelines, at the time the treaty was concluded, would be the Guidelines that might have been in the minds of the negotiating parties; versions of the Guidelines issued later would not have been available. However, jurisdictions use the Guidelines in other ways (eg some follow a process of continuous ambulatory interpretation). This approach will adopt any new or changed meaning as the Guidelines are revised.

2.10   In practice, things are a little more blurred.

2.11   There is a tendency for the latest version of the Guidelines to be applied by tax advisers and tax Inspectors, with no regard to when the actual transaction under audit took place. This could lead to difficulties if there has been a change in the Guidelines; even if that is not appreciated when agreeing a position, it may still come to light during a claim for relief of double taxation that arises from any transfer pricing adjustment when the second jurisdiction considers the claim.

2.12   More importantly, for the most part (though not exclusively), the revisions and improvements to the Guidelines do not actually change their meaning; they improve the clarity of the existing Guidelines. In so far as that is the case, the use of an incorrect version of the Guidelines does not cause any unfairness. For example, a 2013 decision of the Finnish Administrative Court (KHO 2013:36) concerning 'location savings' decided that assistance could be drawn from Chapter IX of the Guidelines (published as new material in 2010) in deciding the correct transfer pricing for a transaction that took place years before; the reasoning being that this material simply explained the arm's-length position which had always applied. Therefore the later Guidelines, though not creating a precedent, might illuminate better the correct interpretation of the arm's-length principle and, if so, those concepts can be applied to transactions that took place before the revised Guidelines were written. At the present time, this point is perhaps more important than it has ever been because of the significant changes to the Guidelines brought about by the G20/OECD's BEPS initiative (the 2017 Guidelines). For example, Chapter VI of the 2010 Guidelines, which deals with intangibles, could be described as being 'commendably brief' at just 39 paragraphs; so 'brief' that, in practice, it offered little help to transfer pricing practitioners. By contrast, the 2017 version of Chapter VI, written in response to Action 8 of the BEPS initiative, comprises 212. Insofar as this new material amounts to no more than a better explanation of how to apply the arm's-length principle as it was understood in the 2010 Guidelines – and much of it will meet this test – in some countries it will be the case that those concepts can be used to test the arm's-length nature of pricing in earlier transactions even if they cannot be cited as precedent. However, where new concepts are created which amount to a change in understanding or practice it is likely that the revised Guidelines could not be applied to tax returns submitted before they were written. In a 2018 judgement of the Supreme Administrative Court of Finland (KHO 2018:173) it ruled that contradictory to Finnish Tax Authority's published guidance to the effect that BEPS guidance could have retroactive effect, the Finnish Tax Authority should apply in tax audits the version of the OECD Guidelines that was available at the time of filing the tax returns for the year(s) in question.

THE ARM'S-LENGTH PRINCIPLE

2.13   The OECD Guidelines set out, in paragraph 1.8, why the arm's-length principle is the preferred method of pricing related party transactions. This majors on parity of treatment between associated and independent enterprises, and states:

> 'Because the arm's length principle puts associated and independent enterprises on a more equal footing for tax purposes, it avoids the creation of tax advantages or disadvantages that would otherwise distort the relative competitive positions of either type of entity. In so removing these tax considerations from economic decisions, the arm's length principle promotes the growth of international trade and investment.'

2.14   Having made this brave claim, the Guidelines do go on to recognise that there are difficulties applying the arm's-length principle, notably in the following circumstances:

- when there are no readily available comparable transactions, such as when the cross-border business in question is in highly specialised goods or services, or unique intangibles;

- when MNEs engage in transactions that would simply not be entered into by independent parties. The example cited is of the sale or licence of intangibles, which groups might feel more able to contemplate when buyer/seller or licensor/licensee are related rather than third parties, or where the seller or licensor may well jib at the loss of control of the intangible;

- when a MNE has to justify its pricing to a tax authority years after the event;

- when relevant comparable data is very hard to find; and

- when it is clear that a MNE group is enjoying advantages simply not available to independents, for example economies of scale or the benefits of business integration.

2.15   Having acknowledged these problems the Guidelines conclude that the arm's-length principle is better than any other approach, such as global formulary apportionment (paragraphs 1.15 and 1.32). It is fair to say that there is usually some form of proxy and/or some practical economic model that can be used to overcome even the hardest pricing problems. If a transaction can credibly be entered into, it can also be priced.

2.16   The arm's-length standard was adopted as the OECD Committee on Fiscal Affairs felt that there were no realistic alternatives. The one non-arm's-length approach that has been mooted is global formulary apportionment. Formulary apportionment has been used by some local tax jurisdictions, most notably the state of California, and it is still put forward from time to time by academics and other interested parties both in the United States and in Europe as a way of resolving the problems of allocation of taxable profit, of transfer pricing documentation requirements and of double taxation. Under global formulary apportionment, total consolidated profits would be allocated among associated enterprises in different countries according to a mechanistic formula based on some combination of costs, payroll, assets and sales. The OECD Guidelines devote several pages to a rejection of this method. OECD's main objection is the difficulty of implementing the method in a manner that ensures single taxation while protecting against double taxation. To do so would require at least the following:

- global agreement to use the method in the first place;

- global agreement on how to measure the global tax base of an MNE group;

- global use of a common accounting system; and

- global agreement on the apportionment formula(e), including the weighting of the various constituent parts.

Without these it would be impossible, should one country make a transfer pricing adjustment, to tell who was the counterparty and who, as a result, should give a corresponding adjustment. There might indeed be a number of possible counterparties, all of whom might be candidates for giving some measure of relief.

2.17   Likewise, without a broad consensus on how to apply the method, one could imagine taxable profits dropping quietly between the cracks of one country's interpretation and another's, thus rendering the idea impotent in dealing with the very matter for which currently it is being actively promoted by some – the elimination of non-taxation of MNE profits.

2.18   It is worth noting that global formulary apportionment has a certain superficial attractiveness. There are, however, issues; differences in accounting systems (movement towards international accounting standards might offer an answer here) and measuring the global tax base. Perhaps the real point is that a broad international consensus is needed to preserve the benefits of fair, single taxation and no double taxation. For that to happen countries would all have to agree the relative value contributed by natural resources, people, intellectual property, and the many other contributors to profit in a MNE; competing interests have so far shown that not to be possible. The arm's-length principle has achieved global consensus for the applicable approach where nothing else has.

2.19   It is worth pausing to consider how easy it would be to succumb to the superficial attractiveness of global formulary apportionment. An approach sometimes put forward is 'contribution analysis'. The idea behind this approach is that it is possible to look at each aspect of the business and to assign a profitability to it, such that the entire profit of the enterprise is allocated to each part of the business. Some argue that the credibility of this approach is now enhanced because of the need to explain the 'value chain' in the Master File of the transfer pricing documentation (keep in mind that not all countries have adopted the Master File/Local File approach to transfer pricing documentation). Though it is possible to undertake this exercise whilst abiding by the arm's-length principle – by analysing profit contribution by reference to third-party activities and profits – the analysis is sometimes undertaken in the form of a purely econometric exercise which applies human judgement and economic theory to allocate profit to different parts of the enterprise. Without reference to the actions and profits of third parties, with due comparability, the fundamental requirement of the arm's-length principle is not met. (Note that contribution analysis can, with appropriate reference to third-party actions and profits, form part of the work in a profit split approach, as described in the Guidelines at paras 2.119–2.120.)

2.20   It is possible that a purely econometric approach to contribution analysis might have a place in some transfer pricing circumstances (eg a bilateral advance pricing agreement (APA), where both tax authorities and the taxpayer agree that there is no potentially comparable data and that a departure from the arm's-length principle is required), if the transfer pricing law of both territories will accommodate such a departure. However, without the explicit agreement of all potentially interested parties, this is a dangerous road to walk.

SETTING PRICES VERSUS TESTING PRICES

2.21   It remains a mystery to the author why there is any doubt on this point at all, but doubt there is in the minds of some. Often one reads of, or hears, assertions that 'the OECD Guidelines require associated companies to set prices in the way they would have been agreed upon by independent parties acting at arm's length'. They do not. The OECD Guidelines do not tell businesses how to transact or set their transfer prices. OECD pricing methodologies are there to test, for tax purposes only, the outcome of MNEs' transactions and pricing policies. The commentary on Article 9(1) of the Treaty (quoted in **2.2** above) says this clearly enough:

> '… its paragraph 1 provides that in such cases the taxation authorities of a Contracting State may *for the purpose of calculating tax liabilities* …' (emphasis added)

This does not mean that hindsight can be used by tax authorities or by MNEs. Transfer prices frequently will be determined ahead of time by reference to best available forecasts; this is fine, and it is not appropriate to require transfer pricing adjustments computed in the light of actual, unforeseen (later) events.

2.22 Perhaps the mistake arises because, in many instances, MNEs do indeed use OECD methodologies to calculate their transfer prices ahead of time – the idea being that conformity with OECD principles at the price-setting and planning stage is a sensible way of ensuring (as far as possible) conformity with OECD principles at the tax return filing and subsequent tax authority audit stage. There are advantages to this approach. For example, in most jurisdictions transfer pricing adjustment of a tax return is possible only to increase the tax due. Failure to trade with an associated business using arm's-length prices would lead to an imbalance of profit between them, and only the under-rewarded business might be able/required to adjust its tax return. The over-rewarded business might be required to pay tax based on the excess profit that it has reported in its accounts, leading to double taxation of the group might would be dealt with through a claim for relief, if available, under an appropriate bilateral Double Taxation Agreement or a multilateral convention such as the EU Arbitration Convention. Bilateral tax conventions containing a Mutual Assistance clause are not available between all countries, when they exist access to them is sometimes refused, when accessed countries do not always agree and eliminate double taxation, and where they do the process can be lengthy and costly to the taxpayer. The cost and time required to pursue such a claim can be avoided by trading at arm's-length prices in the first place and thereby not suffering a transfer pricing adjustment at all.

2.23 So, in summary, it really does not matter how prices have been set – the MNE may have just 'guessed' a price (although we certainly do not recommend that as a course of action!); what we test is the outcome in the tax return from that price and, if the MNE was 'lucky' and chose the correct arm's-length price, there is no transfer pricing adjustment. Although many intra-group services are priced on a cost-plus basis, and software licence rates are set by reference to comparable uncontrolled prices, and so forth, this does not alter the fact that MNEs have considerable freedom in how they set their prices; however, in preparing documentation to support the prices for corporate tax purposes, the methodology used to test the arm's-length nature of the pricing or profit should be founded in one or more of the approved OECD transfer pricing methodologies described at **2.61** below.

2.24 Why is this so important a concept? If a MNE adopts an arm's-length methodology in setting prices and that produces, in due course, an arm's-length result, the question is, of course, irrelevant. However, where a tax authority audits a business, it is not uncommon to find that both sides concentrate on the methodology used to set the price, rather than the out-turn. Much time and effort can be wasted by both sides in attacking or defending the methodology used to set the price; wasted because, even if the methodology was not at arm's length, it did not need to be. All that work may leave unresolved the question of whether the price that was selected (no matter how it was selected) was at arm's length.

THE HEART OF TRANSFER PRICING: COMPARABILITY

2.25   Before beginning to unpick the various OECD pricing methods in detail, it is essential to pause to consider comparability. In the first edition of this book comparability warranted '… a few words …' but over the years – and with increasing pace – comparability has become a significant issue not only for transfer pricing practitioners and tax authorities, but also for the OECD. In response to this, more detailed consideration was given to this area in the second edition and that proved to be warranted when the OECD, in its BEPS initiative, applied considerable time and resources to refining its commentary in this area. In fact, the revised material deletes and entirely replaces the 2010 Section D of Chapter 1 (identifying the features of the tested transaction): 140 'new' paragraphs to emphasise the importance of comparability.

2.26   Comparability has always been at the very heart of all of the OECD methodologies to test the arm's-length nature of the transfer pricing of a MNE. At its simplest – and at the same time at its most profound – transfer pricing justification is being able to point to the behaviour of third parties and say, 'this is how they price it, and therefore so can I'. For that statement to be true, however, the third parties must be involved in a transaction that is sufficiently similar, in economic terms, for their behaviour to be relevant as a benchmark against which to test related party prices or behaviour. It is necessary to test that similarity, demonstrate that comparability exists and thereby show that the third-party data is evidence against which the related-party pricing can be measured and tested. We use that word 'evidence' deliberately. The work undertaken (by taxpayers and tax authorities) should be of sufficient quality that it would be accepted as evidence under the 'rules of evidence' applicable in the courts of the countries to which the transfer pricing work relates. Anything inferior to that would, quite rightly, be dismissed in any later controversy over the filed tax return.

2.27   Where transactions between associated enterprises and independent parties are not identical, that may not matter. Transactions that are not 'identical', but which do not differ in a way that has economic significance, would still be acceptable as comparable transactions. Even where there is an economic significance to one or more of those differences, they can be examined and, where possible, adjusted for. These adjustments serve to align the comparable with the transaction under review, and so create a benchmark.

2.28   It is important to appreciate that the application of the arm's-length principle is not the simple application of formulaic steps in a process. Judgement must be exercised to determine the comparability of transactions, so that accurate adjustments can be made to reflect any differences that have economic effect. A record should be included in the transfer pricing report evidencing the basis on which that judgement has been made. Equally importantly, a potential comparable should not be rejected merely because one can identify something that is different from the tested party; one must show that the difference identified has economic significance. (Note: there can be many differences between a potential comparable and the tested party but these are of no consequence unless they have an economic effect (see Chapter D 1 OECD Guidelines)).

2.29 In determining comparability and making adjustments to data, the OECD Guidelines indicate that a number of general factors should be considered as a source of potential economically significant difference:

- *Characteristics of property and services* – for example, the quality, volume, and reliability of goods, the nature and extent of services and, in the case of intangible property, the nature of the property, the form of the transaction, and the anticipated level of profitability.

- *Functional analysis* – compensation paid between third parties usually reflects the functions performed, assets employed and risks assumed by each party to the transaction. So, to work out whether third party and intra-group transactions are comparable, a functional analysis is needed, the purpose of which is to identify and compare economically significant activities and responsibilities taken on by the third party and associated enterprises. The same analysis should cover risk, since reward is intimately linked with risk. In broad terms the more limited the exposure to risk, the more limited will be the reward (though this limited reward is likely to be steadier than the fluctuating returns associated with the assumption of more and higher risk).

- *Contractual terms* – an analysis of contractual terms is really part of the function and risk analysis outlined above. Where there is no contract or other written agreement, terms can be inferred from the behaviour of the parties and general principles; where there is a written contract, it is important that there is a good match between what the contract says and how the parties behave in practice.

- *Economic circumstances* – by which the Guidelines mean market conditions: geographic location of market, size, competition, availability of alternatives, government regulation, costs of labour and land and so forth. Differences in any of these will put a dent in comparability.

- *Business strategies* – businesses will very likely approach their markets in different ways, with varying degrees of innovation and risk taking. The adoption of a market penetration scheme can also have a significant effect on a transfer price. Contentions that a MNE is following a market penetration strategy should be carefully thought through, as tax authorities usually regard them with a degree of scepticism. Market penetration strategies will always involve one or more parties taking something of a hit in early years in the expectation of profits later. So the contract and other evidence of the parties' relationship must be consistent with this. Cases have been found where a distributor agrees to incur marketing expenditure on such a scale that it cannot make a profit during the lifetime of the contract which, it is arguable, is a contractual position that no third party would agree to. Credible projections (and not just 'projections') of growing profits over a reasonable timescale will be required, as will evidence of lower end prices and/or higher marketing spend and effort.

2.30   It can be seen from this that establishing true comparability is a serious matter that is often far from straightforward. It is not something that can be approached in a 'mechanical manner'; a practitioner well-versed in comparability matters relating to transactions in goods could not apply the same concepts thoughtlessly to an intangibles licence, because the things that drive comparability are different in these two transactions. In addition, a skilled practitioner will not reject a potential comparable just because they have found a difference but will then assess that difference to see if there is economic effect. Nevertheless, however difficult it may be, the process must be gone through by both MNEs when testing their prices for their tax returns and the tax authorities auditing them. In this respect the final sentence of paragraph 1.40 of the Guidelines is illuminating: 'Therefore, in no event can unadjusted industry average returns themselves establish arm's length prices.' It is probably right to say that all tax authorities use industry-average data as a diagnostic tool in choosing MNEs for audit; one can understand that. However, that is the rough and ready beginning of the dialogue with the taxpayer, not the end of it.

2.31   In the preceding paragraphs there is a concept that has not always been appreciated in transfer pricing work to date, one that has led to inaccurate work and irrelevant arguments. The process outlined so far is intended to ensure that the comparable data is as closely aligned with the economics of the tested transaction as possible. Therefore the process should not be applied blindly, but with considerable thought. Differences between the tested party and third-party data have to be 'economically relevant' to require adjustment, not simply differences. The author has seen transfer pricing reports that identify 'differences' between the tested party and third-party potential comparables and go on to claim adjustments for them without demonstrating that these differences are economically relevant. A simple example is to consider the process to compile a comparable data set from a database source to evidence the pricing of the toll-manufacturing service provided by an associated enterprise based on a measure of the return achieved on total cost base of the manufacturing entity. (There are other ways to measure the arm's-length nature of the return achieved by a toll manufacturer, but this example was drawn to make a particular point.)

2.32   A database search for 'toll manufacturing' is unlikely to generate any results as businesses involved in toll manufacturing do not have a distinct industry code or business description. Hence there will be a general search for manufacturing, then it's necessary to screen for matters that may result in economic differences and reject companies that fail the screen; independence, business start-up, different industries, turnover, a very low level of employees (removing owner-managed small businesses), etc. When the process is complete there will be a manageable number of independent businesses concerned with manufacturing in the same industry who have broadly similar levels of turnover, intangibles and staff. Should any business that holds significant levels of raw materials or stock now be screened out as the comparables are sought for a toll-manufacturing activity?

2.33 There may be a knee-jerk decision to take such action because of an emotional reaction to the difference between a manufacturer that buys raw materials in its own name and one that does not. When that step is taken, suppose that it's found that the data set now contains so few companies that a comparable range cannot be established; the typical reaction is to relax one of the earlier screens – typically the industry screen – to boost the number of companies. The step missed out in this example was to analyse and conclude whether stock holding is actually an economically significant difference when considering the profit achieved as a function of full cost. If it was not economically significant, then the additional screening introduced a step not warranted by the OECD Transfer pricing Guidelines. This, then, caused the data issues and led to the relaxation of other, earlier, screen criteria that may have been economically significant and therefore are required.

2.34 Suppose that instead the reaction to the question of stock holding had been to follow the OECD Transfer pricing Guidelines. It is relatively simple to test whether it is necessary to screen the manufacturing data set for stock holding, by plotting stock holding against profit margin as a function of full cost to see if stock holding is a profit driver for this index. In a real case dealt with by the author, the result of that test plotting net cost plus against stock-holding is shown in Figure 2.1 below.

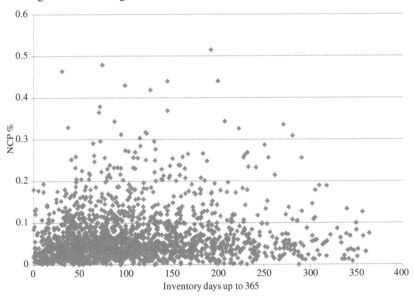

Figure 2.1 – Net cost plus vs stock-holding

2.35 As can be seen, there is no correlation between the holding of stock and the profit achieved by a manufacturer when expressed as a function of full cost in this case. Therefore, there is no justification for removing stockholding companies from the comparable data set in the report being prepared, based on full-cost plus.

2.36   The example above does not illustrate that stockholding is not a profit generator for a business; the activity of stock holding most certainly is a source of profit for the enterprise. What the example shows is that when considering one particular index (full-cost plus) there is no economic difference (in that specific industry) between the margin earned by stockholding and non-stockholding enterprises.

2.37   The particular difficulties of comparability and 'industry average' data are returned to in Chapter 6, dealing with intangible property.

OTHER PRACTICAL ISSUES

2.38   The Guidelines highlight a number of other issues that should be taken into account in applying the arm's-length principle. These are all practical issues that should be observed both by MNEs in analysing and documenting transfer pricing arrangements and by tax authorities in auditing them.

Transaction undertaken

2.39   In paragraph 1.121 of the OECD Guidelines, there is a clear statement to the effect that the transaction actually undertaken should be respected by the tax authorities, with disregard or substitution of the transaction for tax purposes being permitted in only exceptional circumstances described in 1.122–125. Some regimes, notably the United Kingdom, have specifically adopted the Guidelines as an aid to interpretation of their domestic law, yet arguments have arisen as to whether UK transfer pricing rules permit the re-characterisation of transactions without reference to the OECD Guidelines. Prior to the adoption of the 2017 Guidelines, the 2010 Guidelines in paragraph 1.65 permits only two circumstances in which a tax authority may, exceptionally, re-characterise the actual transaction undertaken for tax purposes. These are:

- where the economic substance of a transaction differs from its form. The classic example of this is thin capitalisation: investment in an associated enterprise by way of interest-bearing debt that exceeds the amount that could have been borrowed at arm's length and therefore has the economic substance of equity; or

- when the arrangements made differ from those which would have been adopted by those acting in a commercially rational manner **and** the transaction is structured in such a way that it is impossible to price it. The example given is of a sale up front for a lump sum of intellectual property rights arising from future research to be carried out under a long term contract. Such a lump sum could not sensibly be determined before the work had been carried out, and therefore it would be more appropriate to regard the contract as a continuing research agreement.

Other than these, there are no instances where the current Guidelines permit either MNEs or tax authorities to replace transactions actually undertaken with ones that they prefer; however, read on.

2.40 The G20/OECD BEPS initiative has produced revised material to update the OECD Guidelines which are now included in the 2017 Guidelines. These new ideas impact the above statement in two specific areas: the circumstances where a transaction can be replaced; and the use of an alternative transaction as a means of testing the price at which the actual transaction would have taken place.

2.41 The revised paragraph 1.121 of the Guidelines continues to stress that the 'accurately delineated' transaction should not be disregarded, save in exceptional circumstances. However, paragraphs 1.122–1.125 set conditions to depart from the actual transaction which are easier to meet than those under the 2010 Guidelines (the 2010 paras 1.64–1.69). Under the 1995 Guidelines (para 1.37), a transaction could not be disregarded if it could be priced. Under paragraph 1.65 of the 2010 Guidelines, the phrase used is '… practically impedes the tax administration from determining an appropriate transfer price'. It can be argued that the 1995 and 2010 texts amount to the same thing. However, the current 2017 Guidelines say '… thereby preventing the determination of a price that would be acceptable to both parties taking into account their respective perspectives and the options realistically available to each of them at the time of entering into the transaction'. In particular, the guidance now cites the pre-tax position of the whole group as being potentially relevant to the question of applying re-characterisation. Hence it is very likely that MNEs will face more assertions of re-characterisation simply because a tax authority does not like the arm's-length price that the actual transaction creates. Although additional guidance is given in paragraph 1.124 of the 2017 Guidelines on how to re-characterise, it is difficult to see how the warnings (at para 1.122) about double taxation, contentious argument and the use of re-characterisation can be heeded. Achieving a price for a transaction by means of re-characterising it into a completely different transaction, such that the resulting price is 'preferred' by one tax authority, is almost certain to be a hypothetical transaction and price that are unacceptable to the other tax authority.

2.42 Although not technically 're-characterisation', it is worth noting here that a result can be achieved under the revised Guidelines which has little practical difference. The concept of 'options realistically available' is used to suggest that a party would not pay more for a good or service than the price that it would have paid to achieve the same position by another means. This phrase was introduced into the OECD Transfer pricing Guidelines by the adoption of Chapter IX, on business restructuring, in 2010. At paragraph 1.38 of the 2017 Guidelines, the phrase is used as part of the identification of the 'accurately delineated transaction', but paragraph 1.39 applies it to the comparable transaction used to price the arm's-length value of the actual transaction. This is a subject to which we will return in Chapter 6, where we consider the transfer pricing of intangibles.

2.43 Finally on this subject, one of the key parts of the recent Australian judgment in *Chevron Australia Holdings Pty Ltd v COT (No 4)* [2015] FCA 1092 concerned the interpretation of 'consideration' in the Australian transfer pricing legislation, specifically whether the consideration given by the company for the funds borrowed could be taken to encapsulate more than just the price (ie the interest rate). The Australian court found that adjustments can be made to other factors in the loan terms (such as security and financial covenants) which have an impact on the arm's-length pricing of the loan. The finding that such other factors would have been present in the *Chevron* case meant, in that case, that the interest rate applied was deemed excessive when considering what would have been agreed between independent parties dealing at arm's length.

2.44 This could have important consequences for multinational corporations (MNCs) when analysing whether their internal financing arrangements are 'at arm's length', and the idea is certainly not limited to financing transactions. It also re-emphasises the importance of finding appropriate comparables, bearing in mind all factors considered in arriving at the terms of a loan. We await the output from the OECD on the transfer pricing aspects of Action 4, due at the end of 2016, to see whether a similar approach is adopted for the revised OECD Guidelines. It will also be interesting to see whether commentary is forthcoming on the question of whether the approach taken in *Chevron*, to effectively 're-write' some of the terms of the loans to arrive at an arm's-length pricing, is simply re-pricing (as found in that case) as distinguished from re-characterisation.

Evaluation of separate and combined transactions

2.45 This is another important point meriting careful thought by both taxpayers and tax authorities. The Guidelines acknowledge that, while it would be ideal to evaluate each transaction separately, there are times when a number of transactions are so closely linked or continuous that they are bundled together and should be priced in aggregate rather than individually (see Guidelines, para 3.9). Examples include pricing a range of closely linked products, and intangible property. Should bundled grants of rights to know-how, patents, trademarks, designs etc be separated – and, if so, would the constituent parts add up to a different value from the whole? In many cases it is impractical to unbundle and price in this way. There is a value in having the whole package together that is different from the value of the various parts, hence it is neither possible (nor appropriate in view of the overriding arm's-length principle) to fragment a bundle of rights that, in reality, cannot be used independently and scatter them among a number of associated parties simply to reduce their total value (and hence the amount of income that they might be capable of generating).

2.46 Paragraph 3.11 of the Guidelines does talk of the need to unpack some rights bundles, but the examples given are of rights that are quite different in character (eg patents, know-how and trademarks bundled in with the provision of services and the lease of facilities). This does not constitute permission to disaggregate the various intellectual property rights. Nor does it sanction the breaking out of franchise fees into intangible and service elements. A true franchise will always consist of service and intangible elements licensed together as a package, just as happens between unconnected parties.

Use of arm's-length range

2.47   This is a familiar concept, supported by observation, common sense and the 2017 Guidelines (see paras 3.55–3.59). A range of arm's-length prices generally exists because inefficiencies in the market, good and bad deals and a variety of other factors mean that competitors in the same market do not generally have the same price or the same profit. There is simply no single 'right price'

2.48   The Guidelines are clear: where a taxpayer's pricing is within range there should be no adjustment (see para 3.60) even if tax authorities frequently claim that they are interested in achieving 'the right place within the range'. Where pricing is outside the range and cannot be justified on the grounds of special circumstances, then the recommendation in the Guidelines is to adjust to the most appropriate part of the range. There is a compelling argument to move to the upper or lower reach of a consistently reliable range, whichever is nearer. However, local transfer pricing law or customary practice may provide differently.

Multiple year data

2.49   Again it is standard practice and common sense (but not a systematic requirement) to look at the position over a number of years before concluding that any given result is out of line. Reviewing performance over a number of years gives insight into market and product cycles, launches and other exceptional circumstances and allows a view to be taken on profitability on the contract over time.

Losses

2.50   An independent enterprise would be incapable of sustaining losses forever, but independent data shows that there can be circumstances in which losses are sustained for a number of years. An associated enterprise will often find its transfer pricing policy under scrutiny if it is consistently making a loss, particularly where the group as a whole is making a profit. If the losses arise because of an obligation to make or sell all group products, even though some are incapable of realising profits in that market, then this arguably may be a service provided to the group (or to particular members of it) requiring compensation by way of a service fee. This argument has often been used in the United Kingdom, where it is not unusual to find distributors returning consistently poor results owing either to an inability to reach critical mass or high costs. However, the subsidiary is not closed down because the group wants a 'shop window' in the UK.

2.51   At the same time, factors such as heavy start-up costs, temporarily unfavourable economic conditions or a policy of market penetration should be taken into account when assessing comparability and performance. They do not mean that a transfer pricing adjustment is necessarily required.

Government policies

2.52   Government intervention such as price control, subsidies, anti-dumping duties and exchange controls may all have a bearing on the price attached to an uncontrolled transaction and should be taken into consideration as factors that may affect comparability. The Guidelines (see para 1.73 onwards) note that these are all factors that will affect independent companies doing business in the same market. One would expect these to be taken into account when prices are set along the supply chain. The impact of this can be seen in the decision of the Danish court in *Denmark v Water Utility Companies*, Case No 27/2018 and 28/2018 (an asset valuation case, rather than transfer pricing, but the point is well made). In that case the discounted cash-flow method was found to be inappropriate as a means to establish the value of assets due the overall restriction imposed by the government on the prices charged to customers for their water supply.

2.53   The Guidelines recognise that, sometimes, governments take an asymmetrical approach to certain intra-group transactions. For example, one jurisdiction might expect a royalty of x% and the other might block payment of part or even all of it. The Guidelines comment that, where the same asymmetry is not applied to transactions between third parties, there is no simple solution.

Intentional set-offs

2.54   Where an associated enterprise has provided goods or services in return for goods or services from an associate, such set-offs need to be considered as if the trade had occurred between independent parties. The Guidelines find it easier to countenance set-offs where the flows are similar in character to one another than a general agreement between parties to balance out quite different kinds of business. However, as long as the individual flows can be priced with some confidence, there is no reason why such set-offs should be rejected out of hand.

2.55   Recognition by tax authorities of intentional set-offs is normally limited in practice to transactions between the same two legal entities and does not extend to cases in which three or more companies in different tax jurisdictions net off the effect of a number of transactions in which they are all involved.

Use of customs valuations

2.56   The Guidelines openly encourage cooperation between customs and tax authorities to prevent taxpayers from using one valuation for customs purposes and another for direct tax.

USE OF TRANSFER PRICING METHODS

2.57   Introducing the chapter on methods and methodologies, the Guidelines (see paras 2.1–2.11) make some fairly open-minded comments on how such methods should, in broad terms, be used. The key point is that the method selection should always be aimed at finding the 'most appropriate method' for a particular case. Applying an inappropriate method will lead to a non-arm's-length price and would therefore be incorrect and a breach of the arm's-length principle. They also introduce a 'Typical process' (Section A.1).

2.58   Tax authorities are reminded not to make small or marginal adjustments and not to be so overly rigid in the standard set for comparability that they close the door on useful and illuminating information. Moreover, MNEs are permitted to use just one method and should not be expected to prove why they did not use others. At the same time, in difficult cases, the use of several methods in conjunction is encouraged as a practical way of resolving what might otherwise prove to be uncertain and problematic valuations.

2.59   These remarks do need to be seen against the backdrop of Chapters II and III of the Guidelines as they were originally drafted. In earlier versions of the Guidelines there was a clear hierarchy of the various methods which to some extent limited these opening observations. Nonetheless, even then, the warning against too narrow-minded an approach was a welcome reminder that transfer pricing is, in the end, as much an art as a science. In the 2010 amendments to the Guidelines, much of that hierarchy has been swept away (see **2.60** below). Though there is a clear preference for Comparable Uncontrolled Price, once it is established that this method cannot be used there is now more leeway to apply the most appropriate methodology. This does not mean a move away from science and reason to pure artistry, rather it means that transfer pricing practitioners must be 'professional' in their selection of a methodology and must record the evidence which led them to conclude that the chosen methodology was indeed the most appropriate one.

2.60   As a result of the G20/OECD BEPS initiative, the revisions to the Guidelines adopted into the 2017 Guidelines have made further strides in this direction. The hierarchy of methods is less important, although there continues to be a preference for a true comparable uncontrolled price (CUP), but other methods now rank equally. There is also an acceptance that, in appropriate circumstances, other valuation methodologies may be acceptable (for example, see para 6.212 of the Guidelines).

TRANSFER PRICING METHODS

2.61   The point was made (in **2.23** above) that, subject to company law or practical constraints, MNEs can use any method or mechanism when setting inter-company prices. However, most tax authorities now require taxable profits and allowable losses to be calculated as if intra-group business had been carried out on arm's-length terms. Testing conformity with the arm's-length principle in this way may be possible using only one method, but where there are different transaction types that may not be possible. In most cases, the variety of goods, services, debt and intangibles that are transacted by an enterprise with one or more associated enterprises requires the use of more than one of the methods set out in Chapter II of the OECD Guidelines.

2.62   The Guidelines group the approved methods into two categories:

- traditional transaction methods (Chapter II, Part II); and

- transactional profit methods (Chapter II, Part III).

Notice the emphasis on transactions – the OECD's intention is always to track the return on a particular transaction or group of transactions, not overall results however achieved and of whatever component parts composed.

2.63   Within the first group – the traditional transaction methods – there are three methods comparing prices or gross margins. These methods are:

- comparable uncontrolled price (CUP) method, which offers a direct price comparison; and

- resale price and cost-plus methods, which make comparisons at gross margin level.

Transactional profit methods compare the profit arising from controlled transactions with that generated by transactions between third parties.

2.64   Until the 2010 edition of the Guidelines, there was a clear expression of a preference for traditional transaction methods, in particular, the CUP method. However, even then, the Guidelines recognised that shortage of data may render traditional transaction methods ineffective. As such, in 2010 this moved to 'in exceptional circumstances', and in the 2017 Guidelines this has become 'appropriate circumstances'), transactional profit methods or other methods not described in the Guidelines may be used to establish a transfer price, as long as they provide the best basis for applying the arm's-length principle.

2.65   Let us look first at the traditional transactional methods.

The CUP method

2.66   This offers a direct comparison between an intra-group transfer price (otherwise known as the price of a 'controlled transaction') and the price charged for the same or similar property or services transferred between third parties. There are two possible types of comparison:

- *Internal CUP* – the comparison is between the price charged in the controlled transaction and that charged in a transaction between one of the parties to the controlled transaction and an independent enterprise.

- *External CUP* – the comparison here is with a transaction between two third parties, neither of whom is a party to the controlled transaction.

The use of an internal CUP will almost always be favoured since, all other things being equal, the circumstances of the controlled transaction will more closely mirror those of the uncontrolled transaction.

2.67   Reliable application of the CUP method will usually require either that there are no economically significant differences in the transactions being compared, or that the effect on price of any differences that do exist can be accurately accounted for by way of an adjustment. (The OECD Guidelines discuss comparability in relation to comparable uncontrolled transactions in para 3.24 onwards of Chapter III 'Comparability Analysis'.) In the open market, even a small change in the circumstances of a transaction may have a material impact on price. As such, the overall effectiveness of the CUP method depends on the nature and reliability of any adjustments made to take into account the differing circumstances of transactions.

2.68   Where it is possible to locate comparable uncontrolled transactions, the CUP method is the most direct and reliable transfer pricing method; therefore in such cases the OECD considers it preferable over all other methods. Product comparability is absolutely key, in particular physical features such as size, weight, appearance, along with volume, reliability, storage requirements, regulatory requirements, and the like. Also significant are other contributors to the overall economics of the deal such as the market, delivery and payment terms, etc. Where an independent enterprise buys or sells the same product as is supplied in the controlled transaction and sufficient data on the uncontrolled transaction is readily available, the CUP method will always be the most suitable method of applying the arm's-length principle. Examples of situations in which the CUP method may be used include:

- the interest rate charged on a loan between related parties;

- industries where CUPs are more prevalent, for example, the software industry where products are often licensed to third parties; or

- the price charged for the transfer of a homogenous item, such as a traded commodity.

Often, however, adjustments cannot be made for differences in transaction terms or market cycle and, consequently, the CUP method will not provide a reasonable basis for comparing transactions. Furthermore, in a large number of cases it is simply impossible to identify third-party pricing information to derive a CUP. In such circumstances the most appropriate method, depending on circumstances, may be the resale price method or the cost-plus method.

2.69   These two methods operate at one step removed from a direct price comparison; which one might be used in any given circumstance depends on the nature of the transaction.

2.70   A brief word on terminology: in the United States the terms 'comparable uncontrolled transaction' (CUT) and 'comparable uncontrolled financial transaction' (CUFT) are used in specific and limited circumstances. CUFT speaks for itself, but it is worth pointing out that CUT is used more narrowly in US transfer pricing legislation than it is in the OECD Guidelines, and tends to refer specifically to comparable prices for intangible property (usually royalty rates).We return to the CUP method to review comparability for transactions in intangible property in Chapter 6.

The resale price method (RPM)

2.71   The Resale Price method (RPM) takes the price at which a product is resold to an independent entity after being initially purchased from an associated entity and reduces it by an appropriate gross margin: the 'resale price margin'. The resale price represents the amount of income out of which the reseller in the open market would seek to cover its direct and indirect costs, in addition to making an appropriate level of profit. It takes into account risks assumed, assets utilised and functions performed by the reseller. Subtraction of the resale price margin and adjustment for other costs associated with the purchase of the product (eg customs duties) leaves the arm's-length price, as would be charged between independent parties.

2.72 The reference to making an appropriate level of profit (see 2017 Guidelines, para 2.27) has led to a long, occasionally heated and sometimes tedious debate as to whether the RPM is really some form of thinly disguised profit method. It is fair to say that some tax authorities have certainly appeared to think so, focusing on the bottom line and not appearing to care about a good match at gross level if there are no operating or net profits to be had. Probably the right way to look at this is that no business will put up with losses for a long period of time: it will either give up trying, or be forced to close down. A reasonable gross margin should offer the chance of a decent profit over time; but it need not do so every year. Occasionally, there will be factors that hit the profit and loss account (below gross margin level) that are nothing to do with transfer pricing and that interfere temporarily with the ability to make the reasonable profit referred to by the Guidelines. Where this diminution of profitability is short term and can be explained by commercial factors, tax authorities should not take this poor bottom line performance as discrediting an otherwise acceptable gross margin comparison; at the same time, MNEs should recognise that they cannot rely on apparently comparable gross margins that produce persistent losses.

2.73 The RPM requires a sale to a third party, so is not suitable where goods are sold to an associate rather than into the open market. It is most effective in situations where the reseller adds little value to the property transferred and where only a short time elapses between the reseller acquiring and reselling the property. The RPM is less reliable where the reseller adds substantially to the value of the transferred property by way of further processing to the goods or through intangibles associated with the reseller.

2.74 Care needs to be taken to account for the skills and assets used by the reseller, and the rights he enjoys. In general, the contribution of greater skill or valuable intangibles should attract a greater reward. Paragraph 3.32 says 'Thus, where uncontrolled and controlled transactions are comparable in all characteristics other than the product itself, the resale price method might produce a more reliable measure of arm's length conditions than the CUP method; ...' However, in paragraph 2.35 there is a statement that might easily be misinterpreted:

'Another example where the resale price margin requires particular care is where the reseller contributes substantially to the creation or maintenance of intangible property associated with the product (e.g. trademarks or trade names) which are owned by an associated enterprise. In such cases, the contribution of the goods originally transferred to the value of the final product cannot be easily evaluated.'

33

2.75   Sometimes it is argued that the interaction of a distributor with customers necessarily creates 'goodwill' and so the local distributor 'owns' that local marketing intangible. With a little thought it becomes obvious that this argument is incorrect; as all distributors interact with customers they will all take the same role in generating goodwill, and so the correct compensation for that is already included in the comparables. Looking to third-party arrangements, the local distributor does not become entitled to any additional reward for a marketing intangible unless its activities, qualitatively or quantitatively, go beyond that expected of a distributor. This is discussed in more detail in Chapter 6 of this book.

2.76   Another potential reason for non-comparability would be unusually high expenditure on product promotion, although the Guidelines (at para 2.37) balance this by suggesting that justification would be needed for expenditure that seems unreasonably high. So, for example, it might be the case that abnormally high marketing expenditure is incurred as a service to the legal owner of a trademark, in which case some or all of the expenditure might be reimbursed on a cost-plus basis, leaving the RPM to cope with the distribution function. The converse may also be true, of course: excessive marketing expenditure might mean that the reseller is, in effect, owner or part owner of the intangible in question IF that would be the consequence of such behaviour as between unrelated parties.

2.77   The Guidelines also note (at para 2.28) that the method is suitable for determining brokerage fees, which are usually calculated as a percentage of sales whether the broker is acting as agent or principal.

2.78   All the circumstances surrounding a transaction need to be known and examined and, as described above, adjustments should be made for any differences that would significantly affect the resale margin in the open market. Functional comparability is more important than product comparability, because while specific prices would tend to equalise only where one product could be a direct and suitable substitute for the other, a gross margin represents gross compensation for the performance of specific functions. Hence, for example, one could understand a comparison between the gross margin to be made on blenders with that on toasters, even though one would not expect the price of a toaster to be the same as that of a blender. Nevertheless, some attention must be paid to product comparability. It would not, for example, be appropriate to compare the gross margin achieved on selling tins of beans with that made by a reseller of heavy plant such as mechanical diggers.

The cost-plus method

2.79   This begins with the costs incurred by the supplier of property (or services) in a controlled transaction for property transferred or services provided to a related purchaser (see Guidelines, para 2.45). An appropriate mark-up is then added to remunerate the supplier for functions performed, assets utilised and risks borne. The mark up should be calculated by reference to similar transactions either between the associated enterprise and a third party, or between non-related parties (analogous to internal and external CUPs, described at **2.66** above).

2.80 Cost-plus should only be used where costs are consistently a key driver of profit, and as a result the link between costs and profit is clear.

2.81 Once again, the comparability of transactions is important and it is likely that adjustments will have to be made to account for differences. One issue that often arises is efficiency and this is covered in paragraph 2.48 of the Guidelines. The conclusion reached is that it is not appropriate to deprive a company of its efficiency savings by failing to make adjustments when applying the cost-plus method. The flip side of the same coin is that the cost-plus method can be seen as offering an incentive for an affiliated enterprise to increase its cost base because, in absolute terms, an increase in costs will lead to an increase in profits. This can encourage inefficiencies in both manufacturing operations and service activities. Rigorous budgeting combined with the use of mark-ups based on budgeted costs and other performance measurements can assist in controlling costs. As between unconnected parties, customers constantly press suppliers to be more efficient and to pass-on any savings by way of reduced product price, so it would be incorrect to claim that the cost-plus margin should always rise through efficiencies and so the actual situation should be considered carefully (Guidelines, para 2.49).

2.82 Comparability of cost base is also crucial. This means accounting for differences in both the make-up and reporting of the cost base. Make-up is really an issue of function: is a particular cost incurred by one company but not another because of a key functional difference which either discredits the use of the method or (at the least) necessitates the making of an adjustment? Reporting comes down to the allocation and description of costs in one jurisdiction as against another. Bearing in mind that the cost-plus method is a gross margin method (ie the comparison is made between mark-ups on the costs of production or service provision only, not on the general operating overheads of the entity as a whole), it is important that costs have either been reported in the same way, or that adjustments have been made.

2.83 Typically, the cost-plus method is used for the provision of intra-group services or the provision of manufactured goods under contract:

> '(the cost plus) method probably is most useful where semi-finished goods are sold between associated parties, where associated parties have concluded joint facility arrangements or long-term buy-and-supply arrangements ...' (Guidelines, para 2.45)

Where associated enterprises perform highly sophisticated services, it is often argued by tax authorities that a higher mark-up should be applied. This analysis sometimes fails to differentiate between the cost of providing the service and the risks assumed in doing so. The mark-up should be derived by analysing the mark-up of independent entities providing similar types of service. The analysis of independent entities must take account of the risks of performing the services in question. The greater the risks, all other things being equal, the greater the mark-up that should be charged. Notwithstanding the risk factor, the value of a highly sophisticated or value added service will also be reflected in the cost base, which is then marked up. For example, some payroll type functions could be seen as low-risk functions even though they are performed by a highly paid company accountant. The mark-up to be applied for that service should be derived by analysing the mark-ups of independent accountants providing similar payroll services. The high salary will result in a high absolute charge when a percentage basis is applied to the total cost base.

2.84   There is more on this in Chapter 4, at **4.2**.

2.85   Transactional profit methods may be used to approximate arm's-length conditions where such methods are the most appropriate to the circumstances of the case. Such methods compare the profit arising from controlled transactions with that generated by transactions between third parties, and come with some serious health warnings (see Guidelines, paras 2.4–2.7). They are not to be used just because of lack of data and they must be used in a manner consistent with Article 9 of the OECD Model. There is no justification in seeking more tax from a MNE simply because its profits are lower than average. So what are the sanctioned profit methods and how – in cases where they are, of course, the most appropriate method – are MNEs and tax authorities to use them?

Profit split

2.86   The transactional profit split (or 'profit split') method is particularly useful where the role of the associated enterprises in a transaction are so interrelated (eg with respect to economically significant risks) that they cannot be evaluated separately. A transactional profit split method may also be found to be the most appropriate method in cases where both parties to a transaction make unique and valuable contributions such that third parties might set up a joint venture or partnership and agree to some form of profit split based on their contributions. Step one is to identify the profit to be split. This might be the total profit arising from the arrangements, or a residual amount that cannot be easily assigned to one party or the other. A residual of this sort would almost always be associated with the use of high value, quite possibly unique, intangibles. Step two is to split the profit in line with the expectations that would have been captured in an agreement made between third parties. In general terms, the profit will be split by reference to the contributions of the parties; and those contributions will be identified by means of a functional analysis and valued as far as possible by either available external data or sound economic theory and practice, or both.

2.87   'Sound', incidentally, should not be read as being necessarily limited to 'safe' or 'established'. As MNEs enter into a wide variety of complex and innovative commercial transactions and arrangements, sometimes new ideas are required from economists and tax specialists to capture properly the true value of each party's contribution. Such ideas must inevitably grow out of interpretation of the material facts and of the relations between the parties and out of fundamentally sound economics and reliable data; nevertheless the final analysis of more complex arrangements may not fit easily into any of the comfortable old transfer pricing boxes to which people have become used.

2.88 That said there is never an authority to depart from the fundamental basis of the arm's-length principle; that transfer pricing is tested by reference to what happens between unrelated parties. No matter how superficially attractive an econometric analysis appears to be, it must be based on arm's-length comparability.

2.89 How might profit be split in practice? The ideal approach for goods and services may sound odd and even paradoxical. It is to reduce the profit to be split to the minimum possible. This is achieved by identifying all the 'basic' functions (manufacture, distribution, service provision, etc) and allocating a return to them using normal methods. Once this exercise has been carried out, some residual, non-basic, contributions will be found to remain, along with some residual profit or loss that must be split between the parties, taking into account their relative contribution to the venture. The basis of split will sometimes be based on a direct observation of how profit is split between independent parties who engage in comparable transactions. Often that is not possible and a valid economic analysis, still rooted in observable third-party transactions, will be required. Thus the solution so found should adhere to the cornerstone of the arm's-length principle and yet pass the smell test of common sense, even if it is not possible to point to something exactly like it in the open market place.

2.90 The residual profit (or loss) is allocated by considering factors such as the nature of any intangible property contributed and the relative bargaining powers of each party. Models can be set up to replicate the bargaining process.

2.91 This does not exhaust all possible ways of splitting profit. Other ways might include:

- each party receives the same return on the capital it employs in the arrangements. This is predicated on the possibly unrealistic assumption that each is bearing the same level of risk. Where this is not so, adjustments may be required to account for differences;

- splitting profit by reference to discounted cash flow. This can be a method in its own right, or be used to share out the residual discussed above. Credible benchmarks will be needed when setting the risk premium, and once again the Guidelines utter strong words against the use of an industry-wide approach (see Guidelines, para 2.129); and

- using the same proportions as independent enterprises engaging in comparable transactions. This engagingly simple idea will normally be thwarted in practice because there will be no such comparable transactions to be found, otherwise, one supposes, one of the transactional methods would be used. However, a useful reference may be joint venture agreements.

2.92 Perceived strengths of the profit split method include:

- less reliance is placed on comparability with observed third party transactions, and so the method remains useful even if no such transactions can be found; though there must still be a reference to observable third-party behaviour at some level; and

- both parties to the arrangements are examined, and so profit is unlikely to be allocated in such a way as to leave one or other in an extreme or improbable profit position.

2.93 Perceived weaknesses include:

- the external market data used to identify the contributions of the parties is not so closely linked to the relevant transactions as is the case with other methods. Operating at one step removed, as it were, gives an air of greater subjectivity to the application of the method in practice;

- safe application of the method requires the production of considerable data from more than one jurisdiction, so there may be issues of data availability;

- certainty is required that revenues and costs have been reported on consistent bases by all parties to the arrangements. This might mean special efforts being made by the parties to re-state their books, or to modify their internal systems appropriately; and

- it can be challenging to remain true to the arm's-length principle and measure, at some level, the profit split by reference to the transactions of unrelated parties.

2.94 In 2018, the OECD released updated guidance on the application of the profit split method. Transfer pricing practitioners should consult that material in addition to the material above.

The Transactional Net Margin Method (TNMM)

2.95 This was originally intended to be the method of absolute last resort but, in practice, it became almost overnight the most popular and frequently used of all the OECD methods (in some jurisdictions, but not all – see below). Perhaps its popularity stems, at least in part, from the fact that for years before the Guidelines finally got round to accepting it, great numbers of people had been using it anyway. The United States called it the Comparable Profits Method (CPM) – they still do; CPM is not, of course, officially the same as TNMM, since CPM cuts straight to the bottom line, however complex or multi-faceted the businesses of the comparables and tested party might be, in a way that the OECD finds frankly distasteful. TNMM, by contrast, is a method of greater taste and refinement and there is something akin to elegance in the way in which it – well – cuts to the bottom line.

2.96   The point is that in a large number of cases data reliable enough to permit the safe application of one of the other methods is simply not available, and so for years before the acceptance of TNMM both MNEs and tax authorities had been solving difficult cases on the basis of profitability, usually over a number of years. So, for example, solutions were found under which distributors might take a few years to start up and then would make an operating margin in the region of 2%. The United States were honest about this and called it CPM; everyone else played a game of simultaneously sneering at the US while solving by reference to operating profits or all costs plus.

2.97   The TNMM examines the operating profit (ie the profit after direct and indirect costs) from controlled transactions as a percentage of a base such as sales, costs, or assets. Ideally the operating profit should be established by reference to profits earned by the same taxpayer in comparable uncontrolled transactions. However, if that is not possible, comparable transactions between wholly independent entities can be used. Comparability between controlled and uncontrolled transactions should be established, as ever, through a functional analysis.

2.98   The TNMM should consider only the profits attributable to the transactions under review. This might necessitate separating the profit and loss account into streams where the company engages in a variety of different controlled transactions. By the same token, comparables must be selected carefully to retain only companies whose business is homogeneous and whose transactions are the same as, or similar to, those under review.

2.99   Advantages of the TNMM include:

- use of it is common, as previously described;

- as the TNMM focuses on only one party to a controlled transaction it is a relatively simple method to apply. There is, for example, no need to ensure that all parties' books are stated on a consistent accounting basis; and

- an operating margin is likely to be less susceptible to functional differences in comparing transactions than are the gross margin studied in the resale price method and the price in the comparable uncontrolled price method. It is an observed fact that different businesses might show a wide range of gross margins but be broadly similar at operating level.

2.100   Weaknesses include:

- for many years, not all OECD countries accepted it, even though it had been sanctioned by the Guidelines for many years. This led to a certain amount of creativity on the part of MNEs in those jurisdictions in dressing up what is really a TNMM to look like another method – and not just in those jurisdictions, of course, but in other countries which are the counterparty to transactions involving those jurisdictions, to maximise the chance of obtaining competent authority relief in the event of double taxation. This point has become less of a problem over time, but there are still one or two examples left;

- a comparison made after operating expenses might fail to account for relevant factors that have nothing to do with gross margin or particular prices, such as operational inefficiencies, a redundancy programme, fluctuating marketing spend, etc;

- it might be difficult to be certain that the operating profit has been calculated consistently, (ie that items such as depreciation, reserves, provisions, other operating income, etc have been treated in the same way); and

- there may be difficulties in identifying the counterparty or parties for the purposes of making corresponding adjustments to relieve double tax. This would be so where the company sits in the middle of the group supply chain, or where it buys from or sells to a number of group companies.

Cutting to the bottom line does not do away with the need to consider many of the factors affecting comparability already mentioned, for example threat of new entrants, competitive position, management efficiency and strategy, availability of substitute products, maturity or otherwise of the business, differing cost structures, and so forth. Adjustments will have to be made to account for such differences. Sometimes it is argued that the use of a range takes care of this, but it should be obvious that for the purist this cannot be so. A range does not in itself take account of unique features (start-up phase, innovative strategy decisions, etc). What it does offer is a spread of possibilities which can be of use in resolving a tax authority audit. How? Information on comparables is limited, so it is hard to decide whether or not the enterprises chosen as comparables face the same issues as those being debated in the audit, and so the range can be said statistically to lay off the risk of reaching a demonstrably wrong conclusion. It is worth noting that this risk is reduced further if multiple year data is used, since this will enable proper account to be taken of any short-term economic factors.

Comparable profits method

2.101   This was referred to in our discussion on TNMM. Is the TNMM, when it comes right down to it, essentially the same as the US comparable profits method? Strictly, no it is not. The CPM benchmarks the profitability of companies as a whole, rather than on a transaction-by-transaction basis as the TNMM does. Sometimes, by accident rather than by design, the two methods would reach the same answer because the comparable sets chosen consist of companies with either homogeneous or one-product businesses. But often this is not so, and the CPM has incurred the wrath of the Guidelines and of many individual OECD countries. However, as a practical matter, it can be observed that, when it comes to resolving double taxation issues arising from transfer pricing adjustments, competent authorities, especially those in mature transfer pricing jurisdictions such as the UK, do try to reach pragmatic solutions without getting hung up on mere labels.

RECENT OECD DEVELOPMENTS

2.102 There is a tremendous amount of activity at OECD in the transfer pricing arena right now. The OECD BEPS initiative has led to the creation of guidance in the 2017 revised Guidelines in the areas below:

- intangibles;

- timing issues;

- bilateral safe harbours; and

- profit split.

There is additional work ongoing at the time of writing to consider guidance on the transfer pricing of financial services transactions.

Timing issues

2.103 Arising out of the work on intangibles but then extending more widely, the OECD looked at: (i) the time that comparable information is available to taxpayers in assessing whether their prices are at arm's length; (ii) tax authority acceptance of year-end adjustments; (iii) the use of post-transaction date information to assess reasonableness; and (iv) specific issues in respect of the valuation of highly uncertain intangibles. This material is also dealt with in Chapter 6.

Bilateral safe harbours

2.104 The OECD has amended guidance on the use of safe harbours and in doing so removes the 'somewhat negative tone' that does not reflect the practice of OECD member countries (particularly in respect of smaller taxpayers and less-complex transactions). The OECD continues to encourage countries to agree 'bilateral' safe harbours, given the potential advantages of simplicity and ease of administration, which avoids some of the downsides of providing unilateral safe harbours with no reciprocal treatment in counterparty jurisdictions. However, in the 2017 revised Guidelines the OECD has rewritten Chapter VII of the 2010 Guidelines entirely. This contains, at Section D, new material concerning 'low value-adding intra-group services'. This guidance provides a practical transfer pricing solution, for suitably qualifying services, including the guidance that an appropriate mark-up on the qualifying cost-pool will be 5% (see Guidelines, para 7.61) which would not need to be justified by a comparability study. However, this approach has to be adopted by a country, and so care should be taken to ensure that it has been so adopted before applying it in a particular instance.

THE REST OF THE BOOK

2.105 It is worth setting out at this stage the basic format for the rest of this book, together with an explanation of how this corresponds with the format of the OECD Guidelines.

2.106 Chapters I, II and III of the OECD Guidelines set out the underlying principles in relation to transfer pricing, being the arm's-length principle, transfer pricing methods and comparability analysis respectively. These have been discussed already. Chapters VI to IX of the OECD Guidelines look at the application of the theory from Chapters I to III in a number of different circumstances (eg Chapter IX, which was newly incorporated into the 2010 Guidelines, deals with business restructuring). This book takes a slightly different approach by exploring the application of transfer pricing principles on a transaction-by-transaction basis, dealing with tangible goods, services, financing and intangible property in turn, within the following four chapters.

2.107 Chapter IV of the OECD Guidelines sets out administrative approaches to avoiding and resolving transfer pricing disputes, and Chapter V sets out guidance as to the content of transfer pricing documentation that tax payers should hold on file. These are dealt with in this book in Chapters 9 (Documentation) and 10 (Operational transfer pricing), and also in detail in Chapter 11 (Tax audits and eliminating double taxation).

Chapter 3

Types of transaction: Tangible goods

INTRODUCTION

3.1   At the very highest level, there are four types of transaction that members of the same multinational enterprise (MNE) might enter into with one another or, indeed, with any unrelated enterprise. They can transact in:

- tangible goods;
- services;
- financing; and/or
- intangible property.

The next four chapters introduce these types of transaction and the consequences for transfer pricing them in turn. This chapter looks at tangible goods.

3.2   To begin with, there are some definitions to set out, of the terms 'widget', 'supply chain', 'contract manufacturer' and 'toll manufacturer'.

3.3   For some reason, international tax specialists have decided that the codename to be used when trying to explain anything to do with tangible goods is 'widgets'. The term 'widget' originates from engineering and means 'a small mechanical device or control', though 'widget' has since been appropriated into other spheres such as software engineering where it clearly means something else entirely. In the world of tax and economics, the term is used to mean a physical object, unlike a service, a loan, or a licence.

3.4   We are indebted to the world of business consulting for the term 'supply chain'. It means the channel of distribution beginning with the supplier of materials or components, extending through a manufacturing process to the distributor and retailer and, ultimately, to the consumer. It is convenient as a term, first, because it is much shorter to say 'supply chain' than to describe the flow through a business and, secondly, because 'supply chain' carries a high score if you are playing 'Buzzword Bingo' in business meetings. That said, this term is borrowed for the remainder of this book.

3.5   A 'contract manufacturer' is a specialised form of manufacturing entity where the hiring firm approaches the contract manufacturer with a design or formula. The contract manufacturer will quote based on processes, labour, tooling, and material costs. Unrelated hiring companies would usually request quotes from multiple sources and then buy on price and other factors, such as reliability or capacity to deliver. The contract manufacturer acts as the hiring firm's factory, producing and shipping units of the design on behalf of the hiring firm. A contract manufacturer does not own intangibles in the product that is produced and makes to order which means it has little inventory risk. Sometimes the production process is well known (there are no process intangibles owned by the contract manufacturer) and sometimes the hiring firm provides its production intangibles. Occasionally the contract manufacturer may use its process intangibles but the reward for this is usually a slightly higher margin on a similar unit price. Unrelated parties use contract manufacturers in aerospace, defence, consumer goods, and automotive (to name just a few), but they are commonly found in many industries.

3.6 A 'toll manufacturer' is slightly more specialised in that it does not purchase the raw materials used to make the widgets, though it will often purchase consumables required in the manufacturing process (eg electricity, oil and spares for the machines used in production). Toll manufacturers typically bid for work just like contract manufacturers but they play no part in, and enjoy no reward from, sourcing and holding raw materials. Toll manufacturing is less common between unrelated parties but it does happen. In transfer pricing terms the value added by the manufacturing entity in either contract manufacturing or toll manufacturing is quite close and so unless there is an overwhelming reason to choose toll manufacturing in an intra-group scenario it is often best avoided; there can be significant complexities to raw material procurement in a toll manufacturing structure and customs duty, import licenses and other controls are particularly important.

3.7 Action 7 of the OECD Base Erosion and Profit Shifting (BEPS) initiative has led to agreed changes which have been included in the 2017 OECD model tax treaty and explanatory notes. In addition, Action 7 (and other BEPS actions) have led to over 100 jurisdictions concluded negotiations on the Multilateral Convention to Implement Tax Treaty Related Measures to Prevent Base Erosion and Profit Shifting ('Multilateral Instrument' or 'MLI') in November 2016, that will swiftly implement a series of tax treaty measures to update international tax rules and lessen the opportunity for tax avoidance by multinational enterprises. The MLI already covers 87 jurisdictions and entered into force on 1 July 2018. Signatories include jurisdictions from all continents and all levels of development and other jurisdictions are also actively working towards signature.

3.8 Depending on the specific countries in question and how/whether they have updated tax treaties or adopted certain provisions of the MLI, this may add more complexity to contract and toll manufacturing arrangements in future, compared with that to which we have been accustomed. In particular, the restrictions proposed on the application of model article 5.4 (which eliminates a permanent establishment under article 5.1 in the case of stock holding) are potentially far-reaching and may lead to a permanent establishment of the principal entity when raw materials or finished goods are stored at a facility which is 'at the disposal' of the non-resident. Although countries have the flexibility to retain exceptions for stock holding, it is essential that the possibility of permanent establishments existing is properly assessed in all cases, and especially in scenarios where other group companies operate in the same country, given that countries have the option of introducing an anti-fragmentation rule which is included in the MLI.

3.9   In a simple (though not untypical) business model, a group involved in the production and sale of tangible goods might organise and carry out its business by separating manufacturing operations from sales operations. This can be for several reasons, the most obvious of which being that perhaps they manufacture in a small number of jurisdictions but sell in many. A business model utilising specialist manufacturing companies yet making sales to third-party customers through dedicated reselling and marketing companies must provide for the transfer pricing of goods as they pass through different associated companies along the supply chain.

3.10   There are many variations in the ways that a multinational might structure its business model and supply chain which vary in complexity; potentially involving invoicing companies (eg for the management of currency risk) or agents acting as intermediaries in the sale of goods. To aid this discussion three examples of a supply chain for tangible goods transactions are set out in Figure 3.1 below. As will be demonstrated, the transfer pricing issues surrounding the trade in tangible goods centre on the allocation of key functions and risks among the various group companies along the supply chain.

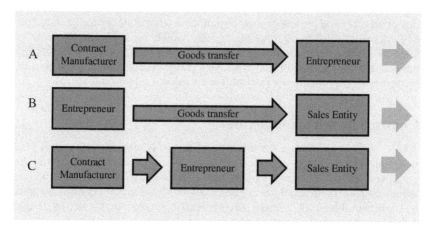

Figure 3.1 – Three supply chain models for tangible goods transactions

3.11   Like the legend of the Phoenix, however, all end with beginnings; and, in our case, the newly introduced term 'delineation of transactions' signals finally the passage to focusing more on the economically relevant characteristics of a transaction and the end of relying heavily on the contractual terms. Therefore, in assessing the allocation of functions and risks in the three scenarios illustrated in Figure 3.1 above, the actual transactions should generally be delineated for purposes of the transfer pricing analysis in accordance with the characteristics of the transaction reflected in the conduct of the parties, rather than relying on the written contracts which may be inconsistent with what actually happens in practice. The newly introduced provisions of the OECD Transfer pricing Guidelines suggest that, where there are material differences between contractual terms and the conduct of the associated parties, 'the functions they actually perform, the assets they actually use, and the risks they actually assume, considered in the context of the contractual terms, should ultimately determine the factual substance and accurately delineate the actual transaction'. It is therefore essential that taxpayers revisit existing contracts, to ensure they reflect a complete picture of the transactions and ensure that these have not been incorrectly characterised or labelled.

MANUFACTURING

3.12   All types of manufacturers apply processes to raw materials to create a 'widget' (in this example). This is true from simple contract or toll manufacturing (see Figure 3.1A) through to complex manufacturing operations bearing full risk exposures and using internally developed product intangible property (Figure 3.1B). From a transfer pricing perspective, the amount of profit to be allocated to the manufacturer depends on the operational model employed by the multinational group, in other words, how the multinational conducts its business between the various group companies, sharing functions and risk between them. The analysis of functions, risks and assets to answer this question is called a 'functional analysis'. This process is fundamental to transfer pricing. A functional analysis provides the information for determining the tested party and provides the information on comparability for the selection of evidence of third-party transactions from which the arm's length nature of inter-company prices can be tested. This can be illustrated by considering the position for the type of manufacturing entity at each end of the spectrum, starting with the operation which adds least value.

Contract or toll manufacturer

3.13   The supply chain for this type of business relationship is illustrated in Figure 3.1A above. A typical contract or toll manufacturer would be employed by the business entrepreneur to undertake well-defined widget manufacturing or assembly processes. The only difference between contract and toll manufacturing is their involvement in procuring raw materials that will form part of the finished goods or packaging but the transfer pricing methodology that is most applicable to this business model is not affected by that. It is likely that a contract manufacturer will not bear any risks associated with currency, inventory or selling the finished goods. Payment terms would likely be based on budgets which, quite rightly, allow the manufacturer to be more, or less, profitable depending on how well they have performed (perhaps with a year-end adjustment to actual, though as this verges on a non-commercial licence to spend, it is not the model most commonly advised), and the risk of unfulfilled orders would lie with the purchaser rather than the manufacturer. Other than possibly some process know-how, the contract manufacturer will not own or develop any valuable intangibles. Transfer prices would often be set on a 'per unit' fee, or a return on assets or a return on costs. Even the risks associated with fixed costs may be ameliorated with long-term contracts and guaranteed volumes.

3.14   The level of reward would be driven by the functions, assets and limited risks borne by the contract manufacturer and would reflect the depreciation of fixed assets employed. These are, in effect, the opportunity costs of providing the contracted service. In testing, or indeed setting, the price to be charged by such a manufacturer – and so the reward that it makes – the most likely approach is a benchmarking exercise in which comparison is drawn between the return on costs achieved by the group company and that of a sample of independent, but otherwise comparable, manufacturing companies operating (as far as data availability permits) in the same territory. Care does need to be taken in assembling and using such samples because publicly available data rarely discloses the nature of the relevant contractual arrangements. There will, as a result, always be some doubt as to whether like is being compared with like. One answer lies in making adjustments in respect of relevant items such as inventory carried, capital employed, debtor days and such like so that, for example, where the group company is a toll manufacturer, all risk and expense related to inventory ownership is factored out of the comparable set.

Complex manufacturer

3.15   Like a contract manufacturer, a complex manufacturer would typically own fixed assets for the widget production process and carry out manufacturing or assembly work. However, it would also bear inventory, product and other risks. It is also likely to carry out research and development and own its intangible property and it is this element in particular that adds to its complexity. From the perspective of benchmarking transfer prices, it is far more difficult to test the arm's-length return for this type of manufacturer, particularly where embedded intangible asset development and ownership is significant. Here, costs and tangible assets employed are not the only value drivers in play, so payment by reference to them is likely to miss the mark. How to proceed, then?

3.16   A common structural model for multinational groups is the separation of manufacturing and sales/distribution activities. This is set out in Figure 3.1B above. Where the manufacturer is complex, the sales entities would, by definition, be relatively simple with the manufacturer bearing most of the risks of the overall activity. In this case, allocating an arm's-length reward to the sales entities and allowing all the residual – whether profit or loss – to fall to the manufacturer would be the most appropriate approach. This relies on the premise that if prices paid by the sales entity are at arm's length, then the balance received by the manufacturer, whatever it might be, is also arm's length. As ever, care must be taken to ensure that an accurate analysis of the functions of the tested party have been undertaken, as any omissions here will lead to an under-reward for the tested party and the 'mistake value' will augment the residual return.

Centralised business model

3.17   On occasions, both manufacturing and sales companies will be regarded as 'complex'. That is set out in Figure 3.1C above. We can use both of the methodologies applied to Figure 3.1A and C to reward both the manufacturing and sales entities to leave an appropriate reward (the residual profit or loss) for the entrepreneur. We look at how to proceed in such cases at **3.39** below.

3.18 Where different manufacturing plants undertake different stages of the manufacturing, or finishing and packing are carried out by the reseller, the situation becomes more complicated. It is important to conduct a comprehensive functional analysis to ascertain the correct transfer pricing method to be used in the benchmarking process.

DISTRIBUTION

3.19 Sales or distribution entities can take a variety of forms. At one end of the spectrum are commission agents and similar entities that act as an intermediary to the sale of the tangible goods between third parties and the relevant group entity. At the other end of the spectrum, there are fully-fledged sales companies that offer warranties to third parties, take full inventory risk and provide value added or ancillary services related to the goods sold.

3.20 Between these two extremes, there are wholesaler- or marketing-type operations that take title and sell the goods but provide little else in the way of risks borne (eg warranty, consignment arrangements with the affiliated supplier, foreign exchange, etc).

Commission agents

3.21 A typical commission agent acts as an intermediary in sales of goods between third parties and the group company that holds title to them. Agents do not take title to the goods themselves, and normally would not sign or execute the sales contract. Commission agents often employ knowledge of the local market in order to find new business and foster existing customer relationships.

3.22 Commissionaire arrangements have traditionally been used in various centralised business models, particularly where they help to comply with the tax regime of the group parent; for example, US parented groups may achieve compliance with the Sub F rules more easily with a commissionaire selling entity. Many tax authorities have challenged the basis of taxation of commissionaire arrangements, not least a number of European jurisdictions. Perhaps in response to this challenge, commissionaire structures are now a less common choice. BEPS Action 7 introduced important changes to the existing threshold for creating a permanent establishment to tax the trading profits of a company in an overseas country. In the future, depending on specific countries adoption of the MLI and various clauses contained within it, a typical commissionaire (or undisclosed agent, in common law countries) arrangement is highly likely to create a permanent establishment of its principal for tax purposes, even though it does not commit the principal to the customer of the commissionaire.

3.23 Assessing the arm's-length commission to be afforded to commission agents is often problematic. In some markets (eg in commodities markets) comparable uncontrolled prices (CUPs) may be available. In the absence of CUPs, a cost-plus based method can be employed. The rationale is that commission agents bear little risk, as they do not take title to the goods involved in the transactions that they broker. It is essential that the possibility of permanent establishments existing is properly assessed, especially if a cost-plus approach is to be used. A modest mark-up on costs may well reward the function of mediating sales without taking title, but if the 'agent' 'habitually concludes contracts, or habitually plays the principal role leading to the conclusion of contracts that are routinely concluded without material modification by the enterprise', then a slice of profit will be taxed in the territory of the agent and on the agent acting on behalf of the principal.

3.24   It is also possible to calculate commission rates 'bottom up' from observed operating margins. The technique is to identify a set of comparables and calculate from their financials a range of possible operating margins. From this, one calculates what commission (ie top line turnover) is required to give the MNE's agent an operating margin that falls within the range. The ratio of required commission to relevant sales is the commission rate. The benefit of this exercise is that it gives a credible price to be charged as sales are made. A target operating margin, by contrast, can by definition only be achieved with certainty by a year-end adjustment which is not consistent with commercial behaviour and can lead to problems in other areas, such as VAT and Customs declarations (if appropriate).

Commissionaires

3.25   In essence a commissionaire is a local distribution company that makes sales in its own name but is in fact an agent for an undisclosed principal. It is a concept of civil law, as opposed to common law. More difficulties arise on the legal front than in relation to transfer pricing, because of the differing ways in which commissionaires are regarded by common as opposed to civil law countries. In brief, under common law an undisclosed agent may in very specific circumstances be held to bind its principal to third-party customers even when making a contract in its own name. Hence, in common law countries a commissionaire or undisclosed agent has the possibility to create a permanent establishment of the principal in the territory of the commissionaire or undisclosed agent if those circumstances are met, whereas under civil law that is not the case. The UK commercial law upon which this concept, the doctrine of the undisclosed principal, is based is non-contentious, having been considered by the UK courts in several cases. For those seeking further information, the place to start is the judgment in *Rolls-Royce Power Engineering plc and another v Ricardo Consulting Engineers Ltd* [2003] EWHC 2871 (TCC). In terms of benchmarking, the approach for a commissionaire will typically be similar to that for a commission agent.

Stripped buy/sell distributor

3.26   A stripped buy/sell distributor is, as the name suggests, a buy/sell vehicle, which means that it takes title and acts as principal in its own business.

However, there are a range of functions and risks that a distributor may, or may not, tackle; as its name suggests, the stripped distributor carries out fewer functions and bears a lower level of risk than a fully-fledged distributor. The differences are likely to be that the stripped entity places orders only when a third party sale is made, so that title passes in a flash with an attendant beneficial impact on working capital requirements and inventory risk. Contractual arrangements might also be made to minimise credit risk and remove functions such as human resources, marketing, after-sales support, and so forth.

3.27   Once again the benchmarking methods of choice would be the resale price method or, as a fallback, transactional net margin method (TNMM). Although the stripped vehicle will be buying and selling and so enjoying a gross margin out of which to fund its operating and finance expenditures, its level of return might not be significantly greater than that afforded to a commissionaire, depending on how complete the risk and function strip had been. As discussed above in relation to contract and toll manufacturers, adjustments may be required for working capital requirements or to reflect any residual risks taken on to ensure close comparability with the sample of third-party resellers selected for benchmarking.

3.28   Although limited-risk distributors are widely used, in some territories they may still be challenged by tax authorities. However, the final deliverable from BEPS Action 7 does confirm the view, one to which most countries already subscribe, that a buy-sell arrangement does not create a permanent establishment. This is achieved by including in the commentary to the model tax treaty a clear statement of the policy intention that buy/sell distributors, including limited-risk distributors, should not create a permanent establishment of their principals, regardless of how long the distributor would hold title in the product sold.

WHOLESALERS AND MARKETERS

3.29   This type of distributor is discussed briefly at paragraph 2.37 of the OECD Guidelines, namely a reseller which does not add substantially to the value of the product resold (such enhancements might be in the form of further processing, packaging or in the creation and/or maintenance of an intangible asset, such as brands underpinned by a trademark and trade name). The OECD Guidelines do not refer to such distributors as stripped and indeed they might not be; they may well be marketing and reselling vehicles whose function and risk profile puts them somewhere between the stripped buy/sell and the fully fledged distributor. For convenience we will call these wholesalers and marketers.

3.30   Wholesalers and marketing-type entities take title to the goods for resale, carry out marketing functions and often handle transportation of the product. They typically bear market risk (ie risk on their operating expenses) but do not own intangibles related to the products sold. Again, the most typical benchmarking approach here is usually the resale price method, with the transactional net margin method as a fallback if needed.

3.31   As with all transactions, there is no clear hierarchy of methods in the OECD Guidelines and the most appropriate method should be used. That being said, there is still a preference towards transactional methods over profit based methods where both could be applied equally reliably, and within the transaction based methods there is a preference for the CUP method if data is available.

3.32   However, in general, external CUPs can rarely be found. Internal CUPs occur more frequently and can be available in some industries, such as software licensing, although they are still relatively rare in practice as multinationals often employ captive distributors to centralise the supply of their products to a particular geographic market.

3.33   As outlined above, in the absence of CUPs, the resale price method is usually the preferred method to apply to distributors. Economic theory suggests that a distributor would only accept a purchase price that would leave sufficient margin to cover its operating costs in delivering the product to third parties over the long term. However, if companies use the resale price method to set their inter-company prices, there is a risk that if the market price for their goods deteriorates, losses can be generated in the short term. Nevertheless, proper application of the resale price method ensures that both the manufacturer and the distributor in a transaction chain will share the downside (or upside) of any market fluctuation.

3.34   Where applying the resale price method accurately would be impossible, the transactional net margin method is typically used. In practice it is frequently impossible to apply the resale price method with sufficient accuracy, the prime reasons all revolving around non-uniformity of reporting conventions and paucity of publicly available detail. There are no established rules as to what should be reported in the cost of goods sold as opposed to operating expenditure, for example. Again, publicly available financial statements do not reveal enough about the size and constitution of sales forces, terms under which companies buy goods from suppliers, whether they own or lease warehouses, and so forth. The transactional net margin method can, therefore, legitimately be used in such circumstances to provide a respectable solution.

3.35   A further issue that arises is the variation between different types of distributor in their gross profit margin and operating expenditure profile. The interesting observable phenomenon is that almost any sample of rigorously chosen independent distributors will show an operating margin of something like 2% to 6%, no matter what their gross margin or their level of operating expenditure. It seems that the market knows what such operators deserve, and acts to keep gross margin and operating expenses in synch so that whether the reseller is moving high-margin low-volume goods or the reverse, it makes a bearable but modest return and no more.

3.36   Often, therefore, a sample of potentially comparable independent resellers will show homogeneity at operating margin level but not at gross margin. Can high gross margin resellers be used to benchmark low gross margin and vice versa? One simple answer is no, not at gross margin level but yes at operating margin level. So the transactional net margin method is often used to provide an answer here. This might be perceived to be somewhat rough and ready, but it is actually quite hard to find cost-effective alternative answers. Those that have been found, such as the Berry ratio (the ratio of gross profit to operating expenditure), tend to be variations on a single quite simple theme, namely that the market will in general keep distributors of all types in check so that operating margins are a constant with the variables being gross margin and operating expenditure.

Fully-fledged distributors

3.37   Fully-fledged distributors perform the same core activity as the sales entities described above but take on more risk. They typically perform value added activities such as post-sales services and support, and, importantly, can be expected to contribute to the creation and maintenance of intangible assets such as a brand underpinned by a trademark or trade name. In terms of valuing the distribution function, the analysis and issues discussed earlier in this section apply. However, the impact of risks assumed and extra functions performed should be considered in detail when seeking third party comparable data, as these factors have a considerable influence on profitability.

3.38   Sometimes there is no requirement to benchmark such entities because the other party to the transaction performs a simple function such as contract manufacture. The same is true where there are several other group companies involved but they all act as service providers to the reseller, such as providers of research and development, back office services, and the like. The problems come when there is more than one complex entity involved, for instance when the counterparty is a complex manufacturer.

3.39   Such structures are not susceptible to straightforward benchmarking of one side or the other, with the residual all going to one party. A useful approach here is to begin by splitting out all the functions performed by either party, and identifying those that in standard parlance would be considered 'routine'. These can be benchmarked and a 'routine' return assigned to them in the normal way. Best practice is to eliminate in this way as many functions and allocate as much profit (or loss) as possible. There then remain the 'complex' functions and risks, associated mainly with the creation and contribution of intangible property, to which can be assigned the residual profit or loss. How that residual might be allocated is covered in detail in Chapter 7; briefly, the relative contributions of the parties will be weighted or scored in some way, or some kind of observable third party behaviour will be found in the market place and an allocation derived from it. Each party will then have been assigned a mixture of routine and residual returns. The sum of all these should equal the total available to be split in the first place; whether it is sufficient simply to add up the amounts allocated to each party in these various exercises, or whether some further refinement is needed to take account of discounts or premiums to be applied because the value of the aggregates is different from the sum of the component parts, is a matter of judgement.

Chapter 4

Types of transaction: Intra-group services

4.1 Intra-group services are generally not the most exciting part of transfer pricing. In the transfer pricing world, for many multinationals, intra-group services can be the kind of thing that you just can't avoid – like attending the wedding celebrations of a cousin whom you hardly ever see and don't actually like very much. It is your duty, as a good family member, to make the effort.

4.2 The most common kind of intra-group services simply cover the kind of backroom activity that could (if you had chosen that option) have been outsourced to a third-party provider: things like IT, HR, accounting, legal, finance etc. which are neither integral to, nor drive the profits of, the business. Yet, even for this kind of service, there will often be audits from the tax authorities: just how many days did it take to install that new accounting system? Have the costs of preparing consolidated accounts really been excluded? There are a number of reasons for this. For a start, no specific industry knowledge is required of a tax inspector to examine intra-group services. Experience from around the world shows that a lot of tax authority audits start with intra-group services – such audits are often the way in which jurisdictions with new transfer pricing rules or new inspectors within mature regimes learn their trade. Apart from anything else, therefore, paying due attention to this issue will improve a multinational enterprise's (MNE's) chance of an audit being closed quickly and not extended into other more critical areas.

4.3 It is also true to say that some unlikely sounding claims are made in respect of payments for services, and tax authorities know this. How often has a multinational group acquired a stand-alone overseas company or group and immediately it transpires that the subsidiary group cannot get by without spending hundreds of thousands of pounds a year on management services? How likely is it that this is really the case?

4.4 There are three essentials to bear in mind when considering intra-group services:

- Is there a benefit to the recipient company? This is usually considered in terms of service provision versus shareholder costs.

- How should a charge be made? This breaks down into selecting the most appropriate OECD method to use and whether the charge should be 'direct' or 'indirect'.

- At cost or at a profit? This is most relevant when a cost-based charge (either direct or indirect) is made.

It is important to look at these three essentials from the viewpoint of the recipient as well as the provider. While it is true that many audits will be carried out by the provider's tax authority, it is equally true that many audits will be conducted into payments made for services by the recipient, with the attendant risks of a disallowed expense and double taxation. Each of these three essential factors will be discussed in the following sections of this chapter. At the close of the chapter, we also provide commentary on new guidance, recently released by the OECD, on an elective regime for determining a charging approach for low value-added services.

IS THERE A BENEFIT?

4.5   Under the arm's-length principle, the question of whether an intra-group service has been rendered depends on whether the activity provides economic or commercial value which enhances a company's commercial position (ie whether the recipient company has received economic benefit from the services). Paragraph 7.6 of the OECD Guidelines sets out the main test for deciding whether or not a service has been provided:

> '... whether an independent enterprise in comparable circumstances would have been willing to pay for the activity if performed for it by an independent enterprise or would have performed the activity in-house for itself. If the activity is not one for which the independent enterprise would have been willing to pay or perform for itself, the activity ordinarily should not be considered as an intra-group service under the arm's length principle.'

There are some activities for which a recharge should not be made. These include what the Guidelines call 'shareholder activity' and the costs of duplicate services.

4.6   Some attempt is made in paragraph 7.10 of the Guidelines to identify typical shareholder costs. These might include:

- meetings of shareholders of the parent;

- issues of shares in the parent;

- costs of the supervisory board;

- costs relating to the parent's reporting requirement, including consolidation of reports;

- costs of raising funds for its own new acquisitions (as opposed, for example, to fund acquisitions to be made by subsidiaries);

- compliance of the parent company with tax laws; and

- costs which are ancillary to the corporate governance of the MNE as a whole.

4.7   Some of these are open to challenge, if on no other grounds than lack of clarity. What, for example, does 'costs of the supervisory board' mean? It may be that some benefit to the operations of a subsidiary is derived from particular board meetings. Text towards the end of paragraph 7.10 of the Guidelines makes clear that the key point to consider is whether or not the activity is one which the recipient would have carried out for itself. Would it have paid for a third party to carry out the operation if there had been no in-house provider? If so, then a charge is warranted. Indeed, the category of 'strategic management' is often viewed as a shareholder activity and thus not recharged, especially if performed by the board. However, there is a strong argument to be made that, in the absence of parental control, the subsidiary in question would either have to develop itself, or source from elsewhere, strategic and market-related guidance. Thus a charge in some circumstances can be warranted.

4.8   Duplicate services are often suggested to have occurred by tax authorities. For example, a recharge might be made for a central human resources function in a group where subsidiaries also employ human resources personnel. It is common for tax authorities to suggest that there must have been an overlap of service provision, and often only a detailed analysis of functions performed by each party can deal appropriately with such an assertion.

4.9   Despite the ban on deducting duplicate costs, tax authorities should nonetheless accept that some temporary duplication may be valid (eg during a reorganisation; likewise, it is not duplication to seek a second opinion before making an important business decision).

4.10   The Guidelines make interesting comments on when an incidental benefit not amounting to a service is received. Paragraph 7.12 considers situations where services (eg restructuring or acquisitions) relate only to some group members, though incidentally provide benefits to others; such benefits may involve realising synergies or achieving economies of scale. The Guidelines consider that no payment is due in this instance, as an independent enterprise would not ordinarily be willing to pay for these benefits. This guidance is reinforced by the new text at paragraph 1.158 which clarifies that 'incidental' is meant in the context of group membership, and not the relative size of transaction. A distinction is also drawn between a benefit derived from specific activity and one attributable solely to being part of a larger concern ('passive association'). The new guidance at paragraph 1.167 is clear, for example, that enjoying a higher credit rating by reason of affiliation should not be independently rewarded, whereas enjoying a higher credit rating by reason of a parental guarantee might be. Similarly, in the context of intra-group services, basking in the reflected glory of marketing or PR campaigns by another group member (activity that is not intended to benefit other entities) should not be treated in the same way as if specific marketing expenditure had been laid out on campaigns for specified local markets.

4.11   The Guidelines also warn against double charging (eg raising a separate service fee when adequate recompense is already received). Examples might be charging for services, the value of which is already embodied in an existing licence fee, or perhaps charging for loan origination services already captured in the spread on a loan.

4.12   To balance the apparent concentration on what is not a service, paragraph 7.14 of the Guidelines also lists a number of activities that would normally amount to a service, because the recipient would have been willing to pay for them, or perform them itself. For example, these services may include:

- Debt factoring.

- Contract manufacturing.

- Administration of intellectual property.

- Legal services.

- Accountancy.

- Market research.

- Auditing.

- IT support.

- Raising finance.

- Central purchasing.

- Exchange risk management.

- Recruiting.

- Training.

These are all services which a subsidiary could readily make use of in conducting its own business. Paragraph 7.9 of the Guidelines also identifies 'detailed planning services for particular operations, emergency management, technical advice (trouble shooting) or, in some cases, assistance in day-to-day management'. When considering whether an inter-company service falls within one of the categories above, consideration should also be given to the new guidance on low value-added services (discussed at **4.31** onwards below).

4.13   Central purchasing, while mentioned as part of our list at **4.12** above, is also discussed in detail in paragraph 1.160 onwards of the Guidelines. The guidance is clear that any charge for procurement should be carefully linked to the value added by the entity containing the central procurement function, and not to broader group-wide benefits. The paragraphs essentially suggest that procurement benefits might be driven by two factors: (i) the skill of the procurement teams; and (ii) the bulk purchasing synergies that come with being part of a large group. The guidance proposes that recipients would be expected to pay for (i) above, but the benefit created by (ii) should in essence be shared throughout the group with respect to the relevant share of the factor which drives the purchasing synergies (ie share of group turnover). It is easy to misunderstand the thrust of this guidance, to suggest that in all cases a sizeable part, or indeed most, of the reward should flow to the parties that provide the volume, particularly as the example given is one where there is little 'value added' by the central procurement activity. In those specific circumstances the example is correct, but typically a central procurement team will play a much more substantial, and value-adding, role and so may itself be entitled to a sizeable part or, in certain circumstances, the bigger part of the reward. Value is typically added by a procurement team in securing a strategic goal in procurement, by minimising disruption to finished goods by securing flexible alternatives for supply, by increasing the confidence in quality control, by reducing instances of 'rogue buying' (employees failing to follow business guidelines on vendors), and in reducing the cost of buying. In truth, whilst additional volume might secure a price difference when moving from purchase of single units to tens or hundreds of units, the kind of volumes that are typically bought in many industrial settings are such that there is much less room for further discount by reason of price. Therefore, to direct reward to the party that actually adds value to the business, it is critical for transfer pricing practitioners to seek evidence concerning each element of the purchasing value chain, as directed by paragraph 1.160 onwards of the Guidelines.

HOW SHOULD A CHARGE BE MADE?

4.14   As with all transfer pricing, the key is that any charge made must satisfy the arm's-length principle. How a charge should be made can be broken down into two sub-parts: **What OECD method might be used to test, or indeed to set, prices? Must the charge be made directly, or are indirect methods permissible?** Each of these is discussed in turn in the sections which follow.

4.15   Further, according to paragraph 7.29 of the Guidelines, the arm's-length nature of the consideration has to be considered from the viewpoint of both provider and recipient.

What OECD method?

4.16   There is no clear hierarchy of methods for pricing services, following the adoption of the 'most appropriate method' principle (as set out in Chapter 2 of this book). However, there is still a preference towards transactional methods over profit-based methods and, within the transaction-based methods, there is a preference for the CUP method if data is available. In practice, three OECD methods are used in testing or setting the price of services: CUP, cost-plus, and TNMM (with cost-plus as the profit level indicator).

4.17   CUPs are relatively rare as there are generally no requirements for the public filing of service agreements. Unless the company also performs similar services for, or purchases similar services from, unrelated parties, it is difficult to use the CUP method to benchmark services. CUPs tend to pop up in specific areas such as debt factoring, where there is a wealth of information available (eg on the internet) and there is a reasonable degree of comparability between third-party and in-house infrastructures. This latter point on infrastructure is very important when proposing the use of, or examining, apparent CUPs in areas such as management consultancy and tax advice. While it is possible to obtain details of hourly or daily rates, these can vary wildly depending on the structure of the organisation providing services.

Factors such as layers of delegation and quality control, the need to obtain new business, training, downtime, risk of litigation, guaranteed utilisation and so forth are all potential differentiating factors to be taken into account. Nonetheless, it is sometimes the case that the recipient of a service could have gone out to his (or her) local market and obtained the service on more competitive terms, especially if the provider is in a higher cost location than the recipient. The new paragraphs 1.142 and 1.143 of the Guidelines stress the importance of looking at local market comparables. In such cases, if it is clear that the local substitute for the group service provider could have provided the right kind and quality of service, then the local CUP is indeed a CUP and will drive the price down. This can result in the group service provider making a loss on the transaction.

4.18　　Some form of cost-plus is much more commonly used, both to set and to test intra-group service pricing. Sometimes a recharge is made of direct costs only (plus a mark-up), for example in the case of a contract manufacturer. In this case, one would expect the recharge to be sufficient to cover indirect as well as direct costs, even though only the latter have been built into the pricing formula.

4.19　　In many cases, an 'all costs plus' or 'fully loaded costs' method, which is really a form of TNMM, is used. This would be particularly so in the case of small service providers where the distinction between direct and indirect costs is neither easy to make nor especially meaningful.

4.20　　Occasionally a high value-added service or management fee will be calculated as a percentage of turnover. This is not the same as allocating a finite pot of costs by reference to third-party turnover (see **4.23** onwards below). Here we are talking about paying out (say) 2% of sales, such that a bumper year means a higher management charge.

4.21　　There is somewhat oblique coverage of this in paragraphs 7.17 and 7.18 of the Guidelines. These deal with paying fixed amounts by way of 'retainers' for (say) legal fees or IT support – what the Guidelines describe as services provided 'on call'. The payment of a fixed percentage of turnover would seem to fall into this category. The sort of justification it would be wise to put together would include difficulty in calculating the charge any other way, an uneven call for the services in question from one year to the next and a direct link between the service and sales performance. Suppose a group member can call on marketing support, legal services, tax advice or computer support whenever, and to whatever extent, they want. One year they might be launching a new product line, be embroiled in litigation, suffer repeated computer problems threatening key supplier and customer records and be faced with a massive tax authority enquiry into a range of difficult technical areas. In the following two years they may require a rather lower level of support. It might well be commercially justified to commit a substantial amount of money each year just to keep such supplies on tap.

4.22　　Having said that, it is quite hard to get fixed percentages of turnover past the tax authorities if the amounts are substantial. Tax authorities will usually measure the amounts paid out over a number of years by reference to some other method (eg cost-plus). If the answer is sensible over time they may well concede, but if overall they appear to be losing, they will not. They will be particularly unimpressed if it appears that there is no need to have the services on standby at all either because the potential need for such services is remote, or other sources of supply are readily available. The other difficulty with the example given above is that not all the services have an obvious direct link with sales (eg tax advice). This weakens the methodology and increases the prospect of tax authority challenge.

Direct or indirect charging? Tracking time, use of allocation keys, identifying the cost base

4.23   A direct charge is one made for a particular service to a specific affiliate, whilst an indirect charge is one that is imputed through other means (such as where charges are allocated across all group entities on the basis of an appropriate metric – for example, share of group turnover). A direct charge has the advantage of providing greater transparency to the tax authorities, in that the time and costs associated with supplying the service will normally be straightforward to identify.

4.24   In practice, an indirect charge is normally associated with the use of a cost-based pricing method such as cost-plus. Direct charges can be calculated by reference to any of the methods discussed above.

4.25   Paragraph 7.22 of the Guidelines acknowledges that direct charging may well be too difficult in practice. In these circumstances it is fine to adopt some other method, necessarily involving a degree of estimation and approximation and using some apportionment or allocation method.

4.26   While it is very common to use allocation keys when there are multiple recipients of the same services provided by either a parent or a shared service centre, it is best practice to look systematically at the range of alternatives as part of a justification that can be shown to tax authorities. The various possibilities, in order of robustness, are:

- *Direct charge* – have individuals keep time sheets identifying activity, cost code and recipient. This can be very difficult where the personnel are very senior, work for many, or indeed all, group companies and it simply would not be possible to have them keep time sheets. Conversely, where the provider is a group shared service centre churning large volumes of for example, purchase invoices for numerous group companies, allocating time would be too burdensome to do properly and so it comes down to simple guesswork.

- *Direct charge* – have monthly or quarterly estimates of time spent by reference (as above) to activity, cost code and recipient. This can work with senior people and, if so, at this point you are, in effect, raising direct charges, albeit based on estimates. Again, however, the process becomes complex and possibly meaningless in a shared service centre or when there are so many recipients that the only cost-effective way of allocating time on a time sheet would be to guess.

- *Direct charge* – have an annual interview in which estimates of time are obtained. As above, this is likely to largely be based on guesswork.

- *Indirect charges* – identify all relevant costs and allocate them among all recipients using a sensible allocation key or keys. For example, IT support might be allocated by reference to number of computers in use; marketing support or the CEO's strategic advice by turnover; personnel services by headcount and so on. Many groups default to using turnover as the key by which to allocate all costs, because it is administratively simple to do so. Care is needed here, because it is not always the case that the need for and consumption of services is aligned with turnover. The key guides should be homogeneity and common sense. If all beneficiaries have a similar need for the service and consumption broadly tracks turnover then turnover is a good surrogate for a more specific allocation key. Paragraph 7.24 of the Guidelines accepts the allocation key method in principle, stating that 'the allocation method chosen must lead to a result that is consistent with what comparable independent enterprises would have been prepared to accept'.

However the charge is made, it is crucial to identify the cost base correctly. This involves collating all direct costs such as labour, plus the costs of any support staff as well as fixed overheads (eg establishment costs). Also included would be costs bought in from an outside supplier (see **4.28** below).

AT COST OR AT A PROFIT?

4.27   Paragraph 7.35 of the Guidelines states that an independent service provider would normally be looking to make a profit from the services it provides, rather than merely to cover its costs. There might be times, however, when services are provided at less than cost (eg when the market value of the service really is less than cost but the supplier agrees to provide the service to increase its profitability, perhaps by complementing its range of activities); or at cost for a limited period (eg as a support strategy for an affiliate starting up or otherwise trying to break into a market).

4.28   One special instance of passing on costs without a mark-up is mentioned in paragraph 7.36 of the Guidelines. It is not normally appropriate to mark up directly the cost of contracted-out or bought-in services, such as external consultancy services (ie 'pass through' costs). For example, a MNE hires an external consultant to undertake a worldwide project that benefits each member of a multinational group. In this situation, when reallocating the costs of the project to each member of the group, a mark-up should not be applied. The profit margin of the external consultant is already included in the cost and to mark-up the cost again is inconsistent with the arm's-length principle. A common follow-on query that often arises here is what constitutes a 'pass through cost'? Aren't there a lot of profit-carrying third party costs included in the cost base of the service provider? Rent, utilities, etc – essentially anything other than personnel costs may well include some other corporate profit element. To answer this question, we need to assess what comparable entities would do. Rent and utilities would almost always form part of the cost base of any comparable. Where a cost would normally form part of the cost base and be borne, it should be included; and where it would not, it should be excluded, and passed through.

4.29 Finally, in a concession to the US IRS's stated policy of only looking for a mark-up on the costs of providing integral services (ie services that are integral to the business of the provider or the recipient), paragraph 7.37 of the Guidelines states that on pragmatic cost–benefit grounds, charging cost only with no mark-up might be accepted where the effort of adding a mark-up is simply not worth it. This concession is unlikely to be made by tax authorities where the provision of a service is a principal activity of the service provider, where the profit element is relatively significant, or where it is possible to make a direct charge.

4.30 As a matter of practice, mark-ups are most often set by reference to the mark-up on costs achieved by independent providers of comparable services. There is an argument as to what comparables should be used: should they come from the territory of the provider or of the recipient? Normal practice is to draw comparables from the country where the service is performed. The philosophical support usually given for this is that although the recipient would most likely go to his (or her) local market if minded to look for alternative providers, the group service provider is likely to be best placed to offer the service and thus is not in real competition with any putative local providers. In other words, no viable alternative and therefore no CUPs can be found, so we should look to what margin the provider would expect to earn in its market.

LOW VALUE-ADDED SERVICES

4.31 The 2015 BEPS initiative introduced a new section to the current OECD Guidelines on services, to be found in Chapter VII. The purpose of the new section is to set out a frame whereby, should governments choose to adopt the OECD's mandated approach, groups can take a simplified approach to transfer pricing compliance, and thereby lower the associated administrative costs, for some types of services. This approach is 'elective' and only applies to a narrow category of services – those defined by the OECD as being 'low value'. However, it is likely to be grabbed with both hands by many multinationals that are drowning in documentation supporting routine IT charges and that are fed up with endless questions on the precise benefit provided by, for example, their central HR teams.

4.32 At the outset, the new section defines which services are in and which are out. The guidance is clear that, to be 'low value', a service needs to be supportive in nature, and not a key value driving part of the enterprise. Paragraph 7.49 of the Guidelines suggests that all of the following would likely be applicable:

- Accounting and auditing.

- Processing and management of accounts receivable and accounts payable.

- Human resources activities, such as staffing and recruitment, training and employee development, remuneration services, developing and monitoring of staff health procedures, and safety and environmental standards relating to employment matters.

- Information technology services, where they are not part of the principal activity of the group.

- Internal and external communications and public relations support (but excluding specific advertising or marketing activities, as well as development of underlying strategies).

- Legal services.

- Activities with regard to tax obligations.

- General services of an administrative or clerical nature.

The guidance also notes that, just because a service is not in the list above, it does not necessarily mean that it is 'high value'. As paragraph 7.48 makes clear, it is perfectly possible to have a low-value service which does not qualify for the low-value services regime!

4.33 In terms of what services are out, the guidance specifically carves out any activities which make use of intangibles or which manage significant risks. Paragraph 7.47 of the Guidelines sets out a list of services specifically prohibited for being a part of the regime, as follows:

- Services constituting the core business of the MNE group.

- Research and development services (including software development, unless falling within the scope of information technology services set out in the section above).

- Manufacturing and production services.

- Purchasing activities relating to raw materials or other materials that are used in the manufacturing or production process.

- Sales, marketing and distribution activities.

- Financial transactions.

- Extraction, exploration or processing of natural resources.

- Insurance and reinsurance.

- Services of corporate senior management (other than management supervision of services that qualify as low value-adding intra-group services under the core definition outlined above).

4.34 The deal is then set out in paragraph 7.52 onwards of the Guidelines. Multinationals must follow a fairly clearly set out process for recharging the low value-added costs (broadly in line with that set out above in this chapter). A mark-up of 5% is also specified as the rate to apply. In return for following this approach, multinationals receive a number of benefits. Firstly, the guidance suggests that tax authorities should refrain from challenging certain aspects, such as whether the local individual enterprise would have paid for such a service locally itself. It also states that they should not require multinationals to show precise benefits performed by the service-providing entity (the 'individual acts which give rise to the service charge'); rather, it suggests that a tax authority should be content with some general guidance that the function as a whole has added value.

Secondly, the Guidelines provide for a streamlined documentation process for complying multinationals. Paragraph 7.64 suggests that the following is all that is required:

- Descriptive data, including: a description of the categories of low value-adding intra-group services provided; the identity of the beneficiaries; the reasons justifying that each category of services constitute low value-adding intra-group services; the rationale for the provision of services; a description of the benefits or expected benefits; a description and justification of the selected allocation keys; and confirmation of the mark-up applied.

- Written contracts or agreements for the provision of services and any modifications to those contracts and agreements reflecting the agreement of the various members of the group to be bound by the allocation rules of this section.

- Documentation and calculations showing the determination of the cost pool, and of the mark-up applied thereon.

- Calculations showing the application of the specified allocation keys.

4.35 In principle, all countries that follow the OECD Guidelines should permit the election of the approach to low value-added services as described above, however, in practice there will be a need to check local legislation as to whether adopting this approach will conform with the specificities of local requirements (eg the explicit need for benchmarking). Some countries have now enacted specific local legislation in relation to the BEPS low value-added services approach, although the full extent to which tax authorities adopt this guidance either through legislation or by practical application remains to be seen. The suggestion put forward by virtue of the existence of this paper – that some services are simply not worth the effort in continually auditing or that tax authorities would be better off spending their resources elsewhere if companies have signed up to this simplified methodology – must be welcome news to many multinationals. Tax authorities are protected from the risk of significant loss of tax revenues by the ability to include a threshold – perhaps based on a percentage of revenues – beyond which they would not be obliged to accept the simplified approach and could impose a requirement for full functional analysis, comparability analysis, and apply the benefits test (see paragraph 7.63 of the Guidelines).

Chapter 5

Financing

INTRODUCTION

5.1   The transfer pricing of financing transactions is thought of by some transfer pricing practitioners to be a specialist subject somehow separate from the wider field of transfer pricing. That should not be the case, yet three key considerations add an air of mystery to the transfer pricing of financing transactions.

5.2   First, the transaction itself is more difficult for non-financial specialists to understand and the nature of the transaction itself can be open to challenge. There is no disputing whether or not a manufacturing operation has taken place or a sale of goods has been made; for financing transactions, transfer pricing legislation in many jurisdictions allows for the level of indebtedness and the form of the financing to be tested against third-party behaviours even before turning to the question of what interest rate should apply to the debt. Therefore questions of capital, debt, subordination, security, guarantees, and so on must be carefully addressed, to increase certainty that the transfer pricing analysis is undertaken on the 'accurately delineated' transaction.

5.3   Secondly, there is, in many jurisdictions, a multi-tiered approach to the acceptability of tax relief for the cost of finance, typically interest. Transfer pricing considerations deal with whether the quantum of debt is arm's length in comparison to equity funding (often referred to as 'thin capitalisation') and also the related question of whether the pricing of the debt is at arm's length. Whilst challenges to the quantum of debt in the borrowing jurisdiction are common – partly driven by the visibility of debt and interest deductions in tax computations and accounts – there can be less focus on the interest rate charged. There might also be broad limitations on the tax deductibility of interest outside of a jurisdiction's transfer pricing rules. For example, a number of jurisdictions have or have recently introduced a ceiling to allowable deduction based on fractions of 'earnings before interest, tax, depreciation and amortisation', these rules recently being promoted and tightened as an output of Action 4: 'Interest Deductions and Other Financial Payments' (Action 4) of the Base Erosion and Profit Shifting (BEPS) project undertaken by the OECD). Such rules are outside of the scope of the subject of this book.

5.4   Thirdly, when we finally consider the level of interest for a particular debt, this is an information-rich environment given the vast amounts of information on the pricing of financial transactions. Compared to the transfer pricing of goods, non-financial services and intangibles, the focus of transfer pricing work for interest rates is much more on managing and correctly analysing the transaction itself and all of the comparable transactions, rather than dealing with the question of whether comparables for interest rates exist at all.

5.5   These points all make for an interesting and challenging environment. Therefore, transfer pricing practitioners must take into account the full context of territories and tax laws involved and the nature of the transactions themselves. They must consider the arm's-length nature of the form of financing, the terms of the financing (term, security, etc), the amount of financing, and the interest rate applied. To make things even more interesting, the deductibility of interest is an area that has been of particular focus as part of the recent OECD developments in relation to BEPS, as we will detail further in this chapter.

WHAT ARE TYPICAL INTER-COMPANY FINANCING TRANSACTIONS?

5.6   Inter-company financing transactions arise for a variety of commercial reasons where a company requires access to funds. The reasons behind the financing transaction are important, not only in relation to non-transfer pricing tax laws but also because they can have a substantial impact on the types of transfer pricing questions that arise and the correct approach to dealing with them. It is important at this juncture to consider some of the reasons for inter-company financing which set the context for transfer pricing approaches that are discussed in the rest of this chapter.

5.7   At the highest level, funding provided to a group subsidiary for the acquisition of shares in a target company or significant business assets might take the form of debt or equity. Immediately this raises a question of the relative levels of debt compared to equity (ie the capitalisation of the subsidiary) once the funding is in place. This mix of equity and debt should be considered against evidence showing the ratio of debt and equity that would be appropriate for an independent entity to fund such an acquisition. This point has to be addressed before one can consider the appropriate rate of interest that should apply to the debt portion of the funding, as changes to the debt/equity ratio also have an impact on the interest rate that would be paid by an independent entity on the debt that remains; more debt leads to a lower credit rating and to higher interest rates because of the increased risk to the lender.

Acquisition scenarios might see external group borrowings at parent company level being pushed down to the subsidiary making the acquisition. In that case it is appropriate to consider the relationship between the terms for the external debt and those for the internal debt. For example, the parent company may give security to the external lender that often cannot be replicated by the subsidiary when it borrows from the parent. The funding profile of an enterprise which has recently undertaken a major acquisition may also differ quite substantially to the profile of a comparable enterprise in a 'steady state' position, with lenders potentially being willing to tolerate higher levels of debt in an acquisition scenario. One should also consider the question of what should happen to the fees incurred in arranging this external funding and in securing committed further funding, which are often substantial; should they (at arm's length) be passed on to the ultimate borrower?

5.8 For most multinational enterprises (MNEs), acquisition financing transactions are relatively infrequent and large scale. For that reason the transfer pricing issues are carefully considered. If they are not, and the level of and pricing of debt is not dealt with appropriately, it will typically prove to be difficult to fix the problems when they are unearthed later on.

5.9 The ongoing operations of subsidiaries also require funding. Unless the subsidiary finances itself entirely from its own operations, funding is likely to be partly by way of share capital and partly by way of debt (which may be borrowed from an affiliate). This might be the same group entity that injects share capital, but frequently it is not, as many MNEs have a specialist group finance company through which intra-group loans are provided. Again, the question of the arm's-length mix of equity and debt funding may arise, although less frequently and with less potential for significant error when compared to the large, one-off transactions considered in **5.7**. However, the MNE will still need to determine an arm's-length price for any loans. As these transactions are likely to occur much more frequently within groups it is advisable, as with other areas of transfer pricing, for the MNE to have a transfer pricing policy in place to address this kind of debt. This should combine the need to determine the arm's-length mix of equity and debt in the borrower, with the need to determine and apply the arm's-length nature of the interest rate. The additional catch here arises from the practicalities of determining the arm's-length nature of multiple loans in differing currencies and with differing terms to borrowers with different credit ratings. A number of jurisdictions have, in response to Action 4 of the OECD BEPS project, implemented or introduced detailed legislative proposals to implement restrictions on the deductibility of interest based on a percentage of earnings. Consequently, it is likely that intra-group lending will increase, compared to current levels, at the time of writing. The limitations to interest deduction based on legislation arising from Action 4 are relatively blunt and are not founded in any transfer pricing principle. Where external debt is concentrated into a parent, it is likely that not all of that cost will be deductible in computing taxable profits in a territory which has adopted such legislation. MNEs will therefore wish to push down debt to subsidiaries, proportionate to their ability to obtain a tax deduction, and ensure (if they can) that the full quantum of interest paid to external lenders is deductible for tax purposes. Of course, there are other – non-transfer pricing – rules that might restrict or prevent the push-down of debt that must be considered on a country-by-country basis.

5.10 On a short-term basis, subsidiaries within a group may either have surplus cash or require additional cash to fund day-to-day operations. From a treasury management perspective, it can be most efficient for the MNE to have a form of cash pool in place. This mechanism for managing short-term balances has its own subset of issues regarding transfer pricing which will be discussed shortly.

5.11   For both long- and medium-term debt, the transactions described above are based on the concept of a central borrowing of external debt, some part of which is pushed down to subsidiary members of the group. A MNE might take a different approach, where the subsidiary borrows funds directly from a third-party bank with the assistance of a guarantee from, usually, its parent or the ultimate group parent. This approach changes the transfer pricing question because the MNE group must now consider how much should be paid by the subsidiary in return for the guarantee. That question is addressed through a variety of quantitative and technical approaches (see below).

5.12   Aside from these most common forms of loan transactions a MNE has a variety of other options to finance its operations and manage its balance sheet. These include issuing bonds, factoring receivables, entering into finance leases or sale-and-lease-back transactions and hybrid debt instruments. Finally, there is a variety of transactions that tend to be grouped with, and considered to be, financing transactions. These are concerned with the management, or alleviation, of financial or operational risk (swaps, performance guarantees and derivatives all fall into this category). The more straightforward of these transactions are also considered in this chapter.

LOAN FINANCING: THIN CAPITALISATION

5.13   The choice of how best to structure the finances of a company between debt and equity is a topic that has exercised economists and financiers for as long as there have been capital markets. The answer cited by theoretical economists is based on the work of Modigliani and Miller, who concluded that a company should be indifferent to using either equity or loans because the price it has to pay for each will equalise the risk/cost–benefit equation. Academia has its place, but away from theoretical economics, here in the real world, this delightful concept does not generally hold true. There exists a substantial volume of finance literature that considers how much debt a company should take on to maintain the balance between risk and retention of profits in the business. Management teams at MNEs change their view on the ideal balance of debt and equity finance for a business over time; events change markets; and businesses experience different stresses and opportunities.

There is also the question of the tax shield on debt costs, which is a factor in theory (in calculating the post-tax cost of debt) as well as in practice.

5.14   The important issue for transfer pricing purposes in many countries is whether loan capital made available to domestic companies by overseas group members (often the parent or a specialist treasury company) should be accepted as a loan for which an interest charge will be tax deductible for the payer, and most likely will be taxable income of the lender, or re-characterised as equity ('thin capitalisation'), so that 'interest' is neither tax deductible nor (often) taxable income for the parties because the debt burden taken on is higher than would be found in an arm's-length situation. A secondary issue then arises regarding the impact of this re-characterisation from a wider viewpoint (ie will the excess interest simply be disallowed as a deduction or re-characterised as a dividend), which may have a different withholding tax treatment.

5.15 Transfer pricing specialists need to look at how much, if any, of the loan would have been made had the companies been independent, as well as at the rate of interest that independent parties would have agreed. Assessing the amount of debt typically involves a detailed analysis of the borrower's financial and business risk profile, as well as a consideration of the terms and financial metrics (eg debt to EBITDA ratio, interest cover ratio) of comparable lending transactions. This economic analysis will often be industry-specific, especially where there are industry norms that third party lenders would usually apply when appraising a potential investment. For example, there will likely be industry-specific factors to consider for borrowers operating in real estate, insurance or banking, inter alia. The approach to pricing debt is considered further at **5.33** onwards below.

5.16 The issue of how to determine the appropriate level of interest deductibility has been recognised by the OECD as a key item in its plan to address BEPS. For example, it notes that, in an inbound context, excessive interest deductions can reduce taxable profits in operating companies even in cases where the group as a whole has little or no external debt. As a result, Action 4 is one of 15 areas of focus of the OECD BEPS project, and this Action has provided countries with 'best practice' recommendations in respect of how to provide tax deductions for interest whilst tackling BEPS.

5.17 The current approach to thin capitalisation (ie before adopting legislation inspired by OECD BEPS Action 4) varies widely from country to country, and each country has the capability to change its rules, so any list in a book (including the one following next) can become outdated very quickly; always check the current local rule. Many emerging economies, such as India, do not focus on thin capitalisation at all, in some cases because existing regulatory restrictions on borrowing make thin capitalisation rules irrelevant. Other countries, such as Canada, have statutory safe harbours; if the MNE keeps within a prescribed debt-to-equity ratio of 1.5:1 then, for the most part, this will be accepted without challenge. Other countries, such as Germany (and, through the 'earnings stripping' rules, the US), apply a mandatory disallowance when interest exceeds a certain percentage of profits. Others, such as the UK, have no safe harbours and rely on the arm's-length principle to reach agreement on the appropriate level of borrowing.

5.18 The 2015 Final Report published by the OECD on Action 4 in October 2015 noted that an arm's-length test is resource and time-intensive for tax authorities and recommended that countries should not solely rely on this approach when testing levels of deductible interest. Broadly speaking, the OECD recommends that for most industries a fixed ratio rule should be applied which limits tax deductions for interest (and payments economically equivalent to interest) to somewhere between 10% and 30% of an entity's tax taxable earnings before interest, taxes, tax depreciation and tax amortisation (EBITDA). The OECD's report provides a recommended 'common approach', with various options around how such a rule could be applied in practice.

5.19   The OECD's comments to date on Action 4 have resulted in changes to some countries' domestic rules to limit interest deductions; for example, the UK has implemented restrictions of interest based on EBITDA, as has the EU as part of a broader package of reforms arising from the Anti-Tax Avoidance Directive. Other territories (eg Australia), however, have stated that they consider their approach to limitation of interest deduction to be sufficient, even if not fully compliant with the OECD's 'common approach' recommendation.

However, it is acknowledged that the arm's-length principle is still important in determining the amount and pricing of debt in the first instance, before application of any thin capitalisation, or fixed interest cover, ratio. A number of jurisdictions allow interest which is restricted under an Action 4-based interest limitation rule to be deducted in future where there is surplus 'interest capacity', whereas disallowances of interest under transfer pricing principles are generally permanent, and so it is still important to determine the allowable interest under the application of a jurisdiction's transfer pricing legislation.

INTEREST-FREE LOANS: IS A TRANSFER PRICING ADJUSTMENT ALWAYS NEEDED?

5.20   Sometimes, financing is made available by one entity to an overseas group member in the form of a loan without interest. The immediate reaction, looking at the tax affairs of the lender, might be to assert that arm's-length loans are not made interest free and thereby to look to a transfer pricing adjustment to increase the taxable income of the lender, with a corresponding reduction to the taxable income of the borrower, if local law or a double tax treaty allows that. That reaction would be too hasty; the analysis jumped straight to the level of interest, which is not the first step. As noted previously, it is important to first consider the form of the transaction before turning to consider the rate of interest, if any. When faced with interest-free debt, there are three possibilities that a transfer pricing specialist must consider: (1) the substance of the financing is actually equity, hence no interest is to be imputed (this is sometimes referred to as 'quasi equity'); (2) the substance of the financing is a loan, but the thin capitalisation position of the borrower means that no interest would be imputed; or (3) the form of the financing is a loan and the borrower is not thinly capitalised, so interest should be imputed at an arm's-length rate on the debt. Of course, the answer might also turn out to be a combination of (2) and (3). Only when analysis of this first question results in some of the value being ascribed to option (3) should one begin to consider what interest should be applied to that debt.

5.21   The first step is again to consider the form and substance of the transaction: debt or equity? The OECD's 1986 'Report on Thin Capitalisation' notes that the distinction between equity and debt is subtle and that 'hidden equity capitalisation' may occur. At this point, the report concentrates on 'hybrid financing' as a means to take 'unfair tax advantage' through obtaining an interest deduction where, in substance, the finance is of an equity nature but the technical point is equally valid for the lending entity. The point here is that the OECD recognises that it is not just issued share capital that can constitute the equity finance of a company. This point was specifically dealt with at paragraph 191 of its 1979 report 'Transfer Pricing and Multinational Enterprises' and was quoted in the 1986 report 'Thin Capitalisation':

> '191. It is generally recommended that a flexible approach should be adopted in which the special conditions of each individual case would be considered, although it is realised that such an approach would call for sufficient qualified staff to carry out a somewhat sophisticated analysis and could, if cases were numerous, thus raise problems for some tax administrations. A hard and fast debt – equity rule would, however, not be appropriate for the solution of problems raised by the determination of the nature of the financial transaction.'

5.22 The pivotal issue, then, is whether, based on the facts and circumstances at the time that the financing was put in place, the transaction has the character of 'debt' or the character of 'equity'. If the transaction has the character of equity then no payment for use of the funds ('interest') would be appropriate. As the character of the transaction does not change year to year, that position would continue whilst the terms of the financing, and hence its character, remained unchanged. Alternatively, if the transaction has the character of debt, then the question of what interest would be charged between a borrower and lender acting at arm's length must be considered (beginning with an assessment of what could be borrowed at arm's length).

5.23 In some countries it is recognised in business, law and accounting that capital might be made available to a local company in more than one form. Share capital is easily recognised as being 'capital' in nature but, for example, US law recognises 'informal capital contributions', as does the law and business practices of many other countries. Where local business practice allows capital to be made available without the issuing of shares then it is open to MNEs to fund the capital requirement of a local subsidiary using these methods. It may be that a multinational corporation (MNC) has taken that approach and the task for the transfer pricing specialist is to show that the loan should not carry an interest payment as it truly performs the function of capital. Regardless of whether the task is to support the non-payment of interest or to challenge the payment of interest, the first question to address when considering an interest-free loan is therefore whether that financing was intended by the parties to have the character of capital.

5.24 Evidence to test whether financing takes the character of equity or debt might take the following form, though this list is not exhaustive. Anything that speaks to this question is admissible as evidence, to be weighed along with all of the other evidence. The weight afforded to each item of evidence is unlikely to be equal; that is driven by the particular facts and circumstances of each case. This is consistent with the increase in emphasis by the OECD on the economic substance of a transaction over its legal form, considered in more detail at section **5.46.**

Is the loan repayable at a fixed date?

5.25   Equity is not generally 'returned' to the investor at a fixed future date. Therefore a fixed term for the financing is indicative of the nature being that of debt, and not equity.

Was an interest rate contemplated?

5.26   A transaction having the character of debt would intentionally contemplate the charging of simple interest as payment to the lender for use of funds. A transaction that has the character of equity would not contemplate the payment of simple interest, though it might contemplate the payment of something else. Regardless of the term used in the loan agreement to describe the payment, it is important to look at the characteristics of the payment to determine whether it is 'interest' or not. A payment made at the discretion of the borrower, out of the profits of the borrower, at a rate set by the borrower does not have the characteristics of interest at all; it looks much more like a distribution of profit. It does not matter here that the payment is not made; if the parties contemplated that 'interest' would arise on the loan then this is indicative that it has the character of debt even if circumstances – such as a shortage of cash – mean that no interest has actually been paid.

What is the accounting treatment?

5.27   This may be very important as it provides contemporaneous, audited evidence of the intention of the parties as to the character of any funding. The management of the borrowing entity has to decide how to present shareholder funding in its accounts: as either equity or debt. If it is shown in the balance sheet as subordinated debt grouped with capital and reserves and if this accords with local practice for reporting equity funding, this perhaps evidences that the nature of the funding was indeed equity. Sometimes the disclosures in the statutory accounts might include an explanation that the loan is interest free, unsecured, has no stipulated date for repayment and is subordinated. In this way shareholder equity funding is presented to anyone dealing with that entity as equity, not debt. Third parties have the right to rely upon this statement in their dealings with the entity and, as the statement is made with the knowledge of the shareholders, a local court may enforce this position against them also.

5.28   If the result of this exercise is that the financing has the character of equity then the simple legal form of the financing – as an interest-free loan – will not justify the characterisation of the funding as interest-bearing debt. As noted previously, if that is the character of the financing at the time it is first made then this continues unless and until something occurs that demonstrates, through the actions of the parties, that the character of the financing has changed.

5.29   If the result of this exercise is that the financing has the character of debt then the legal form of the loan, as being interest-free, does not prevent interest from being imputed. This is not a re-characterisation of the financing – it was always intended to be debt – but an exercise to ascertain the true nature of the transaction. As a debt transaction the question then remains whether the nil-rate of interest is at arm's length. Here we must next consider the concept of thin capitalisation.

5.30   The logic of thin capitalisation is conceptually straightforward:

- STEP 1: Determine that the character of the financing is debt, or equity. If debt, then

- STEP 2: Establish that no interest was charged in the tax period under review. If so, then

- STEP 3: Impute interest on this debt under transfer pricing rules only if that interest would have been paid by an unrelated party in comparable circumstances. Therefore, next

- STEP 4: Establish that there are boundaries beyond which it would not be acceptable to burden a business with additional debt (thin capitalisation). And finally

- STEP 5: Consider whether the MNE entity would be thinly capitalised if interest would have been charged on this debt. If not, then the character of that debt as between unrelated parties would have been interest-bearing debt and an arm's-length interest charge should be imputed in calculating the taxable profits of the lender, even though no interest was received. If the same exercise shows that the borrower would have been thinly capitalised had an interest-bearing loan been in place then, had interest been charged, that interest would not have been justified for transfer pricing purposes. Clearly, paying interest on this transaction would not be an arm's-length position, and transfer pricing concepts do not provide authority to move a taxpayer to a non-arm's-length position.

5.31   Unlike the quasi equity analysis, which is undertaken at the start of the financing and where the answer does not change unless and until the facts of the financing alter in a way that shows the character of the financing has changed, the thin capitalisation analysis for non-payment of interest must be reviewed in every tax year. If the facts of the business change so that it is no longer thinly capitalised in respect of all or part of the financing then interest should be imputed on the qualifying debt, leaving the borrower to claim under national law (which is not always possible) or a relevant treaty to match this treatment by reducing its taxable profits by the same amount.

5.32   Only if the above process has been carried out exhaustively to show that the financing does not have the character of equity and that the borrower is not thinly capitalised is it then appropriate to look to the amount of the interest rate that should be applied to the debt.

LOAN FINANCING: INTEREST RATES

5.33   Once the character of the financing has been established to be debt and not equity and the volume of that debt has been tested to ensure that it meets the arm's-length test, it is possible to move on to test the interest rate that should be applied to the remaining interest-bearing debt. It is important to approach the transfer pricing of financing transactions in this order as the amount of the debt can affect the interest rate to be applied; setting a rate for interest would be a worthless exercise if the next step is to alter the amount of debt on which interest is to be paid. Any downward interest rate adjustment for the borrower has the same effect as a re-characterisation of part of the principal as equity, in that a smaller amount of interest is deductible at arm's length. As a result, double taxation will arise unless the lender can claim under a double tax treaty to reduce the amount of its taxable interest income; if the adjustment is made under audit, interest and penalties may be due. It is therefore important to have in place a process to consider both the amount of any debt and the appropriate interest rates on all inter-company loans. This is not a straightforward issue: there is a natural tension between the arm's-length approach, which emphasises appropriate pricing on each and every loan and considers the position of individual legal entities, and the practicalities of treasury management, often done on a group basis.

5.34   Some MNE groups may wish to take an approach that is primarily practical (i.e. interest rates for intra-group borrowing are set at some standard level across all subsidiaries and by reference to the rate that the group as a whole can achieve in borrowing from third-party banks, or from the market via a bond issue). A typical approach might be to set a spread margin of, say, 100 basis points over the effective external borrowing rate and then use this consistently on all formal loans within the group.

5.35   In some cases, applying a small spread above an external borrowing rate may be appropriate at arm's length. For example, if a company is effectively only facilitating external funds for another company that has the same credit rating, it may be appropriate to only remunerate it with a small return. This small spread would provide compensation for the financing company's administrative activities and costs, but this approach would only be appropriate where the financing company is not taking on significant functions or risks (eg foreign exchange risk or maturity risk).

5.36   This approach of applying a uniform spread margin will, in most cases, underestimate the relative credit risk associated with the standalone subsidiary compared to the group as a whole. (A simple review of the yield curve for quoted bonds against credit rating shows that once the bond dips below 'investment grade' the interest yield rises sharply, even if the bond issuer still holds a very respectable credit rating and has routine access to the capital markets.) This practical approach treats all intra-group borrowers equally. In other words, a well-established sub-group in a major territory, which may well be able to support standalone borrowing at a low-interest coupon, would then be subject to the same borrowing terms as a smaller, more troubled subsidiary in a new or struggling market. Clearly, a different approach that takes account of the transaction being considered and applies a degree of variation on the interest rate applied, driven by the circumstances of the subsidiary doing the borrowing, is more accurate; documenting the approach taken and its consistency with the arm's-length approach is also important to mitigate the risk of penalties.

It should be noted however that a number of jurisdictions have indicated their view is that the starting point for pricing loan financing advanced to a subsidiary is that the group credit rating should apply. This raises the possibility of transfer pricing disputes between such jurisdictions and those that consider the cost of borrowing that a subsidiary would face at arm's length should be based on its standalone creditworthiness in the first instance.

5.37 As with thin capitalisation, where the level of debt considered to be acceptable by unrelated parties varies by industry, there are a number of examples where different interest rate pricing norms apply. One example of this (there are others) is real estate-backed financing. For transfer pricing purposes it is vital to take such factors into account and not to proceed blindly to calculate an interest rate that is more generally acceptable, but which has no relation to the circumstances of the transaction under consideration.

LOAN FINANCING: PRICING OF SHORT-TERM FUNDING AND CASH POOLING

5.38 Going back to the transaction types defined in **5.6–5.12** above, whilst it might be practical from a treasury perspective to determine individual interest rates in relation to one-off pieces of acquisition financing, this approach is not practical for all ongoing funding, not to mention short-term funding and cash pooling.

5.39 As an example, many MNEs benefit from centralising their cash management to ensure that short-term internal funds are used efficiently and so to reduce the need for external financing. Financing or treasury companies are often set up by MNEs to facilitate the efficient movement of such funds and the short-term nature of these means that, although the pricing of the intercompany balances needs to be assessed on an arm's-length basis, it also needs to be pragmatic for the treasury team to be able to implement. For example, if 50 companies borrow from a treasury company it would be very time-consuming to carry out a full credit rating and pricing analysis in respect of each borrower or loan. Therefore, an alternative approach to estimating the credit risk involved – based on quantitative and/or qualitative characteristics that are typically key in determining credit ratings in the industry under review – might be appropriate if it is sufficiently accurate that the arm's-length principle is not breached (see OECD Guidelines, Chapter III, section C which discusses the need to balance compliance costs against the risk of tax loss).

5.40 An additional consideration that needs to be taken into account in these situations is the overall return that the financing company makes for providing this service to the various group companies, which will be primarily derived from the interest rates applied to the company's deposits and borrowings. The remuneration of the financing company should be based on the risks and functions that it carries out, e.g. does the financing company take on foreign exchange risk on behalf of the companies that it lends to or borrows from? Similar questions have been included in the revised guidance (Actions 8–10) arising from the OECD BEPS project – substance, functionality, cash-box, etc – in considering the transfer pricing of intangibles, dealt with in Chapter 6.

5.41   Historically, in this situation some MNEs have taken the approach of basing interest rates on what they would have received, or paid, on short-term balances deposited or borrowed from a third party bank. This approach has been challenged by tax authorities (eg the Norwegian tax authorities in the 2010 ConocoPhillips case, and the Danish National Tax Tribunal issued its first decision on cash pooling arrangements and transfer pricing in 2014), as this does not take into account the relative credit rating of the companies concerned and the relative contributions of the pool participants when calculating the allocation of the overall benefit derived from the cash pool.

5.42   A key point in pricing cash pool arrangements is often whether there are structural balances in the cash pool; ie deposits or overdrafts which have been in place for a period which is greater than one year. For example, where a participant is consistently in a substantial net overdraft position, it may be appropriate to characterise this as a long-term loan, with the risks and corresponding arm's length return determined accordingly.

This reflects the OECD emphasis on economic substance over legal form in performing a transfer pricing review which was reiterated in Actions 8–10 of the OECD BEPS project. The complexity of cash pooling transactions can lead to tax risks arising from discrepancies between the legal documentation for such arrangements and how such arrangements take economic effect, and so care must be taken to ensure that the actual transaction is accurately delineated.

5.43   The pricing policy applied to cash pool transactions (ie credit rates on deposits and debit rats on overdrafts) often represents a subtle balancing act to ensure that the companies which are party to the arrangements are each participating on arm's length terms overall. The pricing policy applied must ensure that each participant company is at least as well off as a result of their involvement in the arrangement as they would have been on a stand-alone basis. Not only this, but there is a need to ensure that any benefits arising as a result of the operation of the cash pool have been allocated fairly across the group.

As well as the allocation of the cash pool benefit through the pricing of transactions with the pool, there are frequently a number of complementary transactions which take place alongside the operation of the pool, such as treasury support services. Consideration may need to be given as to whether such transactions should form part of the pricing policy applicable to the cash pooling arrangement, or whether it is more appropriate to price these as a separately delineated transaction.

It should be noted that it is common for guarantees or cross-guarantees to be in place in relation to intercompany cash pooling arrangements (particularly in relation to the involvement of any third-party banks). Guarantees are considered in further detail in section 5.55; however it is important to understand what guarantees are in place so as to determine where the risk in the financing arrangement ultimately lies.

5.44 The pricing of cash pooling and wider treasury arrangements can therefore be a complex area from a transfer pricing perspective and the appropriate approach to pricing these will depend on the specific facts of the financing arrangements that have been put in place. Again, documenting the transfer pricing approach undertaken and its compliance with the arm's-length principle is important. The importance of having supporting transfer pricing documentation was highlighted by the OECD's BEPS project as part of Action 13: Transfer Pricing Documentation and Country-by-Country Reporting. In this documentation-focused report, the OECD recommended that certain governments should introduce a transfer pricing 'master file' template which should include:

- A general description of how the group is financed, including important financing arrangements with unrelated lenders.

- The identification of any members of the MNE group that provide a central financing function for the group, including the country under whose laws the entity is organised and the place of effective management of such entities.

- A general description of the MNE's transfer pricing policies related to financing arrangements between associated enterprises.

Matters relating to the master file / local file approach to documentation are dealt with in Chapter 9.

LOAN FINANCING: PRACTICAL PRICING ISSUES

Loan pricing

5.45 In contrast to other transactions which are subject to transfer pricing analysis, there is a huge volume of data concerning transactions between third parties that is in the public domain. It can be accessed through financial data providers such as Bloomberg or base research can be carried out using quarterly published accounts of MNEs or market data feeds. Determining arm's-length interest rates typically relies on either suitably adjusted internal comparables or an external CUP approach. This second approach assesses the arm's-length interest rate on the debt by reference to comparable debt in the capital markets.

5.46 Actions 8–10 of the OECD BEPS project focused on the importance of economic substance over legal form in relation to financial transactions transfer pricing transactions. The commercial considerations applicable to loans between related parties (eg the information available to a lender as well as the likelihood that a lender would in practice recall a loan which is not being serviced) are qualitatively different to those which are applicable to loans advanced on third party terms.

There is therefore an increased probability that the economic reality of a financing arrangement between related parties will not be consistent with the position as documented. For example, it is common for trading balances between members of the same group to be left outstanding long term without interest being charged (and thereby take on the characteristics of a loan). Consequently, it is important to have a full understanding of the actual economic substance of the financing transactions within a group for the purposes of performing a transfer pricing analysis.

5.47   In relation to the point regarding economic substance over legal form, a key area of focus of Actions 8–10 in relation to financial transfer pricing was the use of "cash box" companies. A number of multinational enterprises have operated treasury entities to make loans to other members of the group. These entities are typically cash rich but may not have qualified treasury staff to be able to independently take decisions in relation to the management of risk associated with entering into financing transactions.

Revisions to the OECD transfer pricing guidance have made it clear that, where an enterprise does not have the functional capability or financial capacity to manage the risks associated with the provision of financing, then the enterprise which does in fact manage these risks should be entitled to the return from these financing activities, with the "cash box" company receiving a "risk free" return only.

It is therefore increasingly important for taxpayers to provide support for the ability of a group financing company to continue to be able to manage risk and to be entitled to more than a risk free return.

The point in relation to cash box companies and the right to a risk free return only is also considered in relation to intangibles in Chapter 6.

5.48   Revisions to OECD transfer pricing guidance have increased the focus on comparability of the tested transaction with unrelated-party data used to evidence the arm's-length nature of pricing. For debt, comparability hinges on equivalence (or the ability to make appropriate adjustments, where appropriate) across a number of key factors including:

- *Maturity*. An increased maturity of debt will ordinarily result in an increased cost of funds (although inverse yield curves do occur from time to time and it would be important to identify this by looking at the yield curve at the date of issue of the financing).

- *Currency*. Debt pricing data based on different currency denominated debt must be appropriately adjusted before being applied to the tested debt.

- *Creditworthiness of the borrower*. This can have a significant impact on the appropriate interest rate to apply.

- *Geographic location of the borrower*. The most creditworthy borrower in a given jurisdiction is typically the government, and so the interest rate paid by the government on sovereign debt issuances is usually (although not necessarily always) the "floor" on the interest rates which a local enterprise could expect to pay.

- *Interest payment profile*. The frequency of interest payments required under the agreement, and the option to roll up or payment in kind (PIK) interest should be taken into account when pricing the loan.

- *Seniority of the loan*. If the borrower has more than one loan and the loan being priced ranks behind more senior loans, the credit rating of the transaction under review may need to be notched down to reflect the increased risk of the lenders to the subordinated agreement. This may also be impacted by structural subordination; e.g. the difference in security arising from loans being issued by enterprises at different levels of a corporate group.

5.49   There are, of course, many other factors, such as the respective rights of the borrower and lender to repayment or prepayment, which may need to be taken into account in arriving at a correct arm's-length interest rate. Most of the factors influencing the interest rate are observable and, in the case of new debt, provide a straightforward way to optimise the interest rate. Internal comparables, where they are available, must be suitably adjusted to reflect differences in these factors.

5.50   In the absence of internal comparables, an external CUP approach is required. Creditworthiness, encapsulating a variety of issues such as the level of debt, seniority (ie the ranking of the debt in terms of security compared to other forms of debt or other finance) and the financial performance of the borrower, is the key issue and hence the focus of most analysis. Creditworthiness will be impacted by the amount of debt (ie the higher the leverage, generally the higher the interest rate), but this debt should be limited to the arm's-length amount when running the credit rating analysis; otherwise, the interest rate is likely to be overstated. Therefore, as already noted, even if a taxpayer's tax deductible debt burden is limited by a fixed ratio imposed by a local tax authority, the arm's-length amount of debt (even if it is higher) will continue to be an important factor for pricing the interest rate applied.

5.51   Proprietary models belonging to the main credit rating agencies are often used to estimate a borrower's credit rating for transfer pricing purposes. These are built, maintained and periodically evaluated against actual ratings, by a party whose sole concern is to accurately represent the creditworthiness of businesses and therefore the output from these models is strong evidence for transfer pricing purposes because third parties actually make lending decisions based on these outputs. It is reasoned that if the subsidiary has a standalone credit rating comparable to the credit rating of entities which can be observed raising finance in the market place, then this is arm's-length evidence that the subsidiary could also raise both the marginal amount of debt on a standalone basis and also the interest rate that would be applied to that debt. Naturally key financial data is required to use these models. Current cash flow, balance sheet health and profit and loss account figures are needed; these are considered along with a realistic demonstration of the borrower's current and future ability to repay the loan on commercial repayment terms.

5.52   The 'synthetic' credit rating that results from this analysis can then be compared with information on comparable borrowing taken from market information. There are some interesting considerations regarding which data to use. It may be possible to access information on loan transactions for a given credit rating but caution is advised. The interest rate on a loan from a bank to a customer cannot be considered in the absence of the fees which are being earned by the bank for providing the loan otherwise the true cost of the finance will be understated. Additionally, the loan is only one transaction as part of what is potentially a much wider relationship with a customer and accordingly, the pricing of such loans may not be entirely equivalent to that available to the hypothetical, completely standalone, transaction being considered on an arm's-length basis.

5.53   To avoid these difficulties information on bond yields is frequently used as the source of comparable data. A bond is a fully tradable instrument and the yield on a bond can be expected to fully reflect the market's pricing of risk for a given instrument, without any other considerations.

5.54   Potentially, there is a wide range of options available to price interest rates, such as offer letters from banks, indicating the amount they consider the company could borrow on a standalone basis and the applicable interest rate. Most tax authorities are less than impressed with this type of evidence, taking the view that unless the bank has carried out a full credit assessment and made a formal, unconditional offer of funding, any letter is purely indicative and has little persuasive power. It should be noted that the OECD has specifically commented on the use of bank offer letters and suggests that generally they should not be accepted, on the grounds that a bank offer letter does not constitute an *actual* transaction which can be used as a potential comparable.

LOAN FINANCING: GUARANTEE FEES

5.55   Having a credit rating that is adequate to support the size of an inter-company loan that a company is contemplating and securing an interest rate that the borrower would be happy to pay is not the only option. Sometimes a loan is advanced on terms that are made possible only by someone else (usually a parent company) providing a guarantee. A guarantee in this context is a legally binding promise by another party to pay to the lender interest and/or capital if the borrower should not be able to make the payment. A guarantee therefore improves the credit rating of the borrower in the financing transaction and secures a larger volume of debt and/or a more favourable rate of interest. Although guarantees can be arranged with unrelated parties for some transactions, by far the most common circumstance in which a guarantee is given relates to a group company, often a parent, providing a guarantee in relation to the borrowing of a subordinate group member. This gives rise to the transfer pricing question of how much the borrower should pay to the guarantor for taking on this risk and providing that service; after all, an unrelated party would want to be paid for any guarantee that it gives.

5.56 Where guarantees are given, they may affect the volume of debt that can be secured by an entity and also the interest rate applied to that debt. Aside from that, the arm's-length principle means that it's also necessary to consider whether a guarantee fee should be charged between the guarantor and the borrower. Intuitively, an arm's-length guarantee fee must relate to the advantage secured by the borrower by reason of having the guarantee (ie the volume and price of debt that could be secured without the guarantee compared to the volume and price actually secured with the benefit of having the guarantee, in most cases). In that case the fee that an unrelated party would be willing to pay can be only a fraction of this value-add (as no independent party would pay a sum equal to the entire advantage obtained, let alone more, to secure that advantage). Identifying and quantifying this advantage and then splitting that value between the borrower and the guarantor based on their respective bargaining positions is one way to assess the arm's-length nature of a guarantee fee.

5.57 There are other, more complex, approaches such as estimating the likely cost to the guarantor of providing the guarantee, using binomial analysis, or using CUP data from the credit default swap market. As will be apparent, all of these approaches are driven by an understanding of the basic credit rating of the borrower and guarantor and, as might be expected, credit rating analysis is a necessary step in the process.

5.58 As ever in transfer pricing, it is important to establish the actual benefit received by the borrower. Three scenarios are set out below.

The guarantee may have no value at all to the borrower and so no guarantee fee is due

5.59 Sometimes the credit rating of the borrower is sufficient to support the amount of debt and the interest rate that is applied to the debt without there being any guarantee at all. It is necessary to then ask 'why was a guarantee given?'. This concept is dealt with in more detail in **5.70** below.

The guarantee has not affected the volume of debt taken on but has reduced the interest rate applicable to that debt

5.60 This circumstance might be suggested where the credit rating of the borrower is sufficient to support the amount of the debt, but the interest rate applied by the lender is less than that which would have applied to the financing if it were based on that credit rating. The functional analysis now illustrates that value has been given to the borrower, in the form of a reduced interest rate. Comparison of the interest rate applicable to the borrower's circumstances on a standalone basis with that actually secured will provide a measure of the total benefit secured. As described in **5.56–5.57** above, the guarantee fee would be some part of that benefit based on the relative bargaining positions of the guarantor and the lender.

The guarantee might affect the volume of debt that the borrower could reasonably expect to take on

5.61 In this case there is also an impact on the interest rate that is applicable. In these circumstances it is difficult to apply the same approach as laid out above because there is no easy way to isolate the value provided to the borrower by reference to the financing arrangements it could have achieved without the guarantee; without the guarantee, perhaps it could not have achieved any financing at all. It is often appropriate, where the volume of debt is affected, to take a different approach to testing the arm's-length nature of the value given to the borrower. One approach is to consider the position of the guarantor, rather than the borrower. Looking to the guarantor, it has taken on no actual liability upon giving the guarantee, but it has taken on a potential liability contingent upon the default (or not) of the borrower. In that sense it might be possible to consider the cost of an alternative transaction – an insurance transaction – as a means to assessing the arm's-length nature of the guarantee payment. This is not re-characterisation of the transaction as an insurance payment (which is rejected in all but the most extreme circumstances, see Section D2 of the OECD's 'Transfer Pricing Guidelines for Multinational Enterprises and Tax Administrations') but a potentially acceptable methodology in accordance with the OECD Guidelines.

5.62 The provision of a guarantee can be viewed as an intra-group service. In this case, many of the principles set out in Chapter VII of the OECD Guidelines discussed earlier should be applied. The OECD Guidelines state at paragraph 7.13:

> '... an associated enterprise should not be considered to receive an intragroup service when it obtains incidental benefits attributable solely to its being part of a larger concern, and not to any specific activity being performed. For example, no service would be received where an associated enterprise by reason of its affiliation alone has a credit-rating higher than it would if it were not affiliated, but an intragroup service would usually exist where the higher credit-rating were due to a guarantee by another group member ... In this respect, passive association should be distinguished from active promotion of the MNE group's attributes ...'

The OECD Guidelines provide some insight into the definition of 'incidental benefits' in paragraph 1.158:

> '... the term incidental refers to benefits arising solely by virtue of group affiliation and in the absence of deliberate concerted actions or transactions leading to that benefit. The term incidental does not refer to the quantum of such benefits or suggest that such benefits must be small or relatively

insignificant. Consistent with this general view … when synergistic benefits or burdens of group membership arise purely as result of membership in an MNE group and without the deliberate concerted action of group members or the performance of any service or other function by group members, such synergistic benefits of group membership need not be separately compensated or specifically allocated among members of the MNE group.'

5.63   The diagrams below provide examples of how group affiliation can impact loan pricing in practice. Figure 5.1 assumes that a third party lender ('3P' in the diagram) would allocate a credit rating of 'A' to S, which is higher than S's standalone credit rating of 'Baa' due to the fact that its parent, P, is rated 'AAA'. P is not providing any formal guarantee to the third party lender and it should be assumed that it is also not carrying out any other concerted actions or transactions that have resulted in this 'A' rating. So, in line with the OECD Guidelines, the difference between S's 'Baa' standalone rating and the 'A' rating allocated by the lender should be considered an incidental benefit. This is on the basis that the benefit that S is receiving is purely as a result of S being a member of a more creditworthy group.

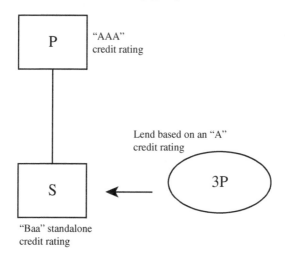

Figure 5.1

5.64   The same facts are reflected in Figure 5.2, with the exception that P is now providing a guarantee to the third party lender. The provision of the guarantee has increased the rating at which the third party was prepared to lend from 'A' to 'AAA'. This additional increase in credit rating is due to P's deliberate action in providing a guarantee, and so S should pay a guarantee fee to P. However, this guarantee fee should only be based on a proportion of the benefit provided by the guarantee itself (ie the difference between 'A' and 'AAA', and not between 'Baa' and 'A'). The difference between 'Baa' and 'A' is still an incidental benefit.

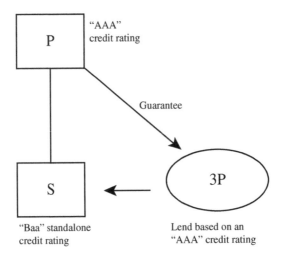

Figure 5.2

5.65   Passive association was discussed in the Canadian courts in the well-known case of *General Electric Capital Canada Inc v The Queen*, 2009 TCC 563. Here, a distinction was made between a purely 'standalone' rating and a 'status quo' rating, which allowed that a subsidiary would receive a certain degree of uplift in its credit rating without having to pay for this benefit. This removes from consideration contentions based on the idea that there could be some form of econometric argument to support the payment of a guarantee fee to a parent when no actual guarantee has been given.

5.66   Whether implicit support should be taken into account in applying the arm's-length principle was also considered in the Australian Federal Court's decision in *Chevron Australia Holdings Pty Ltd v Commissioner of Taxation (No 4)* [2015] FCA 1092 (and subsequently upheld in the appeal court in *Chevron Australia Holdings Pty v Commissioner of Taxation* [2017]). However, the judge accepted the taxpayer's submission that such implicit credit support had 'little, if any, impact on pricing by a lender in the real world'.

5.67   One of the key parts of the *Chevron* judgment, however, concerned the interpretation of 'consideration' in the Australian transfer pricing legislation – specifically, whether the consideration given by the company for the funds borrowed could be taken to encapsulate more than just the price (i.e. interest rate). The judgment found that adjustments can be made to other factors in the loan terms (such as security and financial covenants) which have an impact on the arm's-length pricing of the loan. The finding that such other factors would have been present in the *Chevron* case meant, in that case, that the interest rate applied was deemed excessive when considering what would have been agreed between independent parties dealing at arm's length.

5.68   Another key consideration from the *Chevron* 2017 appeal is that the court noted that, where the group sought to borrow from third parties, the parent company would typically provide a guarantee to keep the cost of debt as low as possible. It was determined that a policy of *not* providing a guarantee to the borrowing subsidiary was not a true 'arm's-length' position; had the subsidiary sought to obtain third party as opposed to related party financing then a guarantee would surely have been provided by the parent.

This has potential ramifications for groups which have a policy of providing guarantees to subsidiaries seeking to borrow from third parties; in the future, tax authorities may well seek to challenge why a parent would not provide a guarantee to a subsidiary which has taken on related party debt to allow it to achieve a lower cost of borrowing overall.

5.69   This could have important consequences for MNCs when analysing whether their internal financing arrangements are 'at arm's length'. It also re-emphasises the importance of finding appropriate comparables, bearing in mind all factors considered in arriving at the terms of a loan. It will also be interesting to see whether commentary is forthcoming on the question of whether the approach taken in *Chevron* – to effectively 're-write' some of the terms of the loans to arrive at an arm's-length pricing – is simply re-pricing (as found in that case) as distinguished from re-characterisation.

5.70   Another situation where the 'passive association versus active promotion' analysis could arguably apply is where the parent company has not bestowed any benefit flowing from the guarantee. Suppose, for example, that the guarantee has been given primarily because of inflexibility in the lending bank's administrative and security procedures. In such cases, one would seek to establish whether the bank would offer the financing on the same terms without the guarantee, albeit that it would 'prefer' to have a guarantee in place, or that a standalone entity with comparable circumstances (except being a member of a group) would have been offered the loan. It may therefore be possible that both the amount of debt and the interest rate are actually unaffected by the guarantee; the borrower has a credit rating that supports the volume and price of the debt without recourse to a guarantee. This is a fact pattern that does arise quite frequently. For example, under the terms of a syndicated loan facility to the group parent, guarantees are required from each major operating subsidiary. In practice, such guarantees would only be called in circumstances where the parent company has defaulted on the loan and the group may be in administration. The primary purpose of the guarantee is to allow the bank to rapidly gain control of the subsidiaries rather than any credit enhancement; and this is essentially an issue of timing.

5.71   Comfort letters are claimed by some as being economically similar in effect to guarantees, so it is argued that comfort letters should be treated as if they are guarantees. Comfort letters may provide value and, if they do, they should be reviewed and consideration should be given to whether a fee should be charged; but comfort letters and guarantees are very different, so the value that each might give is potentially very different. The legal status of a comfort letter and a guarantee is significantly different and this is the basis for a divergence in their respective potential values. Unlike a guarantee, the lender cannot proceed against the issuer of a comfort letter in the event of a default by the borrower. Hence the security created for the lender is significantly less for a comfort letter. That is not to say that a comfort letter does not provide any value to the borrower in all cases. Some third-party banks provide funding to subsidiaries on advantageous terms when they receive a comfort letter from parent companies and hence there is a value given to the borrower. The failure to take on the potential liability that would have arisen in a guarantee does not, however, leave the two situations as being comparable within the guidance in Chapter III of the OECD Guidelines. When one interested party (taxpayer or tax authority) does not accept that point, the pricing of comfort letters becomes contentious. A one-sided view might be that, if a comfort letter appears to be of equal benefit to the borrower, the fee due would be the same as that for a guarantee. The counter view is that transfer pricing should be considered from the viewpoint of both parties to the transaction and the provider of a comfort letter is less obliged than a guarantor. For that reason, the fee for a comfort letter should always be lower than that for a guarantee when both appear to generate the same value for the borrower in terms of debt volume and interest rate.

Non-financial guarantees and intra-group insurance

5.72 The guarantees discussed above are financial in nature. However, non-financial guarantees, and intra-group insurance in general, is an area attracting increasing focus. With respect to insurance there are three broad categories of transactions to consider:

(1) When a captive insurance company (a 'captive') provides insurance to a related party to insure the related party's risks.

(2) Where a captive provides insurance to a related party's customer to insure the customer's risks.

(3) When a group reinsurance company accepts another company's portfolio of insurance risks, which can be by way of a quota share treaty.

Intra-group insurance pricing is a complex area in which transfer pricing specialists often work side-by-side with actuaries in determining arm's-length premiums and ceding commissions. It will not be covered further in this book, although it is noted that the OECD published its view on a common approach for applying fixed-ratio interest deduction limitation rules to this industry in late 2016. In this report it was determined that the application of the recommendations of Action 4 would not be the best way to address the BEPS risk posed by banking and insurance companies. Work by the OECD to respond to the BEPS risk posed by such companies is ongoing.

5.73 Non-financial guarantees may also include performance guarantees to third-party customers. These can occur in any business, but they are more common in industries such as construction. There might also be environmental guarantees given to local governments in industries where there is a significant potential for environmental damage, such as natural resource exploration. The provision, or otherwise, of a non-financial guarantee can often be a commercial deal breaker, and any such guarantee should attract a payment from the benefiting party to the guarantor.

5.74   How to price this kind of guarantee? The most applicable method will vary depending on the facts. A detailed functional analysis should be performed to ensure that there is clear understanding of the benefit being enjoyed by the recipient and any cost/risk taken on by the guarantor. It might be possible to price the transaction using the CUP method if sufficient comparability to third-party data can be proven. If not, then it is often the case that the best available approach will be to adopt actuarial techniques, including consideration of the historical track record for such guarantees being called upon. Appropriate consideration needs to be given to the ability of parallel contracts, such as employment contracts, to induce behaviours similar to those encouraged by the guarantee.

OTHER TYPES OF FINANCING TRANSACTION

Finance leases

5.75   Finance leases are usually employed where the lessee wishes to acquire the rights of use and economic benefits of a specific asset over the greater part of its useful life. Importantly, a substantial proportion of the risks relating to ownership are borne by the lessee, even though title to the asset remains with the lessor.

5.76   Lease payments are spread over the life of the asset. The value of the payments is determined by the net present value of the asset over the course of its useful life. For the purposes of transfer pricing, these transactions fall under the arm's-length principle if the lease arrangement is between related parties. The arm's-length principle suggests that there should be a profit element attributable to the lease payments for the lessor. To achieve this, the net present value calculation should reflect an appropriate rate of return for the lessee.

5.77   The assessment of the arm's-length nature of the fees relating to finance leases usually begins with some form of credit rating analysis. This is unsurprising given that finance leasing is essentially a form of asset-backed lending. As with loan financing, discussed above, specialists have developed financial models to assist in the calculation of lease payments. These models are particularly useful where there is no active market in the asset in question. The leaders in the field model all the elements in lease pricing, including cash flows of the return on equity to the shareholders, interest, depreciation, terminal value and the value of tax allowances.

5.78   One new consideration is the transition to IFRS 16 which broadly requires most operating leases to be brought 'on balance sheet' as finance leases. The impact of this transition is likely to be an increase in the number of finance leases which an entity is required to recognise on its balance sheet, as well as an increase in the overall indebtedness of the enterprise. This in turn may impact on the creditworthiness of an enterprise and the applicable interest rate to its borrowings overall.

It is as yet unclear how increased financing costs under IFRS 16 will interact with local country taxation of leasing expenses and income, particularly as regards restrictions under BEPS Action 4. However, in the short to medium term there is likely to be complexity for enterprises in identifying the transactions (both intercompany and with third parties) which are required to be accounted for as finance leases under IFRS 16, as well as how an arm's length implicit finance cost is to be calculated.

DEBT FACTORING

5.79 Debt factoring is a common way for businesses to manage their cash flow and their borrowings. It involves the transfer of trade receivables to another party in return for the cash value of the accounts receivable, less a fee. Intra-group factoring can take place through a dedicated factoring company, but this need not be the case as any affiliate with cash can factor the debts of another. In practice, debt factoring can be a useful way of managing financial risks faced by the group in its trade.

5.80 Compliance with transfer pricing requirements in most jurisdictions means that the fee for this service should be proven to meet the arm's-length standard. Comparable research into independent companies providing factoring services and analysis of their returns from this activity provides one acceptable approach. Financial modelling that makes use of historical receivables data, funding and service costs and default risk is now common in the transfer pricing arena and it can be equally acceptable.

5.81 Proper differentiation needs to be made between with and without recourse factoring. Factoring with recourse is little more than secured lending; it follows that as with standard loan financing and indeed finance leasing the analysis is going to start from and be centred on credit rating, a key component being the degree of rating enhancement provided by the book of debts factored.

5.82 There is a much lower incidence of non-recourse factoring in the third-party market. The resultant shortage of comparable transactional data increases the need for transparent and rigorous analysis. To be clear on terminology: when debts are factored without recourse they are sold outright, usually along with the obligation to chase and collect (some groups have the factoring company subcontract collection back to the original creditor). Geography and/or the availability of personnel might make this necessary, though where availability of staff is the issue it should be recognised that this can throw the substance of the operation into doubt. The analysis here turns on the quality of the debtor book, likely recovery periods, a full understanding of historical bad debt rates, the likely costs of administration and collection and so forth.

5.83 Finally, just to complete the picture, it is possible to encounter limited-recourse factoring. As the title suggests, this is non-recourse factoring except when certain circumstances arise. Pricing for that transaction would need to follow both of the processes outlined above to ensure that the additional element of risk taken on by the factoring party is added to the simple return calculated for non-recourse factoring.

5.84   It is worth noting that debt factoring is frequently a comparatively expensive form of financing which is often entered into by companies which are undergoing cash flow difficulties. There may be a legitimate question as to whether a company which has sold its receivables to an in-house debt factoring company would have entered into this transaction with a third party.

It is important to consider whether the legal form of the factoring agreement actually represents the economic substance of the transaction taking place.

In *McKesson Canada Corporation v The Queen* (2013 TCC 404), factoring fees paid by McKesson Canada Corporation to a group debt factoring company were subject to a transfer pricing adjustment on the grounds that in economic reality McKesson Canada continued to perform significant functions in relation to the management of these receivables and there were therefore doubts that the factoring company could in fact assume and manage risk in relation to the factoring arrangement. There was also no objective business reason ie a shortage of capital as to why McKesson Canada Corporation had entered into the arrangement in the first place.

This is consistent with two broader points regarding transfer pricing of financial transactions; first, the conduct of the parties must be consistent with the legal form of the arrangement; and also there should be support for the purpose for which a financial transaction has been entered into.

Hybrid debt instruments

5.85   Despite the general decline in interest rates since 2008, cross-border lending within multinational group has remained a key part of many groups' financing strategy. Within this general area, one category of financing that is controversial, for obvious reasons, is the use of so-called hybrid debt instruments. These are funding instruments that are considered to be equity-like by the lender (often in one tax jurisdiction) but to be debt for the borrower (often in a different jurisdiction) according to the applicable national commercial and tax law. Hybrid debt instruments (such as profit participating loans) have a long history in commercial law in some countries, and there are certain sectors, notably banking, where they have been traditionally used for regulatory purposes.

5.86   For completeness, this section considers the pricing questions that arise in respect of such instruments, whilst noting that their use is becoming less common and tax authorities and international bodies such as the OECD are looking to restrict their application. A hybrid instrument may be regarded by law applicable to the lender as having an equity characteristic, and any payments to the lender are considered to be a dividend-like return and are taxed accordingly. The characterisation in the borrower is that of a loan, such that any payments made by the borrower are interest and tax deductible.

This has historically resulted in tax mismatches arising on payments from a jurisdiction which regards a payment under such an instrument as tax-deductible debt and a jurisdiction which regards a receipt under such an instrument as an equity return that is taxed at a reduce or even nil rate.

As part of Action 2 of the BEPS initiative, the OECD made a number of recommendations to target the use of hybrid instruments in tax planning scenarios. In a number of jurisdictions (principally the UK, EU and US as early implementers of anti-hybrid rules), deductions under such hybrid instruments may be significantly restricted or even disallowable entirely for tax purposes. Consequently, there are key tax considerations other than transfer pricing for an enterprise which is considering funding itself through the use of hybrid instruments.

5.87   By definition, the majority of hybrid debt instruments will have some equity characteristics. For example, a hybrid instrument could be some form of profit-participating loan. As such it will normally carry more risk than a simple loan. This may be reflected in greater volatility in the coupon, or greater risk of loss of capital if the borrower becomes insolvent. At arm's length, the lender should only be prepared to take on this additional risk in exchange for a higher return. Accordingly, for financing instruments of this type it is important to analyse these equity characteristics and then to adjust the basic interest coupon, set by use of a credit rating analysis, to reflect them. Again the capital markets provide a good source of comparable data.

5.88   Before leaving this topic it is worth noting that this type of pricing analysis is an important factor when considering whether there is a risk of re-characterisation, or of the application of specific country-based anti-avoidance legislation. These may be encountered in the lender's jurisdiction, or in that of the borrower, or both. Consider, for example, a hybrid instrument with significant equity characteristics but which carries an interest coupon appropriate to a simple loan and where the lender is not compensated for the additional risk. The lender's tax authority might reasonably be considered to have legitimate grounds for re-characterising the coupon as taxable interest as the actions of both the lender and borrower do not evidence the critical features of equity finance.

Other financial transactions and instruments

5.89   A similar analysis applies to other financial transactions and instruments used within a group context. In most cases a credit risk element will be implicit in the transaction. This is true whether it is a finance lease, a guarantee or any other transaction where time is a factor.

5.90   If the financing transaction is more complicated and there is no easy solution from a transfer pricing perspective, there is no defence to claim that these transactions cannot be priced. The markets in such instruments are normally relatively transparent and provide a source of good comparable data. Where the instrument used has a significant impact on the local taxes to be paid there is a similarly substantial sensitivity for both taxpayers and tax administrations to ensure that the pricing is supportable. Equally, the impact on the financing transaction as a whole can be severe if insufficient effort has been put into creating a detailed functional analysis for the financing; paying close attention to the guidance given in Chapter III of the OECD Guidelines is the best way to ensure that there is a solid foundation from which to price the transaction at arm's length.

OECD Discussion Draft

5.91   On 3 July 2018, the OECD released a non-consensus discussion draft entitled '*Base Erosion and Profit Shifting (BEPS) Public Discussion Draft – BEPS Actions 8-10 Financial Transactions*'. The discussion draft follows the work previously undertaken by the G20/OECD in relation to Actions 8-10 of the BEPS Action plan. It contains draft additional guidance for future inclusion within the OECD Guidelines, including a number of key points relating to cash pooling arrangements.

The topics which comprise the Discussion Draft are as follows:

- Guidance on the application of the principles contained within Section D.1 of Chapter I of the Transfer Pricing Guidelines to financial transactions, covering the application of the accurate delineation analysis of financial transactions.

- Specific issues relating to the pricing to be applied to a treasury function, including:

    - Treasury centre services;

    - Intra-group loans;

    - Passive association;

    - Cash Pooling; and

    - Hedging.

- Guarantees

- Captive insurance

Some of the key considerations from the discussion draft are summarised below.

5.92   Prior to pricing a transaction, it is necessary to accurately delineate the capital structure used to fund an entity within a multinational group (ie the mix of debt and equity).

In relation to other intragroup financing transactions, in order to accurately delineate a financial transaction it is necessary to identify all economically relevant characteristics. This includes an examination of the contractual terms of the transaction, but also a functional analysis is always necessary to identify the functions performed, assets used and the risks assumed by each party.

5.93   Cash pool leaders (physical and notional) generally perform no more than a co-ordination or agency function and so remuneration to the cash pool leader should be limited. In situations where accurate delineation of the actual transactions determines that additional functions are undertaken, the pricing of such transactions should reflect this in line with the appropriate guidance.

Members are expected to participate in cash pools on the basis of there being a benefit of doing so (e.g. preferential rates) and would not be expected to be party to the arrangements if there were not sufficient economic or commercially beneficial factors from doing so. The method for allocating the synergy benefit among the pool participants will depend on the specific facts and circumstance of each pool as to the extent to which this benefit

5.94   As part of cash pooling arrangements, cross-guarantees may be required. When considering whether a fee should be payable in respect of this support, it is appropriate to consider the particular facts and circumstances of the situation. There will be certain considerations common to most cash pooling arrangements, including that there will be there will be numerous members of the pool, there may be both borrowers and depositors in the pool, each pool member may have a different standalone credit rating, and the pooling agreement with the bank is likely to require full cross-guarantees and rights of set-off between all pool participants.

5.95   A distinction should be drawn between explicit guarantees and implicit guarantees. In general, the benefit of implicit support arises from passive association and not from the provision of a service for which a fee would be payable. Where a guarantee from a parent company permits a borrower to borrow a greater amount of debt than it could have obtained at arm's length, then it should be considered whether part of the guaranteed loan should in fact be characterised as an equity contribution from the parent.

5.96   The discussion draft touches on captive insurance arrangements, where a multinational group pools risks into a special purpose vehicle which provides insurance to the rest of the group. The key challenge from a transfer pricing perspective is in determining whether the transaction genuinely transfers risk from the insured to the insurer, and in pricing the premium paid to the captive insurer, given that direct comparables may not be available.

Chapter 6

Intangible property

INTRODUCTION

6.1 The Organisation for Economic Co-operation and Development (OECD) published updated OECD Transfer Pricing Guidelines for Multinational Enterprises and Tax Administrations (OECD Guidelines) on 10 July 2017, incorporating updated guidance with respect to the transfer pricing of intangibles (Chapter VI of the OECD Guidelines).

6.2 The revisions to Chapter VI of the OECD Guidelines contain some of the most significant changes adopted by the OECD under its Base Erosion and Profit Shifting (BEPS) mandate, consolidating special considerations for the transfer pricing of intangibles. Broadly speaking, the updated guidance seeks to provide additional guidance in the form of clarification and expansion on the core principles set out in the previous version (July 2010); it is for this reason that many tax authorities will apply aspects of the Guidance to existing transfer pricing audits into previous years. In each particular case you should consider whether it is correct to do so; the 2017 Guidelines are not 'precedent' for the interpretation of the arm's-length principle for periods before they were adopted and so one should test whether the concept being argued is supported from first principle.

6.3 Given the complexity of intangibles as a subject matter, the July 2017 Chapter VI provides a significant increase in the volume of guidance on dealing with intangible-related issues, where previously little of value was given. To put this into perspective, the July 2017 Chapter VI includes 212 paragraphs and 29 examples for dealing with the transfer pricing of intangibles, where previously a mere 39 paragraphs and 3 examples were thought to suffice.

6.4 The core principles of the old Chapter VI can be summarised as follows:

- the Chapter applied to both marketing and industrial intangibles;

- multinational enterprises (MNEs) needed to be careful that they identified true intangible property;

- the arm's-length principle (Chapters I, II and III) applied equally to intangible property;

- it was important to understand, and to take into account, the value of the intangible property to both licensee and licensor; and

- the contribution of both parties to the creation or value of the intangible property had to be taken into account in setting the arm's-length pricing to be agreed between them.

6.5 There is nothing in the old guidance against which we can complain, but it was not actually helpful in any practical way. The new material builds on the core principles identified by the old Chapter VI, and highlights the following:

- the alignment of intangibles-related returns with the important functions related to the development, enhancement, maintenance, protection and exploitation of intangibles (more-easily defined as the 'DEMPE' functions);

- the importance of the parties' actual conduct in determining the ownership of intangibles, including the principle that the legal ownership of an intangible asset, by itself, does not confer any right ultimately to retain the intangibles-related return (a complicated idea, to which we will return following these bullet points);

- the risk-associated return, including the concept that economic control must be exercised over the risks, and the financial capacity that must be available in order to assume the risks; and

- the consideration and appropriate remuneration of the contributions of each party to the transaction (ie a two-sided analysis).

Transfer pricing practitioners should keep in mind here that, rather confusingly, the July 2017 OECD Guidelines often consider where the 'return' associated with the intangible should rest, as distinct from who has the right to receive income from an intangible. This may be a hang-over from earlier rounds of debate at the OECD, when the focus of some meetings that the author attended had been on redirecting the income stream arising from an intangible away from the 'owner' towards another party who had contributed, in some meaningful way, to the creation of value in the intangible. Thankfully, that approach was recognised to be incorrect; intangibles that are 'owned and controlled' (in the terms of the revised guidance) are a form of monopoly created by the law of the country concerned, and the payment for use is, in reality, a payment for the non-exercise of that monopoly right. Looked at in this way (ie taking a commercial view, as we are intended to do under the arm's-length standard), it is clear that the income arising from an intangible will always flow to the party that has the right to enforce the monopoly – by which we mean the 'legal owner'. Therefore, others who have contributed in a meaningful way to the creation value in the intangible must get their reward from the legal owner by way of a separate, secondary transaction. What the Guidance now tells us is that, *net of that additional secondary transaction*, the rewards that can be reaped from an intangible will mainly rest with those who have contributed in a meaningful way to value in the development, enhancement, maintenance, protection or exploitation of the intangible.

6.6   In response to past criticisms that the brevity of the old Chapter VI meant that it did not address, or provide guidance for addressing, the more fundamental areas of the transfer pricing of intangibles, the new material includes a six-step framework for analysing intangible transactions between associated enterprises, and provides detailed guidance on the application of each step.

6.7   The six-step framework for analysing transactions involving intangibles, as prescribed by the new material, is as follows:

(i)   Identification of intangibles – what intangibles are being used or transferred, and by whom are the associated DEMPE functions undertaken?

(ii)   Contractual arrangements – determining legal ownership of intangibles, based on the terms and conditions of legal arrangements.

(iii) Identification and analysis of the parties performing functions, using assets and managing risks related to the DEMPE functions of the intangibles.

(iv)   Confirmation of the consistency between the contractual arrangements and the associated risks undertaken by the parties.

(v)   Delineation of the controlled transaction to determine the DEMPE functions performed in relation to the intangibles.

(vi)   Determination of the arm's-length prices for these transactions consistent with each party's contributions of functions performed, assets used and risks assumed.

Each of these six steps is discussed in the remainder of this chapter.

6.8   In the experience of the author, problems with the transfer pricing of intangibles are frequently traced to a lack of understanding of what intangibles are, who owns them and how third parties transact in them. Even the most difficult intangibles transfer pricing case can be dramatically simplified when the two sides reach agreement on whether or not an intangible exists, who owns it and what rights (ie what monopoly) that intangible actually gives to the owner. The six-step framework quite rightly places this first; it would be a waste of time for everyone involved to argue about contributions to the development of simple know-how when simple know-how (ie falling short of a 'business secret') is unprotectable under the law of the country concerned, and therefore it is not 'owned and controlled' and hence is not an intangible to be charged separately for the purposes of the revised Chapter VI. The existence of an intangible, precisely what it is and who the legal owner is (who exercises the monopoly rights) can be ascertained by following the arm's-length standard (ie looking at how unrelated parties deal with each other). The same is true when dealing with every element of the six-step framework outlined above. After all, it would be a breach of the arm's-length standard if, for example, we found that related parties outsourced a function and we ascribed value to a related party without first checking whether that same function is sometimes outsourced between unconnected parties and, if so, at what price.

Definition

6.9   In order to determine an appropriate method for the transfer pricing of intangibles, it is essential to have a clear understanding of what an intangible actually is. The cornerstone of the arm's-length standard is reference to the actual transactions that occur between unrelated parties acting at arms' length; and the view from business and the profession was that guidance in Chapter VI must not seek to create rights or obligations between related parties that do not exist in commercial transactions.

6.10   The new Chapter VI material refers to an intangible as being 'something which is not a physical asset or a financial asset and which is capable of being owned or controlled for use in commercial activities, and whose use or transfer would be compensated had it occurred in a transaction between independent parties in comparable circumstances'. In this way, an 'intangible' for the purposes of Chapter VI is defined in a way that, in commercial terms, we would call 'intangible property', due to the inclusion of 'owned and controlled' in this definition.

For the purposes of establishing the above, it is suggested that the definition should incorporate tests of being separately identifiable, tradable (or transferable) and valuable, hereafter referred to as the 'three-part test', the logic of which is based in commercial law and practice (and hence affecting transactions between unconnected parties) and which is set out below.

6.11   The commercial origin of this three-part test can be seen in the UK commercial law case of *National Provincial Bank Limited v Ainsworth* [1965] AC 1175 at 1247G–1248A where, in the context of the acquisition of interests in land enforceable against third parties, Lord Wilberforce said:

> 'Before a right or an interest can be admitted into the category of property, or of a right affecting property, it must be definable, identifiable by third parties, capable in its nature of assumption by third parties, and have some degree of permanence or stability.'

This sets out four questions, but the first two can be pulled together into a 'separately identifiable' test, as was applied by Morritt LJ in the UK Court of Appeal case of *Re Celtic Extraction* [1999] EWCA Civ 1835.

6.12   The UK case *Re Celtic Extraction* concerned the legal nature of waste management licences. One question before the court was whether a licence to dump material (that licence, in effect, being an exemption from a statutory prohibition or fine for the act of dumping) was intangible property. A three-part test was simply stated as follows:

- first, there must be a statutory framework conferring an entitlement on the holder of the property in question to an exemption from a fine;

- secondly, the property in question must be transferable under a statutory framework; and

- thirdly, the property in question must have value.

6.13   The 2012 decision in the UK case of *Armstrong DLW GmbH v Winnington Network Ltd* [2012] EWHC 10 (Ch) concerns the 'theft' of European Union Allowances (EUAs), each of which constitutes a permission to emit a metric tonne of carbon dioxide under the EU Emission Trading Scheme, and which can be traded. It was necessary for the court to consider the nature of the property in EUAs; if they were not capable of being 'owned and controlled' then there was no property, and hence no 'theft' case to answer. The High Court applied the above three-part test to decide that they are intangible property at common law. First, the statutory framework governing EUAs – Directive 2003/87/EC which established the EU ETS – confers an entitlement on the holder of the EUA to exemption from a fine, similar to the right in *Celtic*. Secondly, the exemption is transferable, pursuant to the statutory framework. Thirdly, the EUA has value, as it can be used to avoid paying a fine and there is an active market for the trading of EUAs. Following the principles of this case for transfer pricing purposes, a transaction in EUAs is therefore a transaction in intangible property and should be priced as such.

6.14   As a practical matter, both *Celtic* and *Armstrong* concerned licences issued by a statutory authority, hence the remark in the first test to an exemption from a fine. As is pointed out in the judgment in *Celtic*, the word 'property' is not a term of art, but instead takes its meaning from its context (see *Nokes v Doncaster Amalgamated Collieries Ltd* [1940] AC 1014, 1051 and *Kirby v Thorn EMI plc* [1988] 2 All ER 947, 953). In the case of a UK patent, for example, the first test (separately identifiable) is satisfied by the grant of a patent under the *Copyright, Designs and Patents Act 1988*.

6.15   So it is to the commercial law and practice surrounding intangible property that we must first turn to understand whether something is actually intangible property at all. This is critical to any transfer pricing analysis as, until we have clearly identified an item of intangible property, it is not possible to discern the owner of that IP, how valuable it is, or whether any other party made a significant contribution to its development, enhancement, maintenance, protection or exploitation. The revised Chapter VI states clearly that something that is not owned or controlled would be a matter to take into account in comparability analysis, but not a matter to be considered separately.

6.16   It is relatively straightforward to see how intangibles such as patents or copyright can be identified as intangible property as they have their own legal framework, but what about areas such as know-how or so-called 'soft intangibles', which arise from more nebulous concepts such as 'workforce in place', 'strong performance history' and 'available capacity'? We will consider the identification of such know-how and 'soft intangibles' in the paragraphs that follow (see **6.30** et seq.).

Case Law

6.17   Since the OECD initiated the BEPS project, there has been a significant global rise in transfer pricing controversy, leading to increasing numbers of transfer pricing court cases. Most case law only affects the interpretation of domestic tax law. However, when considering transfer pricing the tax implications for the country on the other side of a transaction are equally important. Transfer pricing laws are therefore based on an international Treaty (the OECD Model Tax Treaty and TP Guidelines) so that the interpretation of transfer pricing law in a country should follow the rules and practice that has developed to interpret international law. Case law from one country that considers the application of principles in the Guidelines or which looks at commercial valuation questions can therefore be cited as support (but not as precedent) in disputes in other countries. As such, examples from case law will be used to illustrate and support many points set out in this chapter.

6.18   Following that rather lengthy introduction and discussion of the definition of an intangible, we now turn to the fundamental questions relevant to the transfer pricing of intangibles and will follow the six-step framework identified as part of the BEPS project and referred to above.

IDENTIFYING INTANGIBLES

6.19   Difficulties can arise in a transfer pricing analysis as a result of definitions of the term 'intangible' that are either too narrow or too broad. It is therefore important to identify and understand the nature of the intangible assets being utilised when determining the arm's-length arrangements for transactions involving intangibles.

Consideration should be given as to whether an intangible asset exists or whether an intangible has been used or transferred. In particular, intangibles that are important to consider for transfer pricing purposes are not always recognised as intangible assets for accounting purposes (and are thus not always visible on a company's financial statements).

6.20   Let us explore further the guidance which is available from commercial law and practice on the identification of intangibles and the rights which they bestow. In the commercial world, there are different classifications of intangibles. 'Intangible' simply means 'without tangible form' and so encompasses both assets and liabilities. For example, risk is an intangible which every business has in some measure and must manage, but it is not an asset; it is a potential liability. The concept of 'business risk' is considered in Chapter IX (Business Reorganisation) of the current OECD Guidelines and it is not considered as an intangible within Chapter VI. However, in the commercial world, this still leaves three different categories of intangibles, as set out in Figure 6.1 below: intellectual capital, intangible assets, and intellectual property.

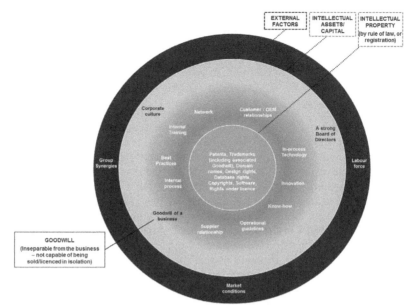

EXTERNAL FACTORS | INTELLECTUAL ASSETS/ CAPITAL | INTELLECTUAL PROPERTY (by rule of law, or registration)

Corporate culture

Network

Customer / OEM relationships

Internal Training

A strong Board of Directors

Group Synergies

Best Practices

In-process Technology

Labour force

Internal process

Patents, Trademarks (including associated Goodwill), Domain names, Design rights, Database rights, Copyrights, Software, Rights under licence

Innovation

Goodwill of a business

Know-how

Supplier relationship

Operational guidelines

GOODWILL
(Inseparable from the business – not capable of being sold/licenced in isolation)

Market conditions

Note: This is not an exhaustive list of all types of intangibles, but provides examples of different types of intangibles. Different laws apply to different jurisdictions and local laws should be considered when undertaking an intangibles project.

Figure 6.1 – Categories of intangibles

Intellectual capital

6.21 For many businesses, intellectual capital is a value-adding part of their whole. However, it is not something that is routinely converted to cash in the marketplace by direct sale or licensing as it cannot be 'owned and controlled'. It is a factor in considering the profitability of the activity which the business undertakes and therefore it is often part of the comparability analysis one would undertake to ensure that a fair reward was earned for the activity. Sometimes, where it can be demonstrated that no reward has been given elsewhere, a 'network fee' is proposed, but these are by no means common in third-party situations. One common third-party fee, where intellectual capital makes a contribution to the size of the charge, is a 'franchise fee'. Intellectual capital does not 'belong' to the current holder and, in a third-party situation, it would not be possible to prevent others from copying ideas or to prevent employees who leave the business from adopting a similar infra-structure design, or taking their tacit knowledge with them. For these reasons it usually does not, in third-party situations, give rise to an 'exit charge' when it leaves the business.

6.22 This is not to say that intellectual capital is not valuable to a business – clearly it is. In many cases, intellectual capital may not give rise to a separate transaction in its own right (such as a copyright royalty) but it should be taken into account in considering the quantum of any charge (such as a franchise fee or a service charge) in which that intellectual capital adds value. Intellectual capital is therefore a comparability matter to identify in a functional analysis and to consider in terms of comparability with proposed third-party pricing evidence.

Intangible assets

6.23   Intangible assets are a stronger form of intangible than intangible capital, but the rights of the holder may still fall short of proprietary ownership and it takes conscious effort to ensure that protection is afforded to intangible assets; if that effort is made then an intangible asset might become intangible property. Intangible assets that fall short of 'property' can be used to improve the value of services or goods and, if they are, they should be taken into account in the comparability analysis when setting arm's-length prices in the same way that has been described for intellectual capital. Frequently, the value created by intangible assets is the driving force behind brand value or goodwill and, in that form, it can be a source of value in that other intangible property licensed to third parties. As a brand licence will generally include a trademark or name (protectable either as a registered trademark or name or through 'passing off'), intangible assets would not be the source of the payment, but they are important in setting the quantification of the fee.

6.24   As with intellectual capital, it can be difficult to prevent others from copying ideas or to prevent employees leaving the business from adopting internal processes or using know how. However, internal processes, for example, can become protectable if they are written down as they can then benefit from copyright. Copyright (which is an intellectual property, as it is a monopoly owned and controlled) then becomes the source of the payment whilst the quality of the intangible asset, the internal process, drives the value of the fee charged.

6.25   Intangible assets may not, in third-party situations, create an 'exit charge' when lost unless effort has been taken to protect them. However, unlike intellectual capital, intangible assets can be and are frequently sold, and therefore if intangible assets are not lost but 'sold' there is likely to be a charge to consider.

Goodwill

6.26   Depending on the context, the term 'goodwill' can refer to a number of different concepts, and this creates a risk of misunderstanding developing between a tax authority and a taxpayer. In theoretical terms, the goodwill of a business is a form of intellectual capital. However, it is important to note that in many countries 'goodwill' is inseparable from the business as a whole; it is therefore not capable of being sold or licensed in isolation and so cannot be treated as a separately identifiable intangible asset. In some countries, the goodwill of a business can be sold together with the registered trademark;

but again, goodwill is a contributor to the value of the property that is sold, which is the trademark.

6.27   Typically, when the phrase 'goodwill' is used in general conversation by accountants, it refers to the difference between the aggregate value of an operating business and the total value of its separately identifiable tangible and intangible assets. Goodwill can therefore be regarded as a quantifiable asset, albeit only when calculated as part of a company's value when sold. Under this concept, the value of goodwill is calculated as the value equal to a business' ongoing concern value, calculated as the value of the assembled assets of an operating business over and above the sum of the separate values of the individual assets. To that extent is it a 'balancing figure'.

In other cases, goodwill sometimes refers to a representation of the future economic benefits associated with business assets that are not themselves individually identified and separately recognised. Alternatively, it might refer to the expectation of future trade from existing customers.

6.28   For transfer pricing purposes, it is important to consider the inherent value of commercial goodwill when determining the arm's-length price for a transaction between associated enterprises involving an intangible asset that derives part of its value from goodwill.

Following the logic above, it is clear that a monetarily significant part of the compensation for the transfer or licensing of intangible assets between independent enterprises may represent compensation for a business' goodwill, recognised under one of the definitions set out above. As a result, when determining the arm's-length price for similar transactions occurring between associated enterprises, such value of goodwill should be taken into account.

6.29   The absence of a single precise definition of goodwill makes it essential for taxpayers and tax administrations to describe specifically relevant intangibles in connection with a transfer pricing analysis, and not to simply use the phrase 'goodwill' without specificity. Only then can we consider whether independent enterprises would provide compensation for such intangibles in comparable circumstances.

The requirement for goodwill and ongoing concern value to be taken into account in pricing transactions does not suggest that the value of goodwill derived for accounting and business valuation purposes is an appropriate measure of the price that would be paid for the transfer or licensing of intangible assets by independent parties. As a general rule, whilst accounting and business valuation measures of goodwill and ongoing concern value may provide a starting point for a transfer pricing analysis, they do not correspond to the arm's-length price.

Know-how

6.30   Whilst there are many things that a business knows how to do, most of these things are also known by their competitors. A bricklayer knows how to build a straight, neat wall of good strength and appearance, and this allows an employer, ABC, to charge customers for construction services. Though this know-how is valuable (in fact, ABC would not be able to earn income without it), it is not intellectual property because the knowledge of how to lay bricks cannot be protected by ABC. For 'know-how' to be intellectual property, it must be protectable. This can only be achieved if the know-how is a trade secret.

6.31 Trade secrets are a particular type of confidential information which, in the possession of departing employees, can still be protected by their former employer. There is no limit to the information that can become a trade secret, but there is no automatic protection. A business must take steps, contractually and practically, to protect the information that it believes should be secret, so that courts will recognise and uphold that protection.

6.32 The United States has a codified approach set out in the *Uniform Trade Secrets Act*. In the US, a trade secret is information that derives independent economic value by virtue of its being secret and is the subject of reasonable efforts by the business to keep it secret. Most US States follow this approach. The Seventh Circuit Court of Appeals considered the steps that a business must take to make mere know-how into a trade secret. See *Fail-Safe LLC v A. O. Smith Corporation* No 11-1354 (29 March 2012), which held that, where information was shared without any contractual restriction being in force to require that information to be kept secret, and it was not used for any purpose other than that for which the information was disclosed, there is no trade secret to protect.

6.33 Trade secrets or 'secret know-how' are, therefore, protectable by law and can qualify under the three-part test set out in **6.10** above. One difficulty that might be highlighted by transfer pricing professionals, particularly those attempting to create guidelines that can be applied to both sides of a transaction and thereby spanning (at least) two jurisdictions, is that IP law varies from country to country. Perhaps minor differences might be tolerated, as we tolerate minor differences in local transfer pricing legislation because the core principle remains, but the difference in protection offered to trade secrets is anything but minor. In fact, the variation in levels of protection offered to trade secrets can be significant. In Member States of the EU, the Trade Secrets Directive[1] aims to standardise the national laws against the unlawful acquisition, disclosure and use of trade secrets.

6.34 This significant variation in the level of protection is the actual landscape that unrelated parties operate within and so, as the arm's-length principle requires that we assess related-party transactions against third-party transactions for transfer pricing purposes, this does not so much pose a problem for transfer pricing professionals and the drafting of effective

---

1   Directive (EU) 2016/943 on the protection of undisclosed know-how and business information (trade secrets) against their unlawful acquisition, use and disclosure.

Guidelines, as provide a real and pre-existing framework within which to test group transactions.

6.35   When know-how falls short of being a trade secret, it is not intellectual property as it fails the three-part test set out in **6.13** above. That does not mean that know-how has no value; rather, it is merely a factor to be identified in the functional analysis and taken into account in considering the comparability of third-party data used to test the transfer price applied.

Soft intangibles

6.36   Let us now apply these tests to so-called 'soft intangibles' by considering a hypothetical example based around a business restructuring of the type contemplated by Chapter IX.

6.37   Suppose that a US-parented global multinational finds that its European business is under-performing. Compared to competitors, management realises that their business is slow to make and implement decisions, has duplicated functions throughout Europe and has an inefficient logistical chain. Management decides that, to retain market position, it has to reorganise and adopt a new, more efficient, business model. It selects a 'European principal' business model, using 'commissionaire' sales entities in several countries as the preferred business model option.

6.38   The US parent effects this change by serving notice on existing subsidiaries, giving notice of its intention to terminate existing licences to use its intellectual property, principally the right to sell in their own name using the parent's brand and trademark. In the United Kingdom, the sales business has historically been operated by a fully-fledged distributor, UK Co, which is offered and accepts the opportunity to become a sales agent.

6.39   The multinational then conducts a transfer pricing benchmarking exercise to assess the level of commission to be paid to UK Co going forward. It identifies potentially comparable companies who are independent, operate in the same economic environment and industry, have almost no stock on their balance sheets (or describe themselves as commissionaires or commission agents) and act in a sales capacity. Let us assume that this shows the range of arm's-length commission to be 0.5% to 2% of sales, and 1.5% sales commission is selected as the appropriate target rate.

6.40   In considering whether the pricing is at arm's length, a question may be raised as to whether or not the transaction would have happened in this form in a third-party situation or, alternatively, whether the commission payable should be significantly higher as the 'soft intangibles' (such as business experience, workforce in place or customer relationships that have been generated by UK Co from its historical operations) would give it the ability to earn a higher reward than is being offered.

6.41   The starting point for this analysis must be that those 'soft intangibles' do not give rise to any intangible property as they are not owned, controlled and transferable separately from another asset such as the business. This is not to say that these intangibles are not adding value to the business, which they clearly are; but that rather than being intangible property in their own right, these are factors to be taken into account in establishing comparability with third-party transactional data which will be used to evidence the arm's-length nature of the price charged.

6.42 Unless very narrowly drawn, the comparables identified in the transfer pricing study would include independent enterprises which are engaged in selling activities similar to UK Co, employing similar assets and bearing similar risks. We must then ask ourselves whether we can assume that, as the comparable companies continue in business, they are both competent at their function and that they have themselves created soft intangibles, such as 'successful customer relationships' or a trained and skilled 'workforce in place'. There is also no reason to assume (without evidence to the contrary) that the customers of the comparable companies will find it any easier to replace them in business than in UK Co's case. If any soft intangibles identified in UK Co are also present in the entities selected as comparables in the transfer pricing study then its impact, if it affects pricing at all, would also affect the prices and the profits of the comparable companies. To this end, the value of the soft intangibles is therefore represented in the arm's-length range already identified. These concepts cannot be used to support an argument that UK Co's reward should fall outside the range of third-party comparables. On an arm's-length analysis, no adjustment to pricing is required at all (see para 3.60 of the OECD Guidelines).

6.43 The impact of soft intangibles on the relative bargaining position of UK Co and the European principal company is also a question often raised, but this has a rather double-edged application. Whilst it could be argued that UK Co, having a large sales team with customer relationships and detailed knowledge of the group's products, would enable it to command a return at the higher end of the range, it also faces a potential exposure to the costs of an unemployed workforce (or to the costs of redundancy payments, should they choose to reduce the workforce) if they do not agree to adopt the new business model. Having the volume of work available is likely to make the European principal more attractive as a business partner than any other option realistically available, and it enhances their bargaining power to drive to a lower price. In many cases a full analysis of soft intangibles shows that the bargaining position remains balanced between the enterprises. Analysis of relative 'bargaining position' or 'options realistically available' which look at only one side of factors breach the arm's-length principle, as expressed in the OECD Guidelines.

6.44 What is the impact of these soft intangibles in third-party transactions? Many businesses have strong customer relationships and those customers would face barriers (time, cost, inconvenience, loss of historical knowledge, etc) to swap to other suppliers but, even so, these soft intangibles do not generally allow charges that are disproportionate to the market rate. In practice, an alternative supplier wishing to break into a relationship may choose to reduce its price to a level which compensates the customer for the inconvenience of changing supplier, which should, in a free market, eliminate the value of that barrier to change. In the commercial world, where such barriers persist because the size or scale makes it difficult for a new competitor to offer lower prices, or there may be some collusion between a small number of suppliers to maintain higher prices, the competition authorities may well intervene but such analysis would be very unusual in a transfer pricing context.

6.45   As noted above, the competition authorities have acted to reduce artificial or unfair barriers in a number of industries, for example customer switching in the (non-investment) banking sector in the UK:[2]

'... we recently required Bacs Payment Schemes Ltd (Bacs) to make changes to the Current Account Switching Service (CASS), a free service that is meant to makes switching your current account significantly easier. These include extending the redirection service, designed to give further assurance to customers that all their payments will be switched from their old account to their new one – and so overcome a key concern about moving banks.' and mobile phones:[3]

'Ofcom Chief Executive, Ed Richards, said: "Ensuring consumers can switch between communications providers by removing unnecessary barriers is one of Ofcom's priorities for 2010/11. Being able to switch quickly and easily between mobile providers is an important part of healthy and effective competition".'

6.46   In conclusion, soft intangibles are not a form of intangible property as they are not 'owned and controlled' but they can be matters that impact pricing and so they should be considered in any functional analysis. The impact of soft intangibles must be considered from the viewpoint of both parties to a transaction, based on substantiated data, and must include the consequential cost of any postulated position. It will rarely be the case that soft intangibles add significant bargaining power to either entity in a transaction in isolation and, in many cases, any soft intangibles that do add value will also be present in the comparable companies identified in the transfer pricing analysis such that the arm's-length range is unaffected. Most importantly of all, for any soft intangibles identified and contended to have significant value for one entity, reference must be made to the impact seen in transactions between third parties. Failure to observe this last step means that the fundamental basis of the arm's-length principle is not observed and this becomes a kind of formulary apportionment. (Paragraph 1.32 of the OECD Guidelines reaffirms support for the arm's-length principle and rejects the theoretical approach represented by formulary apportionment.)

---

2   See https://competitionandmarkets.blog.gov.uk/2018/02/06/retail-banking-remedies/.
3   https://www.ofcom.org.uk/about-ofcom/latest/media/media-releases/2010/quicker-mobile-number-transfers-for-consumers 3.

Intellectual property

6.47   This is a form of intangible asset in which ownership can be asserted and exclusive rights recognised. It is relatively easy to understand how this works for some intangibles, such as patents (where, for example, the right to apply for a patent in the UK is set out in Part I of the *Patents Act 1977* (as amended)), but it is also possible to create intellectual property if you maintain ownership through contract and activity; keeping something secret and sharing it only through a contract which imposes an obligation of secrecy, for example, as the law of confidentiality protects trade secrets. To keep trade secrets protected, you must establish that the information is confidential and ensure that anyone to whom it is disclosed signs a confidentiality agreement. If they then disclose the information, this is a breach of confidence and you can take legal action against them. It is for this reason that 'know-how' makes an appearance both as an intangible asset (unprotectable) and as intellectual property (protectable). Intellectual property carries the enforceable right to prevent others from adopting or using that same idea or even, in the example of patents, from creating independently and exploiting the same idea. In other words, intellectual property is a monopoly over the commercialisation of an idea that is enforced by intellectual property law.

6.48   Intellectual property can be turned to cash by use in the business to create goods or services, in which case it should be taken into account in a comparability analysis when setting arm's-length prices, but it can also be sold or licensed directly. In the latter case, the source of the income is the non-exercise of the right to prevent others from using the intellectual property and so, in third-party transactions, it is the owner of the intellectual property who receives the payment. As intellectual property can generally be transferred only by contract, it will often, although not always, create an 'exit charge'.

6.49   To continue to use the arm's-length principle as the basis of transfer pricing it is crucial to compare related-party transactions with transactions as they would occur when third parties deal with each other. If not, then the arm's-length principle is abandoned and that is no less true for the transfer pricing of intangibles. As noted above, current guidelines indicate that the methods used for setting an arm's-length price for goods and services will be of equal application for the purposes of intangibles transfer pricing. However, there are substantive differences in how intangibles add value to a business, compared to goods or services, and these must be taken into account in assessing which methodology is most likely to best approximate the arm's-length return and how the methodology should be applied. Here it is worth pausing to consider that transfer pricing is not the only reason why it would be necessary to postulate a hypothetical fair price between a willing owner and a willing licensee. Many licence-of-right cases and, in some countries, a proportion of intellectual property infringement claims require an answer to precisely that question. This provides judicial comment on the applicability of different methods and guidance as to how they should be applied.

6.50   There are many useful principles to be observed in commercial cases; here are a selection of some UK decisions:

- There is a preference for using third-party licences (comparable uncontrolled price / transaction) where evidence is available. See *Lilizas Marine UK Ltd v Norseman Gibb Ltd* [2000]: 'One approach, usually the preferred one if circumstances permit it, is to look at comparable licences which have already been agreed.'

- There are court decisions where the same intellectual property is licensed to third parties and those where the potential comparable is a licence to use different IP but those differences can be identified and adjusted for (adjusted comparable). See *Cabot Safety Corp's Patent* [1992] RPC 39.

- Third-party licences which are neither comparable nor capable of being adjusted sufficiently to usefully inform the value of the licence under consideration should be ignored. See *Roger Bance and R Bance & Co Ltd's Licence of Right (Copyright) Application* [1996] RPC 667: the going rate of 5% to 7% being advanced to the court from other licences which were not comparable, the comptroller commented: 'The problem that we face at this point is that while it would be very convenient simply to accept the 5% to 7% figure as a suitable starting point we have no clear justification for accepting that such should be the case'.

- Splitting the profit available to the licensee between the licensee and the licensor is acceptable in the absence of comparable third-party licences (a profit split methodology). See *Gerber Garment Technology Inc v Lectra Systems Limited* [1995] RPC 383.

- Reference to other intellectual property licences in the same industry (comparables search strategy) without identifying comparability differences and adjusting for them amounts to the application of an industry average. This is not acceptable if there is any other way of finding the fair royalty. See *General Tyre & Rubber Co v Firestone Tyre & Rubber Co Ltd* [1976] RPC 197 (HL): 'Before a "going rate" of royalty can be taken as the basis on which an infringer should be held liable, it must be shown that the circumstances in which the going rate was paid are the same, or at least comparable, with those in which the patentee and the infringer are assumed to strike their bargain'.

We can also add here a decision of the US Court of Appeal for the 8th Circuit; *USCA 17-1866 US v Medtronic*, in which a supporting Opinion from Judge Shepherd uses references to the decision of the Court in third-party commercial disputes as a basis to criticise the transfer pricing analysis applied by the Court below. This demonstrates that in assessing whether intangible property exists, who owns and controls that monopoly, how far the monopoly extends, and how to assess the price of a license commercial third-party cases provide significant weight in assessing the arm's-length position.

6.51 The statements above are all completely in line with the old and the new Chapter VI of the OECD Guidelines. They also draw attention to the fact that more elaborate approaches to intangibles transfer pricing, such as the market capitalisation method, may not be well received before a court trying a commercial case because of the potential error inherent in the methodology, and similarly this methodology does not carry sufficient reliability for transfer pricing either. The theory of this method is that the number of shares issued multiplied by the share price plus the value of long-term debt provides the value of the business. Subtracting the fair value of tangible assets will give the value of intangibles. There are significant practical problems to advancing this methodology as 'evidence' before a court. Can we prove that the share price accurately reflects the value of the business or are there other market factors driving price? Have we proved that we identified all of the factors driving value? Have we demonstrated the reliability of the valuation of other assets? Have we identified all intangibles – what, for example, is the role of risk in driving profits and thereby adding value to the business? Have we demonstrated the accuracy of valuation of all intangibles not transferred?

6.52 Distinctions are often made between 'soft' intangibles and 'hard' intangibles, between routine and non-routine intangibles, and between other classes and categories of intangibles. The approach set out in the revised OECD Guidelines for determining arm's-length arrangements makes no attempt to follow this course and it should be avoided.

However, for the purposes of facilitating discussions in determining arm's-length arrangements, the July 2017 OECD Guidelines include the definition of trade intangibles and marketing intangibles.

CONTRACTUAL ARRANGEMENTS – LEGAL OWNERSHIP

6.53 Having identified intangible property, the next step is to understand who owns it. But that in the past has presented conceptual difficulties in some cases.

In transfer pricing cases, arguments about ownership of intangibles have often been focused on who should have the right to receive income, and have used concepts of 'economic ownership', 'beneficial ownership', 'registration' and 'legal ownership'. In fact, that debate was really about who should enjoy the *fruits* of the intangibles (the *profit or loss*), whereas the issue being fought over actually dealt only with who should receive the *income* from intangibles. In transfer pricing terms, ownership of IP – who is entitled to the income – can mean only what it would if unrelated parties had acted in the same way.

6.54 As we shall shortly see, the 'owner' of the intellectual property – where 'owner' means the party accepted in law as the party with rights to the IP – is the only party entitled to charge others for using the IP. That deals with *income*. However, net of payments to others who make significant contributions to the development, enhancement, maintenance, protection and exploitation of the IP, the 'owner' may not actually retain much of that income in the form of profits. In the revised Chapter VI, this is discussed in terms of the 'return' from the intangible, and transfer pricing practitioners should always remember that this is a net position that is achieved by way of also valuing the secondary transaction, and not by redirecting the income stream away from the legal owner.

6.55   One thing that comes from considering 'ownership' separate from 'valuation' is an overt recognition that they are two separate questions. It is important to retain that separation and deal with the qualitative question of ownership – 'who should get the income?' – before turning to the quantitative question of 'how much income should they get?' and then finally the secondary quantitative question of 'net of payments to parties that made a significant contribution to the development, enhancement, maintenance, protection and exploitation of the intangible – how much profit should they keep?'.

6.56   The written contractual arrangements that exist between the parties is the starting place to gain a proper understanding of the transaction, the intangible involved, and its ownership. Though documents (inter-company contracts) may describe the roles, responsibilities and rights of associated enterprises with respect to intangible assets, they might not. Written contracts alone will not provide all of the information we need to perform a transfer pricing analysis. The actual conduct of the parties must be explored and then used in the process of 'accurately delineating' the true contract between the parties. The actual behaviour of the parties will clarify or supplement the terms written in the contract document or, alternatively, replace the written terms if they are different provided that those different actions would have changed the construction of the contract between unrelated parties; to go beyond that is to breach the arm's-length principle and hence would not be supported by OECD Guidelines.

By looking at all of the available evidence – the written contract and the behaviour of the parties – we can consider who the true 'owner' of the intangible is. That is the party who, at arm's length, would be entitled to enforce the monopoly of the intangible and thereby seek income from allowing others to use it. This process is just as it would be if a court was asked to determine the ownership of an intangible between two (or more) competing unrelated parties, and so it is entirely within the limits of the arm's-length standard and it is not a 're-characterisation' of the transaction provided that it is not taken too far.

6.57   So far, we have shown that, in the term 'intellectual property', it is the second word that is important in determining who should be the recipient of income from an intangible. Property is bestowed on someone by reason of law. Intellectual property law does not provide the owner with a right to use the intellectual property, but with a right to prevent others from using it. As between unrelated parties, a royalty is then paid by a licensee in recognition of the licensor not exercising that right to prevent its use. Therefore, we have concluded that the question 'Who gets the income?' is answered by looking to see who has the right to prevent use of the intellectual property. The example set out in the following paragraphs illustrates how asking the right question will sometimes lead to a different answer than asking the wrong question – in this case using the concept of 'economic ownership'.

6.58 **The facts:** Suppose that a company, MIS, was engaged by GSK to write a software package. The terms of this engagement included an agreement that all copyright in the software created would be the property of MIS. That would not be an unusual agreement, and the price charged by MIS would reflect the fact that it would be able to use that same software itself or sell copies of the software to other parties, including competitors of GSK. Suppose, however, that MIS found itself to be unable to complete the project on time without sub-contracting part of the coding to a third party, IPE, who was to be paid at a suitable rate. In that contract, MIS did not include any terms to provide for the transfer of copyright from the author, IPE, to MIS. Upon completion of the project, the finished software was delivered to GSK and then MIS began to sell licences for the software to other parties. In addition to being paid on a contract basis for software writing, IPE also asked to receive a proportion of the additional licence income (not the GSK fee) earned by MIS from selling licences of the software.

6.59 **The question:** As a transfer pricing exercise, if MIS and IPE were related parties, should MIS have all of the additional licence fees or should IPE receive a proportion of the additional licence fees?

6.60 **The economic answer:** Taking an econometric approach, IPE had been paid for its services on an arm's-length basis. The cost and the risk of developing the software therefore fell squarely on MIS; from this, one might conclude that MIS is the economic owner of all future licence income.

6.61 **The arm's-length answer:** The facts used in the example are taken from a commercial dispute heard by the UK Court of Appeal in 2008: *Meridian International Services Ltd v Richards & Ors* [2008] EWCA Civ 609. Copyright arises to the author, which in the case of the subcontracted work was IPE. The failure of MIS to include a requirement for IPE to transfer any copyright in its work to MIS was neither rectified by any 'implied' need to do so because of the sub-contract nature of its relationship with MIS, nor by reference to any agreement that MIS purported to have made with GSK. The 'economic' answer given above is not what happens between unrelated parties; transfer of copyright in the new software would be a factor in testing the arm's-length nature of the reward for the sub-contracting activity, not in deciding ownership of the copyright. Neither would it be appropriate to assert that MIS and IPE 'would have' agreed to transfer the copyright, as it is clear that unrelated parties do not only contract on the basis that ownership of IP would transfer from the contractor to the party engaging the contractor.

6.62 This approach to ownership is closer to what has in the past been considered to be a 'legal test', which is unsurprising since 'intellectual property' is a legal concept in any case. However, this does not mean that the party having legal title to the intellectual property will always get all of the income which the IP generates. In short, the party named on any register of IP is not conclusive proof that they 'own' all of the rights in the IP. Consider the example in the following paragraphs.

6.63   **The facts:** DLN manufactures agricultural crop covering in the UK under the registered trade name 'Gromax'. GPL holds the sole UK distributorship for Gromax and, over the years, GPL has been solely responsible for building the UK client base. In addition, GPL has provided valuable feedback to DLN concerning customer needs and suggested improvements to the product. GPL has also provided suggestions for sourcing raw materials from which the product is made and took steps to ensure the finest quality of product. Over years of trading, GPL has developed a strong reputation as a knowledgeable and helpful supplier of Gromax crop cover. Subsequently the parties fell out with each other and terminated their business relationship. This has led to a dispute about ownership of the trade name 'Gromax' which had been registered by DLN.

6.64   **The question:** Should DLN, holding the registered title to the trade name 'Gromax', be entitled to the goodwill associated with that name, or should GPL, the party that developed all customer relationships, be entitled to that goodwill?

6.65   **The answer:** Starting from first principles, it is accepted under UK law that where a licensee uses a valid trade name or mark then the goodwill accrues to the licensor and not the licensee. The licensee acquires no interest in the name or mark and must cease to use it on termination of their licence. Provided that the licence is valid, it does not matter that the licensee may be held out as the provider of the goods and may, in fact, be primarily responsible for their character or quality.[4] However, there may yet be special circumstances in which the actions of the licensee go beyond that expected of a licensee, and thereby the licensee becomes simultaneous part owner of the goodwill associated with a trade name or mark. In this example, the 'sole' nature of the distributorship and the actions of GPL in creating a customer base, passing on customer suggestions and being interested in the quality of the product do not cross that bright-line test. However, the sourcing of raw materials is an example of the line being passed. In this case, the trade name registration is not overturned, but GPL would be allowed to use the goodwill associated with the trade name (by using the trade name itself without paying a royalty) for a short time.

6.66   Again, in the example above, the facts are drawn from an existing settled commercial dispute: *Gromax Plasticulture Ltd v Don & Low Nonwovens Ltd* [1999] RPC 367. Where the activities of a licensee go beyond that expected of a licensee, either qualitatively or quantitatively, then the right to enjoy the value of the IP might be shared between the licensor and the licensee. This 'bright line' test has echoes in some tax cases, notably the Indian case of *Maruti*

---

4   See C. Wadlow *The Law of Passing Off* (2nd edn, 1995, London: Sweet & Maxwell), para 2.62.

Suzuki ('Maruti' Suzuki India Ltd v Additional Commissioner of Income Tax Transfer Pricing Officer New Delhi WP(C) 6876/2008 (High Court of Delhi at New Delhi, 2010)) and the US case of DHL (*DHL Corp*, TC Memo 1998-461, RIA TC Memo). What is clear is that the party who is entitled to the income is the party to which a court would award the income if the parties were to dispute that point before a competent court. The primary rule is that this will be the party that holds legal title to the intellectual property and that rule will be set aside only if there are circumstances so special that a so-called 'bright line' is crossed, in which case the parties can become simultaneous joint owners of the intellectual property.

6.67   As the law giving rise to each kind of intellectual property is different (patent law is not the same as copyright law, and so on), ownership of intellectual property is governed by the law and the facts relevant to that particular case. Each case must therefore be tested on its own merits and according to the appropriate law and commercial practice.

6.68   The importance of following this process to understand who, as between unrelated parties, would be entitled to enjoy the financial benefit cannot be understated. Let us consider one more example of how a court has decided which of two unrelated parties is entitled to the rights in, and therefore the financial benefit of, IP to reinforce the point.

6.69   Computer programs represent valuable IP in many businesses and the legal form of protection for a computer program is copyright. Copyright has been understood to concern the actual written code, the source code and the object code of the program, rather than providing any protection for its functionality. However, where one party develops a new computer program that contains functionality previously available in a program developed and owned by another MNE group member, it raises debate amongst transfer pricing professionals. The question is whether the developer of the new program should make any form of payment to the developer of the earlier program to recognise some residual value arising from the functionality that is now employed in the new program. The grounds put forward for this view are that the earlier program provided ideas and inspiration for the new work, or that in some way the functionality 'belongs' to the original program owner. The answer to this transfer pricing question again lies in the answer to the question of whether the functionality of the old program is itself protectable as between unrelated parties.

6.70   There is no protection for functionality by reference to simple copyright; as noted above, that looks only to the source and object code. Within the EU, protection is, however, offered to computer programs under *EU Directive 91/250 of 14 May 1991* (the Software Directive). *Article 1.2* of the *Software Directive* provides protection to a form of expression of a program and some have argued that this gives the very protection with which we are concerned. The ECJ was asked to consider whether the functionality of a computer program, or the programming language and the format of data files used in a computer program in order to exploit certain of its functions, could be protected under *Article 1.2* of the *Software Directive*. In other words, is there a copyright protection available to the original program such that there is a residual value that must be licensed and paid for?

6.71   In the 2012 case of *SAS Institute Inc v World Programming Ltd* (Case 406/10), this point was decided. SAS Institute Inc (SAS) markets statistical analysis software under the trade name Base SAS and World Programming Ltd (WPL) produced a competing product. WPL acquired a licence to Base SAS and studied the product to understand its functionality so that it could ensure that it offered similar functionality in its own product. WPL did not access the source code, but it did actively try to mimic the functionality of Base SAS. WPL adopted the same programming language and data file format so that there was end user compatibility between the two products. SAS filed a claim against WPL, based on the argument that WPL had indirectly copied its computer programs and that by studying the functionality of the 'Learning Edition', WPL had breached the licence terms under which it accessed the software. SAS argued that the computer language and the data file format was critical to the functionality of the program because those aspects of the program are used by the application programs and constitute the means by which users of the program exploit its functionality, hence this constituted a form of expression of the program within the meaning of *Article 1.2* of the *Software Directive*.

6.72   The ECJ ruled that *Article 5(3)* of the *Software Directive* gives a licensee of software a right to study and test the functionality of the program to understand the principles on which it operates, provided that they respect the terms and conditions of the licence. However, the licence may not seek to limit the power of the person to act in this way by contract provisions inserted into the licence. Hence WPL committed no offence by studying the Base SAS program it had licensed with a view to understanding and mimicking the functionality of that program. The ECJ also held that the functionality of a computer program does not constitute a form of expression that might be within the terms of *Article 1(2)* of the *Software Directive*. The ECJ also reached the same decision with respect to the programming language and the data file format used by the application programs.

6.73   This ruling means that *Article 1.2* of the *Software Directive* provides copyright protection only for the individual expression of the work. It leaves other authors the freedom to create similar or even identical computer program functionality provided that is not achieved using source code and object code taken from an already existing program which has copyright protection. Any other finding would raise the possibility that a party might monopolise ideas to the detriment of technological progress and industrial development.

6.74   This case tells us about the arm's-length nature of the terms and conditions that can be included in an intra-group software licence within the EU, and it makes clear the answer to the 'residual' value of one software program or platform when its concepts and functionality are included in another, perhaps a 'next generation' offering. It is not possible to argue that one should be able to restrict one group company from adopting into its computer program development the functionality of an existing program owned by a fellow group member, and thus have reason to charge a fee for allowing that use, because it would not be possible to prevent an unrelated party from doing this. The argument, had it been accepted, would have created a non-arm's-length result. Contractual terms in EU licences that claim to make this restriction are invalid, and arguments that such restrictions ought to have been included in an EU contract (when they are not) also breach the arm's-length principle. Provided that no source code or object code is copied, there is no royalty due to the owner of the residual program or platform based on the argument that they 'had the original idea'. Further, any assistance provided by the owner of the old program or platform in helping a new developer to understand the functionality of the old program (but not supplying access to the source code or to the object code) can only be transfer priced on the basis of a service activity, as this 'service' is all that has been given; there is no IP.

6.75 The facts of this case relate to the EU and so, in specific cases involving countries outside the EU, it would be important to review and consider similar provisions.

6.76 In many cases, there are no written legal arrangements conferring the right of ownership of intangible assets between associated enterprises. The absence of written legal arrangements, however, does not negate the concept of legal ownership, nor does it suggest that there is no relationship between the ultimate legal ownership of an intangible and the associated enterprises. As with unconnected parties, the legal owner will be established by considering the actions of the parties that led to the development and (if appropriate) enhancement of the intangible in the light of the law which creates a monopoly over the intangible. In other words, concepts like 'economic owner' have no place in the first process, establishing the owner of the IP. Also in line with unrelated parties, the unwritten contract between the IP owner and any party using the IP is established by the actual interactions, in the light of normal commercial practice.

6.77 Determining the legal ownership and contractual arrangements is an important first step in any transfer pricing analysis involving intangible assets, because it involves the development of a clear understanding of what the intangible is and which party has the legal monopoly, and therefore who has the right to charge others who make use of the IP. The revision to Chapter VI can be a little confusing as it makes a clear statement that bare legal ownership of intangibles (ie legal ownership without performing the associated DEMPE functions) does not confer any right ultimately to retain returns derived by the MNE group from exploiting the intangible. As described above, this does not look to the income flow arising from the intangible but to the net profit retained, after taking into account any secondary transactions under which the intellectual property owner pays others who contribute significantly to DEMPE activities. Net of those payments, the profit retained through the bare legal ownership of the intangibles may be quite similar to an investment return, given the size of the investment and the risk involved.

IDENTIFICATION AND ANALYSIS OF PARTIES PERFORMING THE FUNCTIONS, USING THE ASSETS AND ASSUMING THE RISKS

Functions

6.78 The contributions of the individual members of a MNE group to the creation of intangible value must be determined and appropriately rewarded. The arm's-length principle and Chapters I to III of the OECD Guidelines require the members of a group to receive compensation for any functions they perform, assets they use, and risks they assume in connection with the DEMPE functions. It is therefore essential to delineate the transactions involving intangible assets, by means of an analysis of the functions performed by each party, to understand which members of the group perform and exercise control over the DEMPE functions, which member(s) provide funding and other assets, and which member(s) assume the various risks associated with the intangible. The relative importance of the contribution of each party towards the creation of value in the intangible asset is important in determining the arm's-length price for the transaction, and is largely dependent on the facts under consideration.

6.79 The party assuming responsibility for the function, asset or risk, and therefore entitled to enjoy the profit arising from an intangible, may or may not be the legal owner.

6.80 Taking a step back, the guidance included in the new Chapter VI suggests that, for the legal owner of an intangible asset to be entitled to all of the returns (ie the net profit) derived from exploitation of the intangible, it must perform all of the functions, contribute all assets used and assume all risks related to the DEMPE functions. What if that is not the case?

Where DEMPE functions are undertaken by associated enterprises, they should be appropriately rewarded.

Where DEMPE functions are outsourced to independent enterprises, the associated party that controls the outsourced activity should be appropriately rewarded.

6.81 Where some of the DEMPE functions are outsourced to a related party, it is necessary to consider the arm's-length compensation for those activities. The relative value of all functions that lead to a MNE earning a reward for an intangible may not be the same; in many – or even most – cases, some functions will create or add more value than others. For self-developed intangibles, or for self-developed or acquired intangibles that serve as a platform for further development activities, these more important functions may include, amongst others:

- design and control of research and marketing programmes;

- directions of and establishing priorities for creative undertakings including determining the course of 'blue-sky' research;

- control over strategic decisions regarding intangible development programmes; and

- management and control of budgets.

Once developed as an intangible, other important functions may also include important decisions regarding (a) defence and protection of intangibles, and (b) ongoing quality control over functions performed by independent or associated enterprises that may have a material effect on the value of the intangible.

6.82 Where functions that make a significant contribution to intangible value are outsourced by the legal owner to associated enterprises, the performance of those functions should be compensated. Depending on the facts of the case (with particular reference to control over the execution of those important functions), that reward might be calculable as a margin over the costs of exercising the function (a cost-plus return). Alternatively, it may be correct to reward that party by way of an appropriate share of the returns derived from the exploitation of the intangibles. The facts and circumstances of each case will determine which of these approaches is correct.

The normal approach to setting an arm's-length price applies also to intangibles and so, where it is possible to identify comparable third-party transactions, it would be appropriate to use that data to establish the appropriate arm's-length reward. However, in practice it may be impossible to identify comparable transactions involving the outsourcing of important functions and, in those cases, it may be appropriate to use other transfer pricing methods. Often when comparables are not available, the transactional profit split method might prove to be the most appropriate. In appropriate cases, it might be necessary to use a method not normally considered to be a 'transfer pricing' methodology, and the revised Chapter VI indicates clearly that this is acceptable if that produces the most appropriate approximation of an arm's-length price or reward.

6.83 *Ex-post* valuation techniques are not directly accepted as being the way to calculate the appropriate arm's-length reward for intangibles. However, *ex-post* valuations might be useful in suggesting transactions that *may* be inappropriately rewarded, based on their *ex-ante* valuation. This is a topic to which we return in **6.115**.

Assets

6.84 Group members that use their assets to perform the associated DEMPE functions for a transaction between related enterprises involving intangible assets should receive appropriate compensation for so doing. Such assets may include (a) intangibles used in research, (b) development or marketing, (c) physical assets, or (d) funding; this is not an exhaustive list, and the particular facts of the case will determine whether an asset has been used to add value in this way. Care must be taken to ensure that the 'asset' actually exists. For example, suppose that a US business, A, has a valid US patent concerning a trigger switch, and a related party, B, wishes to use that patent to further develop that switch. The contract entered into between A and B, written under US law, states that B will pay a royalty to A and that contract has no expiration date, being terminable by either party at notice. Several years later, the US patent finally lapses but, according to the contract, B is still committed to pay a royalty to A if it wishes to continue to use the switch. What is the arm's-length payment that B should make?

In the circumstances described, the answer is actually 'nil'. The reason for that is that the facts are closely analogous to the US Supreme Court decision in *Kimble v Marvel Entertainment LLC* [2015] No 13-720. In that case, the US Supreme Court held that upon expiration of the patent there was no intellectual property, such that the 'idea' was in the public domain. Since that was the policy intention of giving a monopoly to the patent holder, to contract in a manner that extends the monopoly is unlawful and unenforceable. As always, please note that this example concerns US law, and transfer pricing professionals would always check the law applicable to a transaction under active consideration. Note that this example is under US law, and for any particular transaction one should check the relevant applicable law.

6.85   The nature and amount of compensation attributable to an entity that utilises assets in transactions involving intangible assets must be determined based on all of the relevant facts, and should be consistent with similar arrangements among independent entities where such arrangements can be identified.

Where a situation arises in which an associated enterprise utilises an asset to perform the associated DEMPE functions, but does not control the risks or perform other functions associated with the activity or asset, that enterprise would not receive anticipated returns equivalent to those received by an otherwise similarly situated party who also performs and controls important functions and controls important risks associated with the activity.

6.86   Consider a situation where funding is provided by a related enterprise; it is likely that the same enterprise controls the risks involved in the provision of funding, as funding and risk-taking are so integrally related (eg the funding party contractually assuming the risk of loss of its funds). In this situation the nature and extent of the risk assumed, which will vary depending on the circumstances, must be considered in determining the appropriate arm's-length compensation. For example, the associated risks of funding are likely to be lower for an enterprise with a high creditworthiness.

Risks

6.87   The bare legal ownership of intangibles does not confer any right ultimately to retain the net profit (called the 'returns' in the revised Chapter VI) derived by the MNE group from exploiting an intangible asset (see **6.57**). The returns accruing to the MNE group must be attributed between the bare legal owner and the associated parties active in DEMPE matters based on the functions performed, the assets used, and the risks assumed by the parties.

It therefore follows that unless a party contributes to the control over the economically significant risks, it would not be entitled to retain the returns derived from risk.

6.88   The identity of the parties assuming risks related to the DEMPE functions is an important consideration in determining the arm's-length price for a controlled transaction relating to the exercise of DEMPE functions. The assumption of risk will determine which entity or entities will be responsible for the consequences if the risk materialises, and therefore who should be compensated for the inherent risk borne and, should they materialise, bear the consequences of that risk.

6.89   Chapters I to III of the OECD Guidelines include guidance for the process used to analyse risk in a controlled transaction.

When determining the arm's-length price of a transaction between related enterprises involving intangibles, it is therefore crucially important to understand the nature of the risks assumed by each party. Particular types of risks, that may have importance in a functional analysis relating to transactions involving intangibles, include the following (although again, this is not an exhaustive list and each case must be considered based upon its own facts):

- risks related to development of intangibles, including the risks that research and development or marketing activities yet to be undertaken will prove to be unsuccessful;

- the timing of the investment (the stage at which the investment is made in the development of an intangible) which ultimately impacts the underlying risk of investment;

- the risk of product / idea obsolescence, including the possibility that technological advances of competitors will adversely affect the value of the intangibles. This is not limited only to advances in thinking in the narrow field of the intangible itself, as the viability of the wider economy in which the intangible is intended to derive profit may change. For example, an exciting idea in 1954 to improve the efficiency of steam locomotives in the UK would seem to be considerably less valuable in 1955, when the Modernisation Plan was announced, and it called for the phasing-out of steam traction (major withdrawals occurred during 1962–1966, and UK steam traction locomotion ended in August 1968);

- infringement risk, including the risk that any defence of intangible rights or defence against other persons' claims of infringement may prove to be time consuming, costly and / or unavailing;

- product liability and similar risks related to products and services based on the intangibles; and

- exploitation risks and uncertainties in relation to the returns to be generated by the intangible.

6.90   As alluded to above, the concept of 'control' is particularly important when assessing the entitlement of each party to the returns derived from an intangible asset.

To contractually assume risk, a party must exercise control over the risk and also have the financial capacity to assume the risk. Although there is no bright-line test to determine control over risk, the factors to be considered include (in addition to the technical capacity to understand and act in mitigating the risk, as well as the activity claimed to be performed):

- which entity takes the decision to accept risks;

- which entity responds to the risks associated with the business opportunity; and

- which entity performs risk-mitigation activities.

The guidance permits risk-mitigation activities to be outsourced as long as the party outsourcing the risk-mitigation activity exercises control over the party doing the day-to-day risk-mitigating activity in the way that one might outsource to an independent party.

6.91   Where the actual (*ex-post*) profitability differs from the anticipated (*ex-ante*) profitability, it may be that the risks assumed by the parties actually materialise in a different way from what was anticipated. For example, where, for unforeseen reasons:

- a previously competitive product is removed from or unable to be sold in a particular market; or

- the development of a competitor's product reduces the level of demand for a particular product or service which makes use of the intangible in question;

it might also be the case that the financial projections on which the calculation of the compensation arrangements are based properly take into account risks and the probability of reasonably foreseeable events occurring. In that case the differences between actual and anticipated profitability reflect the playing out of those risks. In each of the three scenarios described above, the fact that the *ex-post* value differs (even significantly) from the *ex-ante* valuation does not call into question the arm's-length nature of the *ex-ante* value. Only where there has been a failure of financial projections used in the *ex-ante* valuation to take into account foreseeable events, or to analyse correctly the probability of positive or negative events occurring, would the *ex-post* value call into question the *ex-ante* valuation. In other words, the *ex-post* value does not displace the *ex-ante* valuation, but it might raise suspicions about the quality of the *ex-ante* valuation which should be investigated.

The implications of differences between *ex-post* profitability and *ex-ante* profitability with respect to determining the arm's-length arrangements between the parties are considered in more detail later in this chapter.

CONSISTENCY OF CONTRACTUAL ARRANGEMENTS AND ACTIVITIES PERFORMED

6.92   Undertaking the analysis described earlier in this chapter should facilitate a clear assessment of the legal ownership, functions performed, assets used, and risks assumed with respect to the intangible transaction. The contract between the parties is what they agree and intend to be bound by, which is pivotal to understanding the allocation of risk and function between the parties. Although this is often written into a document which we then call 'the contract', the true contract between the parties is, as we have just noted, what they agree and intend to be bound by.

In determining the actual contract, which is the basis of our transfer pricing analysis, we must check that the true contractual arrangements are accurately reflected in the written contract. In short, when we consider the behaviour of the parties, do the written terms of the contract accurately reflect the actual assumption of the economically significant activities and risks? Where discord arises between the written contractual arrangements and the activities performed by the parties, this may indicate that the 'true contract' between the parties is not that which is set out in the written contract. A detailed transfer pricing analysis must be undertaken in order to determine the 'true contract'. This is not a 'recharacterisation' of the transaction; it is simply gaining an understanding of the true transaction and is what happens between unrelated parties, should they come before a court in a dispute over what their written contract actually means.

6.93   **Example:** Suppose a private equity firm, consisting of two associated enterprises, is engaged in investment in the share capital of operating companies. Under the terms of the written contract:

● Company A will determine the investment approach and strategy, will determine which investments to proceed with based on the recommendations given, and will make the actual investment; and

● Company B is a low-risk service provider, undertaking research to determine the best available investments, and makes a recommendation to Company A.

Provided that the actual functions performed by Company B are consistent with the written contract (ie Company B does not set the investment strategy or make the final investment decisions), Company B would be entitled, at arm's length, to a low-risk return for the services provided. Company A, as the main decision-making entity, would be entitled to receive a return that acknowledges the significant risks borne by the company – which might be a profit or a loss, depending on whether those risks actually matured.

However, suppose that the actual activities performed are not consistent with the written contract. In reality, Company B undertakes research to determine the best available investment and also decides which investments to make, based on an investment strategy set by themselves. Company A has no employees, and is only operating as a legal signatory to make investments.

Under these arrangements, the true contractual arrangement between the parties is evidenced by their behaviour. The written terms of the agreement are undermined, and they are supplanted by the actual behaviour if that would also happen in construing a contract between unconnected parties; our analysis then shows that the risks relating to the operation of the private equity business lie with Company B. It therefore follows that Company B would be entitled to receive a return based on the actual activities undertaken, which includes the reward relating to risk, whilst Company A would receive a relatively low return commensurate with its actual role.

6.94 It is important to stress here that the actual contract between the parties, accurately delineated, is only changed from the written and signed agreement if, as between unconnected parties, a Court asked to rule on the contract between them would have reached the same conclusion. For example, suppose that a written and signed license was 'non-exclusive' but for several years no other party had been licensed to act in the same territory. It would not be possible to re-interpret the contract for transfer pricing purposes as being 'exclusive' simply because the Licensor had not, so far, exercised that right to appoint others, because no third-party could succeed in that argument.

DELINEATION OF THE CONTROLLED TRANSACTION TO DETERMINE THE DEMPE FUNCTIONS

6.95 In line with the six-step framework identified as part of the BEPS project, following the identification of the intangibles, determination of the contractual arrangements, identification of the parties performing the DEMPE functions, and an analysis of the consistency of the parties' conduct to the contractual arrangements, the next logical step of the process is to delineate the transaction in light of the actual functions performed, assets used and risks assumed.

To put it simply, after undertaking steps (i) to (iv), is it important to step back and take stock of the controlled transaction, and to look at the arrangements as a whole to ensure that the details and nuances are fully understood.

6.96 Once understood, the controlled transaction should be defined for the purposes of a transfer pricing analysis and an appropriate approach to calculating the arm's-length price should be determined. It should be emphasised that delineating the controlled transaction does not necessarily dictate the use of a particular transfer pricing method. For example, a cost-plus approach will not be appropriate for all service transactions, and not all intangibles transactions require complex valuations or the application of the transactional profit split method. The facts of each specific situation, and the results of the required functional analysis, will guide the manner in which transactions are combined, delineated and analysed for transfer pricing purposes, as well as the selection of the most appropriate transfer pricing method in a particular case.

DETERMINATION OF THE ARM'S-LENGTH PRICE

6.97   In order to determine the value of an intangible asset in a transaction between associated enterprises, the arm's-length price must be determined using an appropriate valuation method.

The critical point to keep in mind when considering valuation methods is that the OECD Guidelines set a framework within which a competent professional works; it does not give rigid and simple answers that can simply be 'looked up' and applied without thought. Everything set out in Chapters I to III is applicable to intangible property, and the new Chapter VI should be considered to be additional material to supplement the application of the concepts laid down in those chapters, not something to be read in isolation. By adopting this approach, it can be concluded that valuation is to be undertaken in the context of the arm's-length principle and it is not a purely theoretical exercise. Why the warning? A story from the author's childhood may help to explain:

> 'My father worked in the construction industry as a plasterer. As a child, before the advent of "Health & Safety", he took me to work with him in the school holidays. I was not much help, being only a child, and spent much of my time simply playing in the builder's sand. One day I watched a joiner who had brought door casings to fit into the building. One aperture left by the bricklayer wasn't quite perfect; a single brick was twisted slightly, it protruded a little and prevented the door casing from fitting.

> The joiner carefully marked the wooden frame and then removed a small section so that it would fit around the brick. His skill with saws and chisels, gauges and planes was remarkable. My father had joined me to watch, so I asked him a question. "Father, why did he not simply knock-off the protruding piece of brick? It would have been quicker and easier". My father answered "Joiners think in wood, bricklayers think in brick".'

As professionals, most of us have trained in something other than transfer pricing: taxation, economics, valuation, accounting, law, corporate finance, etc. The danger is that if we think in that discipline when we approach the question of how to test the arm's-length nature of the price placed on an intellectual property transaction then we may not be meeting the requirements of the arm's-length principle at all. We must not rely on a valuation method simply because it is one used by accountants or by corporate finance (or any other discipline) as that methodology has been designed by those professionals to suit their needs and standards, and not ours.

6.98   Chapter II of the OECD Guidelines provides clear guidance on the selection of an appropriate method with which to test a transfer price. One should choose the most appropriate methodology for the case in hand (para 2.2). However, comparability is key to understanding whether the methodology is being applied correctly. In the remainder of this section we will consider first the comparable uncontrolled price method (CUP) and then turn our attention to other methods for assessing the arm's-length nature of a controlled transaction.

6.99 The author would have preferred the OECD Guidelines to remain at this higher level of analysis with respect to valuation methodologies. To delve deeper into one method – as the revised guidance now does – has two clear drawbacks. Firstly, the analysis of any one method alone risks creating the impression that this methodology is preferred over (all) others, which is very clearly not the case; to delve deeply into any one methodology surely requires that a similar level of analysis is applied to other methodologies that might, in given circumstances, apply. Secondly, textbooks already exist to describe and define how to apply various economic and statistical methods. These books are voluminous, and the material now included in the revised Chapter VI, with respect to using the potential future income stream as a basis of valuation, does not cover the application of this methodology in anything like as much detail. That said, it is appropriate now to note some of the potential short comments on various valuation methodologies.

Comparable Uncontrolled Price

6.100 CUP is the method favoured by tax authorities and tax advisors alike, although there is no longer any hierarchy of methods in the OECD Guidelines, if there is adequate comparability to the tested transaction. We have already discussed the existence of internal and external CUP evidence, and stressed the need for comparability. We have also noted (at **6.97** above) that the guidance in Chapters I to III of the Guidelines applies to intangible property transactions. However, we must understand that the unique nature of intangible property means that we have to be very careful to ensure comparability. Although all intellectual property is unique (as otherwise there would be no 'property' in it), for valuation purposes it can be thought of as fitting into one of two categories which we have labelled 'me too' and 'blockbuster'.

6.101 The 'me too' category covers any kind of intangible property that achieves something that can also be achieved in another, non-infringing way. For example, suppose a business, ABC, makes computer games available on its website free of charge (thereby attracting users to the site and selling advertising space). ABC purchases a non-exclusive right to use computer games written by many unrelated parties and it pays a one-off fee of £2,000 for the licence for each game. Suppose, then, that ABC incorporates an overseas subsidiary to create similar games and thereby reduce (but not eliminate entirely) the number of games purchased from others. The new games written by the subsidiary are each themselves subject to copyright and ABC will need to obtain a licence to use them. However, though each game is separately programmed, and is subject to separate copyright, the games themselves are, in this case, performing a very similar function. Each 'game' is a substitute for another and so the value paid to third parties – £2,000 for a non-exclusive right to use the game – is a comparable with which to test the arm's-length nature of the fee paid in a controlled transaction to acquire a game.

6.102 The 'blockbuster' category is different from 'me too' in that there is no simple workaround to achieve the same economic position. Take a trademark such as 'Deloitte'. Although there are other accounting and professional service firms, and those firms also think highly of their business name and reputation in the market, they are not 'Deloitte'. Hence the licence fee paid to use any of the other names in the accounting and business advisory market tells us nothing about the value of the fee that should be paid to use the name 'Deloitte'. There is not the comparability between the target and the potential comparables that is required by the OECD Guidelines for us to use this information in any constructive manner. Even if we discover the fee paid by every user of all names associated with accounting and business advisors, it still tells us nothing about the value of the name 'Deloitte'; without showing comparability, we have nothing more than an industry survey, which is useless for testing the arm's-length nature of a controlled transaction.

6.103 Having established what kind of intangible property we are dealing with, we should first look for CUPs. Internally generated CUPs are our preferred data source for both 'me too' and 'blockbuster' intangibles, as we are able to see all of the potentially relevant economic circumstances of the different licences and thereby prove comparability, or make suitable adjustments to the data (for an adjusted CUP). If there are no internally generated CUPs, then for 'me too' intangibles only we can look to database sources that might provide additional reference points. We must take great care, however, to ensure that we can demonstrate comparability in the data but, if we can, then this is the preferred way to test the arm's-length nature of the controlled transaction.

6.104 In addition to the matters that we would routinely consider in assessing comparability, we would also want to consider the following:

- *The relevant time period.* Past licensing deals may provide little guidance as to what the market is doing now. Industries change, as does the market perception of adequate return on capital.

- *Financial condition of the licence parties.* Urgency to complete a transaction will not lead to a fair market price.

- *Relevant industry.* Licences for the same technology to be used in different industries will show considerable variation in rates.

- *Country.* International licences are affected by differences in country markets. Whilst it might be reasonable to assume that UK, French and German licence rates might be similar as they are all within the EU, they would have little relevance for Brazil, India or China.

- *Remaining life.* Long remaining life tends to be associated with higher licence rates, and vice versa.

- *Non-monetary consideration.* This might be hidden in publicly available licence data but has an obvious effect on the total licence receipt.

- *Licence terms.* Exclusive versus non-exclusive licence, period, renewal rights, onerous compensation clauses in default, technical assistance given, obligations to spend on publicising the IP and other licence terms affect the level of licence that would be agreed between third parties.

- *Package licensing.* Contrary to the view of the OECD (ie it is best to dissect packages into their constituent parts), package licensing is common and the allocation between the elements in a real third-party deal might not always be clear.

6.105 It is challenging, however, to use external data searches for 'blockbuster' intangibles because it is difficult to show comparability. This point has already been tested before the UK courts in *General Tyre & Rubber Co v Firestone Tyre & Rubber Co Ltd* [1975] 1 WLR 819 (HL). Lord Wilberforce stated:

'Before a "going rate" of royalty can be taken as the basis on which an infringer should be held liable, it must be shown that the circumstances in which the going rate was paid are the same, or at least comparable, with those in which the patentee and the infringer are assumed to strike their bargain.'

The court rejected as evidence the royalty rates paid on two licences advanced by the respondent, as the respondent had not shown how they were comparable to the case under consideration. Though not a transfer pricing case, this nevertheless provides helpful commercial guidance, and we will return shortly to the use of commercial case law in testing transfer prices. The same result can be found in a transfer pricing case, however: the US Supreme Court decision in *Medtronic v Commissioner*, T.C. Memo 2016-112, in which the trial judge rejected the taxpayer's use of comparable uncontrolled transaction (CUT) in two (out of four) instances due to lack of comparability.

Other methods

6.106 If we are not able to find CUPs we must turn to other methods. As indicated above, we can use any valuation method that is appropriate, but we must be sure to 'evidence' why this valuation method is appropriate and that we have applied the technique with appropriate rigour. Just as with CUPs, if we cannot show how the methodology tests the transaction in question then we do not have 'evidence' at all (see **6.105** on this point).

6.107 In this respect, the US case of *Uniloc USA Inc et al v Microsoft Corporation* 4 January 2011 (US Court of Appeals for the Federal Circuit) is instructive and both reinforces the point and shows that it is not simply a UK phenomenon. In this commercial case, the US Court, hearing an infringement claim, needed first to determine the likely royalty that would have been agreed between a willing licensor and a willing licensee. A calculation of royalty using the '25% rule of thumb' method (whereby 25% of the value is assumed to be returned to the licensor as a royalty) was put before the court but was found to be 'fundamentally flawed'. The US Court looked at examples where this 'rule' had been used in US cases, and also at criticisms of the rule, to hold that there was no scientific basis behind the '25% rule of thumb'. As this methodology held no evidential value, it was inadmissible as evidence before any US court for any litigation purposes under rules established in *Daubert v Merrell Dow Pharmaceuticals Inc* 113 SCt 2786 (1993), not just inadmissible as evidence in this particular case. More recently in the US Tax Court in *Medtronic v Commissioner*, T.C. Memo 2016-112, and further to **6.105**, the trial judge also rejected the IRS' use of an aggregate comparable profits method as a means to value a royalty.

6.108   One key theme of the revision to Chapter VI of the OECD Guidelines is the focus on the functions performed, assets used and risks borne by the parties related to the DEMPE functions in the creation of value for an intangible asset.

In order to consider the actual activities undertaken, and therefore the options realistically available to the parties, the perspectives of each of the parties to the transaction must be considered. The new Chapter VI provides guidance on considering the perspectives of each of the parties to the transaction, and suggests that a comparability analysis focusing only on one side of a transaction generally does not provide a sufficient basis for evaluating a transaction involving intangibles.

In particular, the reliability of a one-sided transfer pricing method will be substantially reduced if the party or parties performing significant portions of the important functions are treated as the tested party or parties.

6.109   However, while it is important to consider the perspectives of both parties to the transaction in conducting a comparability analysis, the specific business circumstances of one of the parties should not be used to dictate an outcome contrary to the realistically available options of the other party.

For example, the revised guidance indicates that a transferor would not be expected to accept a price for the transfer of either all or part of its rights in an intangible that is less advantageous to the transferor than its other realistically available options (including making no transfer at all), merely because a particular associated enterprise transferee lacks the resources to effectively exploit the transferred rights in the intangible. That does not mean that the absence of resources to effectively exploit the intangible should be ignored, merely that one should assess the options realistically available to it, given that lack of resources to exploit the transferred rights in the intangible.

Similarly, a transferee should not be expected to accept a price for a transfer of rights over one or more intangibles that would make it impossible for the transferee to anticipate earning a profit using the acquired rights in the intangible in its business. Such an outcome would be less favourable to the transferee than the realistically available option of not engaging in the transfer at all.

When considering the phrase 'options realistically available', the key word here is 'realistic'. In the course of disputes, it is unfortunately not uncommon to find that one side defends its case by proposing alternatives that are not realistic, and sometimes they are not even legal or enforceable. Any suggestions of alternative options should therefore be subject to critical analysis.

6.110 The process of undertaking a two-sided analysis, to consider the relative contribution of each of the parties, is set out in detail later in this book.

The transactional profit split method, one approach to undertaking a two-sided analysis, and in particular the residual profit method and the total available profits method, is introduced in Figure 6.2 below and discussed in detail in Chapter 7.

6.111 There follows shortly consideration of several valuation techniques commonly used in different professions and in third-party licensing situations from the viewpoint of their evidential value in transfer pricing. It should be remembered that any and all valuation techniques have their limitations, and each method contains elements that are critical to the successful application of the method. Some of the methods dealt with here are fundamentally sound for transfer pricing purposes if they are applied correctly, whilst others are unacceptable under any but the most specific circumstances. It is critical that, in transfer pricing work, evidence is provided as to why a particular valuation technique is appropriate (in the circumstances of that case) and how this particular technique provides an accurate valuation. Before reviewing these methodologies, it is appropriate to consider the lifecycle of IP in order to give context to the value of data based on the historic cost of creating the IP and the potential future income stream of the IP.

6.112 Consideration of the lifecycle of investment / return for a successful IP development is important, as spend / income changes with time. Figure 6.2 below sets out a theoretical revenue life cycle for a successful IP. This illustration ignores spending on IP that does not prove to be successful.

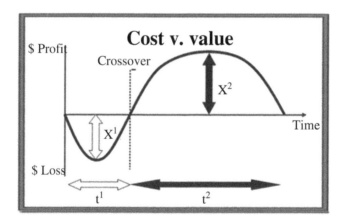

Figure 6.2 – IP cost and income over time

6.113 IP development begins with expenditure. Over time (t1) this expenditure results in an IP asset that creates income and gives rise to profits over a life represented by the time period t2. As time progresses, what we know about the revenue potential (cost and income) of the asset changes. To begin with, we do not know how much it will cost to develop the IP (the area of X1).

6.113 *Intangible property*

Later in life we may know the historic cost of creating the IP but have little appreciation of how much profit it will generate (the area of X2). This chart makes three points.

- For any sale or licence in the time period represented by t2, the actual costs incurred to develop the IP are unimportant. The sale price will be determined by reference only to the expected income (area x2) over the time remaining in t2, possibly limited by the cost of taking another option to acquire IP of similar impact and value.

- For a sale or licence before development work is completed, the cost incurred to date might be a driver. The risk of failure to complete the IP is high and the future income stream is more uncertain. It may be that a suitable return for the work completed to date would be the fair reward for the seller / licensor.

- For sales during t1, the switch from cost-reference to potential income-reference is driven by the risk remaining that the IP will not be successful/ commercial. The switch takes place before the IP begins to generate any income (the crossover from cost to income in Figure 6.2).

6.114   Comments on some valuation methodologies:

Adjusted CUP/CUT	This methodology takes similar, but not necessarily identical, IP transactions and makes adjustments for any economically significant differences.
	In practice, it can be difficult and expensive to apply, and often impossible to apply outside of 'me too' intangibles (as discussed in **6.100–6.102**), unless the same IP is licensed to a third party. As more differences are identified between the controlled transaction under consideration and the comparable transaction, the statistical margin of error increases rapidly as more and more adjustments are made to compensate. However, a variation of this is to identify the methodology applied repeatedly to generate third-party royalty rates and then apply this same methodology. If you can demonstrate that you have understood and taken into account all of the appropriate economic drivers of that methodology, then third-party licences based on that methodology are adjusted CUPs.
Rule of thumb	This approach, which is frequently raised as a more simplistic measure, suggests that the royalty to be paid for use of IP will generally be 25% to 33% of the gross profit derived by the licensee from its use.

This is not a scientifically based approach and suffers from numerous failings, including a failure to: define 'gross profit'; acknowledge that the IP may or may not lead to increased operating costs; acknowledge that the risk sharing might lay more heavily on one party or the other; or determine what a fair rate of return for using the technology might be.

Despite its many shortfalls, the rule of thumb approach is used extensively in industry due to its pure simplicity. However, following cases such as *General Tyre & Rubber* and *Uniloc*, it cannot be relied on for transfer pricing analysis as it will, at best, provide only a 'ballpark' range into which many licence fees may fall. In low-value cases, where information is limited and the cost of getting better data cannot be reconciled with the ultimate likely licence value, this method is commonly used to set the licence fee but, on audit, it is unlikely that the taxpayer will have any admissible evidence at all with which to support their transfer price.

Industry norm

This method looks to the level of royalties that are typically set in a particular industry and uses that data to set the rate.

This approach does not set out to locate specific comparables, but merely provides a benchmarking of licences for any technology in a particular industry. From a transfer pricing viewpoint this is unlikely to be considered to be sufficiently specific. From an economics viewpoint it has many of the faults associated with the 'rule of thumb' approach, plus the additional sin of failing to take into account whether the licensee will make a profit from using the IP and so it does not consider the transaction from the viewpoint of both parties.

Interestingly, any error in setting a royalty by a party is likely to be replicated and reinforced over time as others copy. It is possible for such a faulted rate to then become a major determinant of future royalty rates. Similarly, the methodology completely ignores changes in the market and industry that ought to have moved royalty rates on from past benchmarks.

In practice this methodology is another useful 'ballpark' indicator. It is often used in tax audit defence of related-party licensing, in the form of a database search that makes no effort to test the critical elements of the licence and hence prove comparability. It therefore does not meet the arm's-length standard and it is unlikely to be acceptable to most tax authorities.

5% of sales	Whether this is a variation of 'rule of thumb' or an observation based on 'industry norm', the '5%' methodology is still unacceptable for transfer pricing purposes. The most common rate of royalty used in practice across many different industries is actually 5% of sales, though there is no data to support why this should be so. Like the 'rule of thumb' referred to above, this method does not meet the arm's-length standard and it is unlikely to be considered supportable by a tax authority. This 5% licence rate is found across several different (but not all) industries, regardless of the life stage of the industry.
	In practice, this can again provide a 'ballpark' answer before any serious work begins and in third-party licensing situations the methodology has a similar appeal to the 'rule of thumb' method. Neither, however, have found support in cases of litigation and so for related-party licences they have little merit as justification for a royalty charged.
Return on R&D	This method attempts to ensure that the creator of the IP makes an adequate return on their investment.
	Though instantly attractive in related-party situations (data is available to show the amount of spend, the remaining life can be calculated and return rates can be obtained), this method is applicable only to early-stage IP, as explained above. There is little, if any, valid correlation between the amounts incurred on developing an intangible and their ultimate value to the business. This method is sometimes misapplied to challenge a licence which has been set based on another, more acceptable, methodology. However, if the licence income is insufficient to provide the desired return from the IP, that is one of the risks that the IP creator / owner assumes.
Historic cost	The historic cost method is superficially attractive as historic cost data is usually readily available. See 'Return on R&D' above and 'Replacement cost' below.

Replacement cost	Cost of replacement can be an effective valuation method, but only for IP that is not 'blockbuster'.

This method is harder to apply where the value of the IP is reliant on a composite of activity or is not certain to be recreated regardless of spend. A common error is to assume that the historic cost of creating this IP is the cost that would be incurred to create a replacement, but the advance of technology, the impact of blocking IP and the trends in the market will all affect this in practice and should all be considered. That said, as we are instructed to look at realistically available alternatives as a way to understand the value of the transaction, there is strong ground for saying that a licensee or transferee would not pay more than the cost of recreating the IP itself. For 'me too' IP there would certainly be an option of creating new IP. The analysis of replacement cost should look not only at the actual costs (people, assets, external costs) but also at the lost opportunity; if the net present value of the actual replacement costs and the licence fee are equal, but the licence is available now whilst the new IP would take three years to develop, there is an opportunity cost to include in calculating the replacement asset cost.

Market approach	There are a number of methodologies based on the concept that the total value of an enterprise, less the value of tangible assets, will create a theoretical value for the IP, from which a proportion can be allocated to the specific IP being considered, and a licence fee can be calculated by means of calculating a return on that asset value. This approach is rarely applied with sufficient vigour to be considered sufficient evidence in transfer pricing cases, as there are a number of very subjective aspects to this approach.

First, valuing the enterprise itself is a subjective exercise. Even where there are listed shares issued in a market, the capitalisation that this represents does not necessarily equate to the true value of the underlying business. Turning next to the subtraction of the tangible asset value, the book values shown in the accounting records will rarely reflect the true value of those assets, and so another subjective exercise – or, more likely, series of subjective exercises – must be performed.

The figure arising from the subtraction of the asset value from the total enterprise value does not represent a true reflection of the total value of the various intangible assets. For one thing, that figure includes the reward for risk in the business and so we would have to deduct it; but how would we value the return for risk?

Assuming that we did manage to get to a value for all the intangible assets, how do we identify (let alone quantify the value of) all of the individual intangible assets in the business in order to isolate the value of the one in which we are interested? Every staff instruction book, template and advertisement is copyright, not to mention the software copyright, design rights, database rights and so on that exist in every business. All of this will have to be identified and valued so that it can be removed from the remaining total that represents the value of the single intangible in which we have an interest. In almost all cases, the identification task alone will be impossible.

If we are able to complete these tasks, we have a value for the intangible. We can extrapolate a licence fee from this value if we know the useful life and the discount rate to be applied, following the economic principle that the value of the asset and the potential income stream that it might generate are equal. Considerable disagreement can arise concerning both the useful life and the discount rate (see 'Decapitalisation of IP value' below).

In summary, this method has little validity when trying to establish an arm's-length value for transfer pricing purposes. It is even more prone to error when applied to any industry experiencing short-term volatility. From the above critique of the method, it will be appreciated that incorrect application will almost invariably significantly overstate the value of IP.

Decapitalisation of IP value

In the same way that IP value can be calculated from a known income stream that is / will be generated, one can decapitalise a known IP value to determine the appropriate royalty rate.

This methodology relies upon knowing the actual value of the IP, together with considerable amounts of further data relating to the useful life of the asset, further expenditure needed to support the asset and the correct discount rate to apply. In practice, the methodology is often misused due to an underestimation of the intricacies of the valuation model to determine value from income.

In theory this method should be one of the strongest for setting royalties, but it requires a significant amount of data and it must be accurate. Even if those hurdles can be crossed, as the asset value is of fundamental importance to the process it is only as robust as the valuation of the IP. A recent purchase of IP from a third party, for example, may appear to generate a hard value for the IP. However, the financial press contains many articles covering stories where it is apparent that the price paid for IP was excessive (or sometimes, though much less often, a bargain).

Price comparison

The price comparison approach comes in two forms.

Where the same product or service is available without the IP (eg unbranded product versus branded product), a comparison of the volume and price less the additional cost of the IP can illustrate the profits that the IP creates. In this way the methodology becomes a profit-split calculation. In this example, it is important that care is taken to ensure that the comparison product is 'unbranded' in the eyes of the consumer; often there is still a brand adding value, such as the supermarket's own name, that reduces the accuracy of the method.

This method is sometimes used by IP valuers to identify a royalty rate from a wider search by looking at the price point for the goods or service. That may be sufficient for some purposes, and it might be indicative of a ballpark royalty rate, but it has insufficient evidential value for transfer pricing purposes.

Depreciated cash flow

Depreciated cash flow (DCF) of a licence income stream is a valuation method used in many cases to calculate the value of an intangible from a known licence income. It is more difficult to apply this method to a business in order to calculate the value of the licence. In those circumstances, see 'Residual profit method' and 'Profit available method' below.

Differential profit analysis

Based on the approach of the court commonly used in IP infringement cases this method compares the operating profit that is derived, including the benefit arising from the infringement and the profit that would be expected to be earned in a 'normal' situation. The difference between the two is then awarded to the complainant as a recompense for the infringement. To apply this method the operating profit that would be earned without the infringement needs to be calculated. This is rather difficult and, in practice, the court often accepts the 'normal' operating profit of that industry, ie., an industry average.

This method also ignores the balance sheet and hence fails to allow the licensee a reward for investment in new, specialised plant, etc. However, this would also have featured in any third-party licence negotiations.

Finally, in non-infringement negotiations the user would not pay all of the profits to the licensor as they would expect to retain some benefit from the use of the licensed property. Hence the 'excess profit' calculated needs to be split between licensee and licensor (often achieved using the 25% 'rule of thumb' which has been discredited in the courts) so without further subjective adjustment this methodology is not generally acceptable for transfer pricing purposes.

Residual profit method

This approach takes the profits of a business, applies a reasonable return in respect of all of the assets and functions other than IP and concludes that the residual (the difference) must relate to the value afforded by the IP licence.

This method can be difficult to apply because of the huge amount of data and assumptions that will arise in most businesses. Also, as noted above, not all of the residual profit would be paid to the owner of the IP as a licence fee as there would be no benefit in entering into the arrangement if the licensee retained none of the benefit. This methodology therefore presents us with the problem of how we split the residual profit and it is difficult to see how third-party data could be obtained to demonstrate that split. If we turn to econometric concepts, such as bargaining power, we have a methodology which at no point references what might happen between unrelated parties. We have stepped away from the arm's-length principle into a theoretical, econometric exercise. This might be acceptable for the negotiation of an advance pricing agreement (if all of the parties agree), but it is not evidence of the arm's-length nature of the licence fee.

Profits available method

The profits available methodology is the purest in economic terms. It is a form of total profit split, which accords with OECD methodologies, and considers the viewpoint of both the licensor and the licensee. Using a full profit split avoids the problem inherent in 'residual profit split': that there is no third-party data available to show how the residual should be split between the licensor and the licensee and uses the data available from court cases to show how the total profit is split between licensor and licensee. The methodology does not rely upon comparable or benchmark public licence rate data searches and so has none of the weaknesses inherent in that process.

The data used relates to the actual and potential markets for the IP, the cost of entering into and trading in those markets, and the risks of the business (which drive capitalisation rates). All of this data is available, though collating it can be a costly process. The split of total profits can be evidenced from the splits that are agreed or imposed by courts in considering actual third-party commercial disputes.

The methodology is frequently used by the UK (and other) courts to settle the question of a fair royalty between a willing licensor and a willing licensee and so, by applying this method in the way that the courts do, we have adjusted comparable transactions in every case that has been settled by the court. Many of the court cases relate to royalty rates for commercial disputes relating to patents (eg 'licence of right' cases) but the methodology is not restricted to use only with respect to patents; it can be applicable for any IP. (See *Blayney Trading as Aardvark Jewelry v Clogau St David's Gold Mines Ltd and Others* [2002] Court of Appeal (Civil Division) Case No A3/2001/1755.)

The methodologies above do not represent an exhaustive list of all potentially applicable methods. Although not a single one (save for CUP / CUT) is recommended beyond all others (subject to adequate comparability), the object in writing this section is to impress upon the reader the need to use all of their skills to apply any valuation methodology with sufficient rigour for it to attain the quality of 'evidence'.

6.115 In the case of *Medtronic, Inc. & Consolidated Subsidiaries v Commissioner of Internal Revenue* [2018] US Court of Appeal Case No 17-1866, Medtronic, a medical device company, produces and markets class medical devices. Medtronic's parent company, Medtronic US, and its distributer, Medtronic USA, Inc. (Med USA) are located in the United States, and its device manufacturer, Medtronic Puerto Rico Operations Co. (Medtronic Puerto Rico), is located in Puerto Rico. Medtronic allocates the profit earned from its medical devices between Medtronic US, Med USA, and Medtronic Puerto Rico through its intercompany licensing arrangements.

In 2002, Medtronic used the CUT method (using an agreement between Medtronic and Pacesetter regarding patent and licence use in 1992) to determine royalty rates paid on its intercompany licences, allocating large proportions of their profits to the Puerto Rican subsidiary. Medtronic argued that as their Puerto Rican subsidiary bore the majority of any potential liability arising from manufactural defects, it was entitled to a commensurate rate of return on Puerto Rican operations.

6.116 The IRS asserted that Medtronic US allocated non-arm's length profits to Medtronic Puerto Rico. Applying the residual profit split method the

IRS determined that 90% of Medtronic's relevant profits should be allocated to US operations with only the remaining 10% to those in Puerto Rico. Put simply, the IRS argued that the reported royalty rates were too low and eroding the tax base in the US.

In order to resolve this difference in opinion, and without any admission of error on either side, a Memorandum of Understanding was agreed upon setting out 'compromise' royalty rates to be applied in 2002 and in the future, provided that no significant changes to the 'underlying facts' took place.

However, in 2005 and 2006 the IRS determined that the most appropriate method for determining an arm's length price on intercompany licencing agreements was the comparable profits method, rather than either of the CUT or residual profit split methods, or the rates set out in the memorandum. Applying the comparable profits method, the IRS assigned Medtronic Puerto Rico a routine manufacturing return, allocating significantly higher royalty income to Medtronic US (where the royalty income is subject to higher US tax rates). Over 90% of the system profit were therefore assigned to Medtronic US and Medtronic filed a lawsuit.

6.117   The Tax Court rejected both royalty rate valuations, claiming that neither produced a true arm's- length result, and performed its own analysis, eventually determining that Medtronic was correct to use a CUT methodology, but with some adjustments. The Tax Court thereafter issued an order concluding that Medtronic had an income tax deficiency in 2005, but that it had an income tax overpayment in 2006. The Commissioner then filed an appeal, seeking a recalculation of the arm's-length royalty rate.

The Court of Appeal subsequently deemed that the Tax Court did not give proper consideration to the fact that (1) the Pacesetter-Medtronic agreement rose out of litigation, (2) included a lump sum payment and (3) included cross-licences and (4) excluded certain intangibles. The Court of Appeal therefore used the Pacesetter-Medtronic as a starting point for its CUT analysis, then making a number of significant and broad adjustments to account for differences between the Pacesetter-Medtronic agreement and the Medtronic licensing transaction.

From this, we can take that Tax Court preferred to assess the arm's length nature of licensing transactions by reference to direct pricing evidence from comparable transactions. The *Medtronic* judgment sends a clear message to taxpayers and transfer pricing professionals, namely that a solid and detailed CUT analysis and presence of third party evidence can, in many respects, convince the courts and reduce the ability of tax authorities to allocate routine returns to offshore licensees.

HARD TO VALUE INTANGIBLES

6.118   The value of an intangible is often uncertain at the time of transfer, as later events and developments will affect its subsequent ability to drive income or reduce costs. Significant differences may then arise between the anticipated, *ex-ante*, and the actual, *ex-post*, valuations of an intangible because the projections on which the valuations are based are not followed precisely by subsequent events. Where this is the case, an intangible is considered to be hard to value, and thus is a 'hard to value intangible' (HTVI).

The term 'HTVI' covers intangibles or rights to intangibles for which, at the time of their transfer between associated enterprises, i) no reliable comparables exist, and ii) the projections or future cash flows or income expected to be derived from the transferred intangible, or the assumptions on which the financial projections are based, are highly uncertain.

6.119   In June 2018, the OECD released guidance for 'Tax Administrations on the Application of the Approach to Hard-to-value Intangibles' under BEPS Action 8. The guidance was subsequently incorporated as an annex to Chapter VI of the OECD Guidelines. The revised Chapter VI sets out to provide a common understanding for tax administrations and is intended to improve consistency of approach across jurisdictions and therefore reduce the risk of double taxation and enhance tax certainty. The guidance includes a number of examples to clarify the application of the HTVI approach in different scenarios and addresses the interaction between the HTVI approach and the access to the mutual agreement procedure under the applicable tax treaty.

6.120   The revised Chapter VI prescribes guidance for the application of the arm's-length principle for an HTVI. Under this approach, a tax authority or taxpayer may be entitled to use the ex-post outcomes to adjust the ex-ante pricing. The provisions are intended to prevent worldwide groups from artificially moving profits to lower tax jurisdictions by transferring intangibles between group members, while protecting tax authorities from any negative implications of information asymmetry arising from the difficulty in objectively valuing the assets.

6.121   In evaluating the *ex-ante valuation* of an HTVI, the tax administration is entitled to use the *ex-post* evidence about financial outcomes to risk-assess the arm's-length nature of the pricing arrangements, including any contingent pricing arrangements. It is therefore of significant importance that the pricing of an HTVI at the time of transfer is fully assessed by using robust forecasts and considering the effect of timing on the pricing of the intangible asset.

Where this approach implies that the HTVI was transferred at an under or overvalue compared to an arm's length price, the revised value may be taken into account for tax purposes. The approach may not be used where the transfer is covered by a bilateral or multilateral APA.

TIMING

6.122   One question that regularly arises is 'when' in time the test of arm's-length nature of the transaction value should take place. This is an important question as the passage of time will change the facts that drive a valuation. A simple example to illustrate this point follows.

6.123   Suppose that on Friday Mr A wants to buy a lottery ticket for the draw which takes place on Saturday. Despite his best intentions, he fails to find time to make a purchase. Mr B has 10 tickets, and offers to sell one to Mr A. How much would Mr A pay for the ticket? If we test this now, on Friday, the answer will be close to £2, the original price of a ticket. Mr B might extract a premium from Mr A – if Mr A is sufficiently driven to have a ticket that he will pay a premium – but in cash terms the price will still be close to £2. However, if we test the same question for the same ticket on Sunday morning, the passage of events (the Saturday night lottery draw) has changed the value of the ticket in the eyes of the parties. Either the ticket did not win, in which case it is worth nothing; or, if it did win, then the value of the ticket is based on the winnings, less a certain sum if Mr B does not want the publicity. Although this is a rather overly simplified example it illustrates a point that is equally true for IP. The example also makes it very easy to observe that the *ex-ante* valuation of the ticket (at 'close to £2') was not incorrect at the time of the transfer (before the draw) and that subsequent events (the ticket winning, or not) do not change the past as it was impossible for either party to have reliably predicted the 'win / lose' subsequent event. In this case the potential for the ticket to win was understood by all parties and had been priced-in to the initial ticket sale by the operator of the lottery. A winning ticket produces an *ex-post* value that is significantly different from the *ex-ante* valuation and, under the revised guidance, that difference would be cause for a tax authority to check the validity of the *ex-ante* valuation. However, the evidence gathered during audit will show that, as the sale took place before the lottery draw, neither Mr A nor Mr B could anticipate the future event, and therefore the *ex-ante* valuation was indeed 'at arm's length'.

6.124   The above concept is not restricted to *ex-ante* and *ex-post* valuations of an HTVI; the same concept is important in selecting the most appropriate valuation method for all IP and then in determining the facts upon which to apply that method. When we discussed the lifecycle of IP (see **6.111–6.113**), we recognised that the methodology used to assess a fair value of the intangible would change from one that considered cost to one that considered future income, as the risk profile of the licensee and licensor changed. The data known to the parties, and the risk profile of the parties, continues to change over the whole life of the IP and so (just as in the lottery ticket example above) the point of time at which the pricing is tested will affect the outcome of the valuation exercise, even if it does not change the methodology that one applies. For this reason it is crucial to select the correct time at which to set the valuation and to use only information that would have been available to the licensor and the licensee at that time.

6.125   The statement above is supported by UK case law (evidencing what actually happens between unrelated parties). In a claim for damages for infringement of confidential information (see *Force India Formula One Team Limited v Malaysia Racing Team (and others)* [2012] EWHC 616 (Ch), the latter racing as 'Lotus' in the subsequent Formula 1 season) the court found there to be an infringement and sought to establish an equitable value for a hypothetical licence that would have been agreed between the parties to gain access to the confidential information. One question before the court was the point in time at which that hypothetical licence would have been negotiated. The point was important to the parties because changing circumstances meant that the value attributable to the licence was significantly different depending on whether the licence would have been agreed at the time of the original use of the confidential information, or later, when the Malaysia Racing Team was accepted as a contender in the Formula 1 race season. The following is extracted from the decision of The Hon Mr Justice Arnold:

'432 The Defendants contend that the date of the hypothetical negotiation is the beginning of August 2009, that being the date when any misuse of confidential information started. Force India contends that the parties would not have concluded a deal at that point, but rather would have postponed finalising the negotiation until 14 September 2009 when Lotus obtained its F1 entry. In support of this contention counsel for Force India argued that the value of the licence would only be clear once the parties knew whether or not Lotus had gained entry into F1.

433 In my judgment the Defendants are correct on this point. Prima facie the date of the negotiation is when the misuse of confidential information started. The parties are to be taken to know at that point what use the defendant is going to make of the confidential information. The misuse I have found largely took place in August 2009. Although some of that misuse continued after 14 September 2009, there was very little new misuse after 14 September 2009. Thus the majority of the misuse took place before Lotus had gained entry into F1, and would have to be paid for either way. Furthermore, as I shall discuss in more detail below, the purpose and effect of the misuse was to enable Aerolab and FondTech to arrive an initial model more quickly. It was always intended that the initial model would be the subject of extensive aerodynamic development from October 2009 to March 2010, and thus the design of the initial model was relatively unimportant. Still further, relatively little of the misused confidential information found its way into full-sized parts on the actual racing car. It follows that the value of the licence was not going to be significantly affected by whether or not Lotus achieved entry into F1.'

From this it is clear that the valuation exercise should take place at the time when the IP is used, and the exercise is to be based on the information available to the parties at that time, from the viewpoint of the parties at that time. Subsequent events are not to be taken into account because the licence deal would already have been struck.

6.126 When circumstances are unclear at the time of first use, or change rapidly in the early years after first use, a tax authority might argue that uncontrolled entities would have either delayed their negotiation, or would have entered into a short-term agreement that would have been renegotiated when matters were clearer. The former point is dismissed by the example above, and for the latter point to be valid, it would be for the tax authority to introduce evidence to show that uncontrolled entities behave in that way.

OECD EXAMPLES

6.127 Additional guidance on the transfer pricing of intangibles, including practical commercial examples which may be helpful for both businesses and tax authorities, are set out in the Annex to the new Chapter VI in the revised OECD Guidelines. Care should be exercised in considering these examples as they are intended only to illustrate the concepts contained in the guidance. They cannot be used to support a proposition that conflicts with the guidance.

Chapter 7

Profit split

INTRODUCTION

7.1   Although the profit split methodology is a long-standing method in the 'OECD Transfer Pricing Guidelines for Multinational Enterprises and Tax Administrations' (OECD Guidelines), historically it was not commonly applied by taxpayers as the 'appropriate method' to test the arm's-length nature of intra-group transactions. However, in recent years, interest in the profit split method has increased and this trend has continued in the light of the work of the OECD and G20 countries under the Base Erosion and Profit Shifting (BEPS) project. It is therefore important to understand when profit split may be relevant and, if it is, how it is applied in practice.

7.2   The 2018 revision to Section C of the OECD Guidelines[1] state that 'the transactional profit split method is particularly useful when the compensation to the associated enterprises can be more reliably valued by reference to the relative *shares* of their contributions to the profits arising in relation to the transaction(s) than by a more direct estimation of the value of those contributions'.

7.3   The profit split methodology is considered to be particularly relevant to transfer pricing analysis where more than one party makes a significant contribution to the generation of profits, ie where both parties to a transaction make unique and valuable contributions; as noted in Chapter 6, an example might be in the licensing or transfer of intangible assets. In such a case, independent parties might determine a price for a transaction between them on the basis of their relative contributions, making a two-sided transfer pricing analysis more appropriate than a one-sided method. Furthermore, as noted in the revised OECD Guidelines, the fact that both transacting parties make unique and valuable contributions will mean that, by definition, no reliable external comparable data will be available; consequently, it will not be possible to use another transfer pricing method.

7.4   A profit split is a methodology often applied by the commercial courts dealing with disputes over intangible property. A UK case in point is *Ultraframe (UK) Ltd v Eurocell Building Plastics Ltd* [2006] EWHC 1344 (Pat), where the High Court considered damages for infringement, of a patent and unregistered design rights, based on the concept of the royalty which would

---

1   Revisions to Section C, Pt III, Ch II, of the OECD Transfer Pricing Guidelines, published on 4 June 2018.

have been agreed to allow use of the IP. Is this relevant for transfer pricing practitioners? The judge in that case noted:

> 'The reasonable royalty is to be assessed as the royalty that a willing licensor and a willing licensee would have agreed. Where there are truly comparable licences in the relevant field these are the most useful guidance for the court as to the reasonable royalty. Another approach is the profits available approach. This involves an assessment of the profits that would be available to the licensee, absent a licence, and apportioning them between the licensor and the licensee.'

7.5   This confirms that what a commercial court seeks (the value of a licence between a willing licensor and licensee) and what transfer pricing practitioners seek (the licence that would have been agreed between unconnected parties) is actually the same; that was a point taken in the 2018 US Appeal Court decision in *Medtronic Inc & Consolidated Subsidiaries v Commissioner of Internal Revenue* [No 17-1866 United States Court of Appeals, Eighth Circuit]. Hence these commercial courts provide insight into how a court might view a transfer pricing case, which valuation methodologies are acceptable and which fall short of evidential quality. The excerpt quoted above confirms both a preference for using comparable licences and, where they are not available, the appropriateness of the profit split methodology for determining a reasonable royalty for the use of intangible assets in case of dispute between unconnected parties.

7.6   The minimum standards agreed as part of the BEPS Final Reports on transfer pricing reduce the possibility of using inappropriate comparable uncontrolled price (CUP) or comparable uncontrolled transactions (CUT) for the transfer pricing of intangibles by stressing the need to show comparability. Consequently the use of profit split for pricing intangible asset transactions is likely to continue and, indeed, increase. At the time of writing, this trend has already been observed; the use of a profit split method to price intercompany transactions involving intangible assets is becoming increasingly common amongst taxpayers and tax authorities.

7.7   The driver for selecting an appropriate methodology for transfer pricing purposes is the functional analysis; the analysis of the relevant contribution to the value of the transaction by each party. There is no industry or transaction type where profit split cannot potentially be the most appropriate transfer pricing methodology. For example, this method may be used in situations as diverse as insurance arrangements where control over risk is shared, or for pricing the sharing of savings generated by centralised activities such as procurement.

OVERVIEW OF PROFIT SPLIT

7.8   The profit split method seeks to test or establish the arm's-length nature of pricing by determining the overall profit from a transaction and its division between the parties, based on what unconnected enterprises would expect to realise from engaging in those transactions.

7.9   The OECD's revised guidance on profit split also identifies three particular situations in which the use of a profit split method may be appropriate:

1.   where both parties to a transaction contribute unique and valuable intangibles in relation to the transaction;

2.   where two transacting parties are engaged in highly integrated operations; and

3.   where there is a high degree of uncertainty for each of the parties to a transaction, for example in transactions involving the shared assumption of significant risks, or the separate assumption of closely related risks.

7.10   Where both parties make unique and valuable contributions to a transaction, a 'one-sided' transfer pricing analysis, such as cost-plus or the transactional net margin method (TNMM), does not take into account the balance of risk and the contributions of the parties. It would therefore be inappropriate to treat one of the transacting parties as the 'tested party', receiving a relatively 'fixed' remuneration; it would be more likely that, in these circumstances, unrelated parties would share in the profits (or losses) of the venture. Hence a profit split approach, which explicitly considers both transacting parties (ie a two-sided analysis), would be more likely to be an appropriate method.

7.11   There are many circumstances in which profit split might be considered an appropriate methodology for transfer pricing purposes. Some examples are provided below but this list is by no means exhaustive:

●   Where there is insufficient reliable data to analyse comparability so as to determine an arm's-length outcome by any method other than profit split, noting the point set out in the revised OECD Guidelines that 'a lack of closely comparable, uncontrolled transactions ... should not *per se* lead to a conclusion that the transactional profit split method is the most appropriate method'.

●   Where the nature of the business arrangements means that both parties to a transaction are performing highly valuable functions and bearing significant risks such that appropriate comparables cannot be identified to price one end of the transaction.

●   Where there are a variety of transactions (eg transfers of tangible assets, the licensing of intangible assets and the provision of services) between the associated enterprises, some of which may involve overlaps, and there are no comparables for the combination of transactions. In these cases, profit methods may be a more reliable way to set or review the transfer pricing used in the dealings between the associated enterprises, or to check the findings made using traditional methods if there is doubt about the reliability of the data used or the outcome produced.

●   Where the supply chain is highly integrated and the parties to the transaction share the key risks or provide the key intangibles. This situation may arise, for example, where product development risk is genuinely shared between associated manufacturing entities, one of whom supplies highly specialised components to another group company.

7.12   One of the strengths of the profit split method is that all relevant parties to a transaction are directly evaluated as part of the pricing methodology. Contrast this with one-sided methods which, by definition, consider only one of the parties to a transaction and might, therefore, lead to a result which is inconsistent with arm's-length behaviour, ie an unexplained result for the party not being analysed.

7.13   The profit split method does, however, suffer from notable weaknesses which need to be considered and overcome in a proper application of this method. These weaknesses include:

- the fact that the profit split method does not directly rely on information about independent enterprises (except for one aspect of the residual profit split discussed below);

- difficulties, for both associated enterprises and tax authorities, in obtaining the detailed information required for a proper application of the profit split method; and

- challenges with identifying and supporting the appropriate profit splitting factors (also considered below).

Although the profit split method is rarely applied by independent enterprises as a means for establishing pricing arrangements, it is worth noting that this, in itself, is not a reason to consider the profit split as inappropriate. The revisions to the OECD Guidelines, helpfully, confirm that 'transfer pricing methods are not necessarily intended to replicate arm's length behaviour but rather to serve as a means of establishing and/or verifying arm's length outcomes for controlled transactions'.

7.14   Care should be taken to record the reasons why profit split (or, indeed, any chosen method) is selected as the most appropriate transfer pricing methodology. The reasons, and the recording of those reasons, should be undertaken in a manner that would be considered to be 'evidential'. Referring to another UK case, *General Tyre & Rubber Co v Firestone Tyre & Rubber Co Ltd* [1975] WLR 819, the judge commented that it is for the plaintiff to adduce evidence which will guide the court. The ruling notes as follows:

'This evidence may consist of the practice, as regards royalty, in the relevant trade or in analogous trades; perhaps of expert opinion expressed in publications or in the witness box; possibly of the profitability of the invention; and of any other factor on which the judge can decide the measure of loss.'

7.15   Guidance provided by the courts in both tax disputes and commercial disputes as to the evidential nature of material brought before the court is thus relevant to a profit split analysis. This latter point can be seen in the decision of the US Tax Court in *Medtronic v Commissioner*, T.C Memo 2016-112, in which the trial judge rejected the IRS' use of an aggregate comparable profits method as a means to value a royalty on the grounds that this did not take into account the value contributed by one party, as defined by the functional analysis. The trial judge also rejected the taxpayer's use of comparable uncontrolled transactions in two (out of four) instances due to lack of comparability. In those two cases the court therefore created its own valuation analysis.

7.16   To apply a profit split methodology, there are two broad steps, though we will break this down further shortly:

(1)   Identify the profit to be split. This might be the total profit arising from the arrangements (a 'total available profit' split), or the residual profit that cannot be easily assigned to one party or the other by another means (a 'residual profit' split). A residual profit split approach requires there to be other activities that are 'routine' in nature and which can be accurately priced by way of another transfer pricing method. Commercial disputes settled before the UK courts by applying a profit split commonly look at total available profits due to the added uncertainty introduced in the residual profit split method. In transfer pricing, however, the popularity of the two approaches is, historically, reversed.

Most commonly, the combined profits to be split in either approach are operating profits, ensuring that both income and expenses are attributed to the relevant related enterprise on a consistent basis. However, it is important to consider the accurate delineation of the transaction in determining the appropriate profits to split. As noted in the revised OECD Guidelines, where two transacting parties are independently responsible for economically significant risks which impact their own level of operating expenses (ie they do not share such risks), a profit split based on gross profits may be more appropriate.

Another important factor to consider is whether the profits to be split are actual profits, or anticipated profits. Again the revised guidance from the OECD is helpful here. Where the functional analysis indicates that both parties share the assumption of economically significant risks, a split of actual profits may be more appropriate. On the other hand, if a profit split method is found to be the most appropriate method (eg because both parties contribute unique and valuable intangible assets) but one of the parties does not share in the significant risks, a split of anticipated profits may be more appropriate.

Irrespective of whether the profit is defined as operating profit or gross profit, and whether actual or anticipated profits are to be split, it is essential to ensure that the relevant financial information of the parties is consistent and reflects, only, the transaction being considered. In practice, it can be a significant challenge to make sure that the financial data has been determined under a common set of accounting rules, and that financial information for other transactions involving one or more of the parties to the transaction are excluded from the profit split analysis. It will therefore be important to evidence and appropriately document the decisions taken and assumptions made in determining the relevant financial information to use in the profit split analysis.

(2)   Split the relevant profit identified above in line with the expectations that would have been agreed between third parties. In general terms, the profit is split by reference to the value contributed by the parties; those contributions will be identified by a functional analysis and valued by either available external data or sound economic theory; in practice, it is common to find that both have been applied.

Whilst there is no prescriptive list of profit splitting factors, or criteria to determine those factors, the OECD Guidelines identify three considerations which need to be taken into account. A profit split factor should:

(a)   be independent of transfer prices, ie based on sales earned from, or expenses paid to, independent parties;

(b)   be verifiable; and

(c)   be supported by comparables data and/or internal data from the associated enterprises.

7.17   It is also worth noting that 'sound economic theory' in this context does not mean 'established' or 'commonly used' but an approach that is of 'evidential' quality. For example, splitting profits according to the 'rule of thumb' (25% of profits belong to the licensor, 75% to the licensee) is simple and therefore appealing, but it is not a method of 'evidential' quality (see the US case of *Uniloc USA Inc v Microsoft Corporation* US Court of Appeal for the Federal Circuit 03-CV-044). The 'rule of thumb' will not provide evidence of the arm's-length price under any circumstances. In order to achieve a result which is supportable, an analysis will be required to determine the appropriate split, given the facts and circumstances of the transaction.

7.18   As multinational enterprises (MNEs) enter into a wide variety of complex and innovative commercial transactions and arrangements, sometimes new ideas are required from economists, valuers, business or tax specialists to capture the true value of each party's contribution. Such ideas must inevitably grow out of interpretation of the material facts and the relationship between the parties and out of fundamentally supportable economics and reliable data. In practice, therefore, the profit split methodology is one of the most complex transfer pricing analyses to undertake.

That said, there is never an authority to depart from the fundamental basis of the arm's-length principle: that transfer pricing is tested by reference to what happens between unrelated parties. No matter how superficially attractive a theoretical econometric analysis appears to be, it must be based on arm's-length comparability to meet the fundamental requirements of the arm's-length principle.

APPLICATION OF PROFIT SPLIT

7.19   Profit split methods are transfer-pricing valuation methods that identify the combined profit arising from a controlled transaction which is to be split between the associated enterprises, and then determine an appropriate ratio for that split on a basis that accords with the arm's-length principle. That requires the split to be calculated using evidence of third-party behaviour, or an economically valid basis, which approximates the division of profits that would have been anticipated and reflected in an agreement made at arm's length between independent parties.

7.20   Where data is available from transactions involving independent enterprises, such data can be useful for determining an appropriate split of profits. For example, joint venture arrangements between independent parties, pharmaceutical collaborations, co-promotion, or co-marketing arrangements, and development projects in the oil and gas sector all offer potential sources of information to inform the relevant split of profits under a profit split transfer pricing analysis. In practice, however, it can be difficult to obtain either confirmation of the comparability of such third party arrangements, or the information required to determine the split factor used by third parties; often, therefore, the profit split analysis will need to rely on internal data from the associated enterprises involved in the controlled transaction being analysed, with reference to their relative contributions as measured by their functions, assets and risks.

A five-step methodology for applying profit split to a licence of IP

7.21   The calculation of a licence rate by way of profit split typically follows the five-step process described below. The transfer pricing practitioner is expected to exercise judgement, so if the facts and circumstances of a particular case demand additional steps or a different approach, compared to these five steps, there can be no excuse for not taking that into account in designing the transfer pricing work program.

Step 1: Identify the transaction and assess appropriate transfer pricing methodology

7.22   The first step is to correctly identify and delineate the transaction and confirm whether profit split is an appropriate methodology to price the transaction. We would establish the nature and impact of the IP which is subject to the licence, which of the parties bears the economically significant risks in relation to the IP, and confirm that it is not possible to identify an internal or external CUP/CUT which meets the requisite level of comparability to allow us to reliably price the licence accordingly. We would then document the reasons why profit split is therefore an 'appropriate method' for determining an arm's-length licence fee.

Step 2: Identify the profit to be split

7.23   In this step, we establish the profit to be split. This comprises the licensee's profits from using the IP (income of the licensee less relevant costs of the licensee) and any additional costs of the licensor which relate to the exploitation of the IP, such as its expenses associated with maintaining the IP. Through this process we ascertain the net benefit achieved from the exploitation of the IP. As noted above, there are options to apply either a total available profit, or a residual profit, analysis; care must be taken to analyse the limitations and benefits of both approaches in deciding which to apply. However, the identification of profit to be split begins in the same way for both methods. In the UK commercial case of *Ultraframe v Eurocell Building Plastics* [2006] EWHC 1344 (Pat), the total available profits method was used to determine the split likely to be agreed between a willing licensor and willing licensee, bearing in mind the nature of the product and the market in which the IP was used. This case is instructive as to how to ascertain the relevant profit to be split, regardless of the selection of the total or residual method.

7.24   In summary, one tries to create a unified profit and loss account for the transaction, including all of the profits arising from the transaction and all of the costs but, as noted above, excluding other costs of the parties which are unrelated to the IP licence being analysed. In a simple IP licensing case where the parties only transact with each other, we might take the entire profit and loss account of a licensee and add some costs (ongoing maintenance and protection, for example) of the licensor. In this simple example, income arises to just one party – say, the licensee – but we must be open-minded and inclusive in our analysis because, commonly, that is not what actually happens. We have also assumed that all income of the licensee relates to the IP under consideration, and that may not be true in 'real life' as the licensee may have other products and income streams that are not connected in any way to the IP licence under review. In looking at the costs of the licensor, we must be similarly vigilant; for example, where there is more than one licensee, we should not take all of the maintenance and protection costs into account in this exercise, as those costs also benefit other licensees.

7.25   If we are using a total profit split approach then we have completed this step and we can move to determine the ratio of the split. However, a residual profit split method requires further work to identify the profit to be split – the elimination of any return for 'routine functions'.

7.26   Having ascertained the total profit of the overall activity made by the connected parties (see above), we must now identify, analyse and reward any 'routine' function that either (or both) of the parties perform. This reward is removed from the total available profit, and the remaining balance is then the relevant profit to be split between the parties in an appropriate manner. This introduces additional challenges to the accuracy of the analysis:

(1)   Did we correctly identify all of the routine functions?

(2)   Did we accurately ascertain all of the costs of the routine functions, including any on-costs?

(3)   Did we identify an appropriate transfer pricing methodology to reward the routine functions?

(4)   Did we calculate an arm's-length reward for the routine functions?

In addition, when we come to the calculation of the split ratio:

(5)   Now that we have a reduced profit to allocate in the profit split, how do we find data to drive that allocation?

7.27   In assessing whether to apply a total or a residual profit split approach, the evidential value of the work must be considered. The additional analysis in a residual profit split (as compared to a total profit split) may either increase or decrease the robustness of the work:

* Where routine functions are readily identifiable, costs are easily ascertained and the correct transfer pricing methodology and the appropriate reward (the margin) identified with a high degree of confidence, then as this approach reduces the value of the residual to be split the potential impact of any uncertainty in that split calculation is reduced. In those circumstances the additional uncertainty arising from the routine reward may be less than the reduction in uncertainty arising from the profit split and, if so, the residual approach would improve the robustness of the final answer.

* However, the evidential value of the work can be reduced if the identification of the routine function is difficult, or the allocation of income and cost requires judgement, or the applicable transfer pricing methodology is debatable, or the evidence of the appropriate profit margin suggests a wide range of arm's-length returns. In these circumstances the additional uncertainty caused by the determination and calculation of the routine functions, and their reward, may be greater than the reduction in uncertainty arising from the reduced pool of profit to split. In that case the total profit split approach provides the more robust answer and, therefore, the better evidence.

7.28   A brief comparison of the two methods is set out below:

	Total Available Profit Split	**Residual Profit Split**
Size of profit to be split	Maximised	Minimised
Level of data analysis required	Lower	Higher
Activity of parties	Unique/routine activity taken together	Segregate activity of both parties into routine/ unique
Sub-analysis of arm's-length reward for routine function	Avoided	Undertaken as a preliminary step to isolate the residual profit. The potential error arising from this step is additional to that from the profit split calculation

	Total Available Profit Split	**Residual Profit Split**
Calculation of the split	There can be third-party evidence, or evidence, of how the econometric split should be performed. A split based on pure econometric principles can be acceptable if the above are not available	Third-party evidence is less likely to be found and econometric split is commonly used, based on pure economic principles
Tax audit risks	Limited to the calculation of profit and to the split applied	Calculation of overall profit, the routine activity identification and cost analysis, the reward for routine activity, and the split applied to the residual profit
How commonly used?	More common in unrelated party transactions Less common in related party transactions	Less common in unrelated party transactions More common in related party transactions

Step 3: Split the profit

7.29   Once the most appropriate form of profit split has been selected and the appropriate profit calculated, the next step is to split this profit between the licensor and the licensee. Some of the common approaches are discussed below. In practice, it is often better to use more than one approach so that there is an element of corroboration in the results of the analysis.

Case law

7.30   Guidance relevant to a total profit split analysis can be found in commercial court cases, available in the public domain; cases which attribute the profits generated by IP between a licensor and a licensee. These are examples of what arm's-length behaviours would be in circumstances where a court is asked to split profits arising from the use of IP between a 'willing licensor and a willing licensee'.

7.31   Analysis of case law shows that the split appropriate in any situation will depend on its own fact pattern; the relative values and costs of contributions by each party along with the value-impact of the transaction under examination. Thus, when reading third-party cases, even though an analysis of the actual split found in each case would provide material from which one might create an 'industry average', this would not meet the requirements of the arm's-length principle. Analysis of these cases is therefore appropriate to understand the methodology of the profit split and the factors which influenced the actual split; this can then be applied to the facts and circumstances of the particular transfer pricing case.

7.32   That approach is fully consistent with the arm's-length principle and it accords with the need to produce work of evidential quality. The need for transfer pricing valuations to be evidential in case of any dispute brought before a court is illustrated in the US case of *Daubert v Merrell Dow Pharmaceuticals Inc* 113 S.Ct 2786 (1993) and the UK court's approach in *General Tyre & Rubber Co v Firestone Tyre & Rubber Co Ltd* [1976] RPC 197 (HL). In the latter case, it is worth considering the following statement which was made in relation to the use of a claimed CUT for determining an appropriate licence fee:

> 'Before a "going rate" of royalty can be taken as the basis on which an infringer should be held liable, it must be shown that the circumstances in which the going rate was paid are the same, or at least comparable, with those in which the patentee and the infringer are assumed to strike their bargain.'

7.33   Under the profit split methodology, the determination of the split ratio is chosen based on hypothetical negotiations. The case law in some countries, such as the UK, indicates that this exercise can start from an assumed split which is then adjusted for the specific facts and circumstances of the case by the application of 'scientific, technical, or specialised knowledge … based on scientific and technical grounding'[2]. Thus, this approach will alter the starting estimate to arrive at an appropriate profit split, given the specific facts and circumstances.

7.34   The case law in other countries, such as the US, rejects that idea and requires the analysis to proceed from first principles; however, it is arguable that this is simply to start at a different assumed ratio for the split of profits, either 0:100 or 100:0. It is not clear that the two approaches would lead to a different answer, as cases in both countries apply precisely the same factors to determine the profit split.

7.35   In practice, as the transfer pricing analysis has to be acceptable to the tax authority responsible for auditing each end of the transaction, it is likely to be appropriate to take the more conservative approach of analysing the factors and concluding on an appropriate split of the profits, rather than assuming an initial split and then adjusting (based on the same analysis) to reach the same split. The result may actually be the same, but the ease of explaining it to both tax authorities may well be different.

7.36   In terms of ascertaining the factors to take into account in determining an appropriate split, a seminal court case in the US is *Georgia-Pacific Corp v US Plywood Corp* (318 F Supp 1116 (SDNY 1970)) (the '*Georgia-Pacific*' case). It concerned the infringement of IP and led the courts to establish the

---

2   *Uniloc*, 632 F 3d at 13315 (citing J Weinstein & M Berger, Weinstein's Evidence, para 702[2], 1988).

factors considered to be critical in determining a reasonable royalty rate – in that case, as a base for the estimation of damages.

7.37   Although the *Georgia-Pacific* factors originate from a court case dealing with IP infringement, they were used by that court to ascertain a 'reasonable royalty' as a first step in assessing damages. This 'reasonable royalty' is one which willing parties would have negotiated, and so it is the same as an arm's-length royalty. Therefore the logic applied in *Georgia-Pacific* can also be applied in transfer pricing analysis. The methodology remains valid even if different IP is involved. The factors are relied upon to inform a hypothetical negotiation process between the licensor and the licensee, where each party presents various scenarios to which the factors are applicable and which are supported by direct and circumstantial evidence.

7.38   This same approach is also supported by UK case law, which shows that the methodology is not restricted to patents but can be applied to other forms of IP. In *Blayney v Clogau St David's Gold Mine Ltd and Others* (Case No A3/2001/1755, 2002), an objection was raised to the use of the methodology outside of patents. This was rejected, with the ruling stating that there is:

> '... no reason not to apply it in cases on infringements of copyright. In each case, the infringement is an interference with the property rights of the owner ... [and] though the nature of the monopoly conferred by a patent is not the same as that conferred by copyright [there is] ... no reason why that should affect the recoverability of damages where the monopoly right has been infringed.'

7.39   The 15 factors noted in the *Georgia-Pacific* case are frequently referred to in US cases assessing the respective contributions of the licensor and the licensee. The same 15 factors are routinely considered by the courts of other countries, but without reference to the US case. These factors are detailed in **7.57**.

Internal data

7.40   The clear benefit of using internal data to drive a profit split, from the viewpoint of the taxpayer or advisor, is that the data is likely to be available, notwithstanding the complexities of correctly applying the data, as noted above. Though that sounds rather simplistic, it is very important for taxpayers and advisors to consider the availability of data before setting out on a particular valuation methodology. If data critical to the methodology is not going to be available, it is worth identifying that from the outset, and then record why this methodology cannot be used, before moving to another method.

7.41   Some of the most commonly applied approaches to splitting profit using external data are set out below, although it should be noted that this is by no means an exhaustive list. The OECD Guidelines go to great length to explain that there is no right or wrong answer; rather, the split factor should be based on the functional analysis, taking account of the key drivers of profit from the transaction being analysed:

- costs, eg historic or forecast, relative spend, and/or investment in specific areas such as R&D or marketing;

- assets, eg total value of operating assets or intangible assets, and/or specific categories of assets such as production assets, or IT assets;

- capital employed;

- employee compensation or employee numbers, eg number of 'senior' staff; and

- headcount or time spent.

7.42   Sometimes the split of profits can be determined based on the relative costs of the parties contributing to the value inherent in the transaction. It is not true to say that the output from BEPS Action 8, in the form of revised transfer pricing guidance for intangibles, nor the revised OECD guidance on profit split, argues against this. The OECD Guidelines indicate that there is rarely a correlation between 'cost' of creation and 'value' of an intangible (see paras 6.142 and 6.143, for example). Whilst it is intuitively obvious that there is no correlation between the cost of creating IP and the value of the IP created, when we are looking at how to split the income arising from that IP then it can be more logical to look to the costs incurred by the parties as a proxy for their relative contribution to value. This approach rests on a simple assumption that, in a commercial setting, cash is its own balancing factor; businesses will spend their limited resources in the way that brings best return.

7.43   This approach may have more validity where both sides are working on the same thing. For example, if software is being written by two parties then (without evidence to the contrary, and this should always be checked) it might be reasonable to assume that the relative value of the contribution of both parties is equivalent to their respective costs. More senior people are more highly paid, and a higher volume of people writing the software leads to increased cost. It may be more difficult to support this assumption where the contributions of the participants is significantly different; hardware, software and marketing intangibles may drive value in a single transaction, and the additional aspect of the relative value of each area makes this simple cost-based approach more difficult to support to an 'evidential standard'. In such cases, it may be necessary to risk-weight the costs of each party in order to restore parity; or, of course, it may be more appropriate to use a factor other than cost to split the profit.

7.44   If historical cost of creation is a good proxy to value creation, it is important to consider the amortisation of value associated with that cost incurred at a point in time. Take the simple case concerning two parties contributing to a marketing intangible. The long-run impact of advertising spend to a typical fast-moving consumer goods (FMCG) branded product might be three years. There would also be costs associated with creating the name and art work, and registering the trademark, which will have a longer lifecycle (say, seven years). The allocation of profit between the participants must take into account the different amortisation cycles for the respective costs incurred in each of the areas.

7.45   Another important factor to consider, particularly for analyses which are being used to establish a licence rate (as opposed to test a rate already applied), is whether the profit split factor should be fixed (eg a 60%-40% split) based on an historical analysis of the parties internal data, or variable depending on the parties' future data.

Bargaining theory

7.46   In determining the appropriate split of profits, we must take into account the respective bargaining positions of the parties. Often this is achieved through the application of bargaining theory.

With regards to profit split, paragraph 2.128 of the OECD Guidelines states that:

> 'An alternative approach to how to apply a residual analysis could seek to replicate the outcome of bargaining between independent enterprises in the free market. In this context, in the first stage, the initial remuneration provided to each participant would correspond to the lowest price an independent seller reasonably would accept in the circumstances and the highest price that the buyer would be reasonably willing to pay. Any discrepancy between these two figures could result in the residual profit over which independent enterprises would bargain. In the second stage, the residual analysis therefore could divide this pool of profit based on an analysis of any factors relevant to the associated enterprises that would indicate how independent enterprises might have split the difference between the seller's minimum price and the buyer's maximum price'.

7.47   Further, paragraphs 9.27 to 9.31 of the OECD Guidelines outline the concept of 'options realistically available' to each party in understanding how parties would have transacted at arm's length. Under commonly accepted principles of bargaining theory, the key factors in the analysis include consideration of:[3]

(1)   *Availability of alternatives* – if a party has a number of credible (and it is important that they really are 'credible') alternatives, they will be in a better position than one with few available alternatives to the transaction in question. It is commonly understood that the availability of alternatives is often the most important of all factors in determining

---

3   Muthoo, A., *A Non-Technical Introduction to Bargaining Theory*, World Economics, Vol 1, No 2, June 2000.

the relative bargaining position for the purposes of a profit split analysis.

(2)   *Information asymmetry* – if information asymmetry exists, the party with more or better information will be in a better bargaining position.

(3)   *Commitment* – if a party has not formally committed to anything, it is likely that they will be in a better bargaining position when compared to a party which has openly committed to the transaction prior to finalisation of the agreement.

(4)   *Patience* – if one party has the ability to wait for better opportunities to come along, they are likely to be in a better bargaining position.

(5)   *Risk aversion* – if one party has a greater tolerance for risk, it is likely that the pool of potentially acceptable projects will be greater and, as such, with more choice, that party will be in the better bargaining position.

7.48   Economist John Nash has written widely on the subject of bargaining theory. In a situation where two parties are bargaining, a Nash equilibrium for a bargaining situation occurs at the point where the positions of both parties are maximised simultaneously, ie there are no alternative options in which one party can do better while the other party is at least as well off. The eventual outcome of a bargaining situation is therefore dependent on the relative bargaining power of the parties involved, ie the relative ability of the parties to exert influence over each other.

An analysis of the bargaining position of both the parties (the licensor and the licensee, for example) might therefore form part of the transfer pricing analysis.

Step 4: Determine the licence rate

7.49   In this step, the licensor's share of profit, plus any reimbursement of their costs, is expressed as a percentage of the relevant turnover of the licensee to determine an appropriate licence rate.

Step 5: Check the result

7.50   Expressed simply: regardless of the technical merits of a methodology, if the result is incredible then it is not the most appropriate method. Here is where the transfer pricing professional exhibits judgement in addition to, and overriding, technical competence.

It is critical to sense check the result and ensure that it is credible. It might be possible to create a profit split model which is theoretically sound but which produces a result that is unsupportable. For example, in the UK case of *Arbuthnott v Bonnyman* [2014] EWHC 1410 (Ch), the trial judge rejected as evidence valuations compiled by the applicant's expert witness on this very point; they led to answers that simply were not credible. Although the methodologies had been applied in a technically competent manner, the underlying assumptions used did not withstand the challenge of the court as to their reasonableness in application to the case at hand.

7.51 The transfer pricing professional must apply not only technical accuracy in any methodology, but also judgement and professional scepticism as to whether this is the most appropriate methodology to use. If an acceptable methodology, accurately applied, generates an incredible result then it is not appropriate to use it in that case.

The rule of thumb

7.52 This approach is frequently raised as a more simplistic and realistic approach. It suggests that the royalty to be paid for use of IP will generally be 25% to 33% of the gross profit derived by the licensee from its use, or a 5% royalty on turnover. The rule of thumb has no scientific basis and it suffers from numerous failings, including a failure to define 'gross profit', or to acknowledge that the IP may or may not lead to increased operating costs, that the risk sharing might lay more heavily on one party or the other, or what a fair rate of return for using the IP might be. In short, it has no evidential value at all.

7.53 Despite its many shortcomings, the rule of thumb has been used extensively in industry because of its pure simplicity. It came to the attention of the US court in *Uniloc USA, Inc v Microsoft Corporation* (2011). The Federal Circuit rejected the '25% rule of thumb' in calculating patent damage awards. The Federal Circuit analysed the basis of the methodology and concluded that it did not meet the minimum standard to be admitted as evidence before a US court; it bore no relation to the facts of the case and, as such, was arbitrary, unreliable and irrelevant.

7.54 In low-value cases between unconnected parties, where information is limited and the cost of getting better data cannot be reconciled with the ultimate likely licence value, this method is commonly used to set the licence fee. As between unrelated parties, that may be a fact of life and, if so, it is possible that this would provide evidence that, in a similar related-party case, a licence fee could be set on a similar basis. However, on audit, the rule of thumb is unlikely to provide a taxpayer with any admissible evidence at all with which to support their transfer price. This method is therefore to be avoided.

STRENGTHS AND WEAKNESSES OF PROFIT SPLIT

7.55 Some of the perceived strengths of the profit split methodology are as follows:

● Less reliance is placed on comparability with observed third-party transactions, and so the method remains useful even if no such transactions can be found; but, as noted in the OECD Guidelines, there must still be a reference to comparable data, internal data, or both, and the methodology applied must be verifiable.

- Both parties to the arrangements are examined, and so profit is unlikely to be allocated in such a way as to leave one or other in an extreme or improbable profit position.

- Both parties to the transaction are being examined, in accordance with the guidance from OECD that the position of both parties should be taken into account.

- The data used for the profit split is (usually) held by the taxpayer and hence will (usually) be available, subject to the complexity in ensuring the data is consistent, appropriate and correctly applied.

7.56   However, there are also perceived weaknesses of the profit split methodology. These include:

- The external market data used to identify the contributions of the parties is not as closely linked to the relevant transactions, compared with other transfer pricing methods. Operating at 'once removed', as it were, gives an air of greater subjectivity in practice. This is particularly the case where the analysis contains no reference to third party transactions, prices, or split factors.

- Related to the above, the specific factors used to split profit commonly rely on internal metrics (eg cost, staff numbers, relative value of assets) rather than on third-party data.

- Appropriate application of the profit split method requires the production of considerable data from more than one jurisdiction, so there may be issues of data availability.

- Certainty is required that revenues and costs have been reported on consistent bases by all parties to the arrangements. This might mean special efforts being made by the parties to re-state their books, or to modify their internal systems appropriately. Additionally, it can be difficult to accurately 'carve out' the financial results applicable to other transactions (whether related party or third party) in order to ensure that the data being used for the profit split relates only to the controlled transaction under review.

- It can be challenging to remain true to the arm's-length principle and to measure, at some level, the profit split by reference to the transactions of unrelated parties.

- Inherently, the profit split method will usually rely on judgement at some level. Consequently, evidence of the reasons why the profit split is selected as the most appropriate transfer pricing method, the specific approach being applied, and the profit split factors which have been adopted, will be required and should be adequately documented.

FACTORS IN *GEORGIA-PACIFIC*

7.57 The 15 factors identified in *Georgia-Pacific Corp v US Plywood Corp* (1970) [318 F Supp 1116, 166 USPQ (BNA) 235] are summarised below:

(1) The royalties received by the patentee for the licensing of the patent in suit proving or tending to prove an established royalty.

(2) The rates paid by the licensee for the use of other patents comparable to the patent in suit.

(3) The nature and scope of the licence, as exclusive or non-exclusive, or as restricted or non-restricted in terms of territory or with respect to whom the manufactured product may be sold.

(4) The licensor's established policy and marketing program to maintain a patent monopoly by not licensing others to use the invention or by granting licences under special conditions designed to preserve that monopoly.

(5) The commercial relationship between the licensor and licensee, such as whether they are competitors in the same territory in the same line of business, or whether they are inventor and promoter.

(6) The effect of selling the patented specialty in promoting sales of other products of the licensee, the existing value of the invention to the licensor as a generator of sales of non-patented items, and the extent of such derivative or convoyed sales.

(7) The duration of the patent and the term of the licence.

(8) The established profitability of the product made under the patent, its commercial success, and its current popularity.

(9) The utility and advantages of the patent property over the old modes or devices, if any, that had been used for working out similar results.

(10) The nature of the patented invention, the character of the commercial embodiment of it as owned and produced by the licensor, and the benefits to those who have used the invention.

(11) The extent to which the infringer has made use of the invention and any evidence probative of the value of that use.

(12) The portion of the profit or of the selling price that may be customary in the particular business or in comparable businesses to allow for the use of the invention or analogous inventions.

(13) The portion of the realisable profit that should be credited to the invention as distinguished from non-patented elements, the manufacturing process, business risks, or significant features or improvements added by the infringer.

(14) The opinion testimony of qualified experts.

(15) The amount that a licensor (such as the patentee) and a licensee (such as the infringer) would have agreed upon (at the time the infringement began) if both had been reasonably and voluntarily trying to reach an agreement – that is, the amount an infringer would have been willing to pay as a royalty and yet be able to make a reasonable profit and which amount would have been acceptable by a prudent patentee who was willing to grant a licence.

The above factors are not exclusive, but indicative of what needs to be taken into account. These factors, adapted as necessary to suit the facts and circumstances of a particular case, could be applied to arrive at an arm's-length profit split between the licensee and licensor.

Chapter 8

Business restructuring

INTRODUCTION

8.1   It is a simple commercial truth that a business either grows or it shrinks, it succeeds or it fails; every business is in a constant process of change. Positive change is necessary for any business to remain attractive to customers because the alternative, standing still, is to become inefficient and expensive compared to competitors as they develop. Change is therefore a welcome aspect of business life. Change is normally driven by commercial need, and tax rules are one of the matters that need to be taken into account. Tax rules may prove to be a barrier to change (for example, exit taxation when assets or activities are moved) and they may also help shape the future business design (the location of assets and activity will drive the recognition of profit subject to tax, and the amount of tax paid has consequences for the business). Until recently, the pace of change in the international tax arena had been steady, but over the last few years we have seen a significant increase in that pace of change and this will continue over the next few years. International tax rules are being overhauled; there are changes to international tax rules defining 'permanent establishment' and in the understanding and application of transfer pricing. These changes in taxation rules and standards are being driven by a desire in many countries to adopt an international tax framework suited to current business models and practices, and the process is being coordinated through the OECD in its Base Erosion and Profit Shifting (BEPS) programme.

8.2   Any change in the operating model of a business might have implications for transfer pricing, but often those changes do not lead to a significant change in the arm's-length profitability of a multinational enterprise (MNE) in a particular country. For example, a MNE might decide to concentrate certain 'back-office' services into a single Shared Service Centre (SSC) located (typically) in a country offering lower-cost (relatively speaking) premises and a skilled workforce. Formation of the SSC will reduce employment costs in other MNE entities where staff are no longer required to perform the now centralised activities and those costs will be replaced by a (smaller) charge paid to the SSC. This is unlikely to change any other aspect of the transfer pricing methodologies applied by those entities in setting intercompany prices and it is unlikely that the profitability of that entity will fall – it might even rise slightly. The SSC, being a service provider to the group, will most likely receive remuneration, in the form of a charge (referred to above), sufficient for it to make a reasonable profit, relative to its cost base (ie its transfer pricing methodology might be cost plus, based on its operating costs) so the SSC will not attract significant profit. So, change happened, the business performance improved, there was a transfer pricing impact, but that impact was relatively small and non-contentious.

8.3   However, very occasionally in the life of a MNE there might be significant change; change on such a scale that the whole business is restructured. When this happens, the transfer pricing methodologies previously applied to each country entity of the MNE may become outdated and irrelevant such that a new approach is required. That, in turn, means that the profitability of a particular entity within the MNE might be significantly affected.

8.4   The current OECD Model Tax Treaty can trace its origins back to the 1927 League of Nations model. At that time the character of 'international trade' was very different. The aim of the Model Treaty, back then (and for many, many years after), was to reduce the barriers to international trade so that more cross-border trade would take place. The character of international trade as we know it today has changed dramatically, with almost instantaneous communication and data transfer and with improvements in logistics. These technical developments allowed MNEs to consider new ways of working; activity models that optimised business performance and profitability by centralising control, direction and risk-taking in one place whilst standardising activities that could not be centralised so that 'best practice' runs throughout the MNE.

8.5   In the early 1990s the first businesses transformed MNE efficiency, and profitability, by taking a holistic view of their business and optimising their supply chain networks (the phrase 'supply chain networks' refers to the complex web of suppliers, production and R&D facilities, distribution centres, sales subsidiaries, channel partners and customers). Typically the most efficient commercial structures involved a centralisation of activity away from regional businesses and into a 'principal' company supported by 'contract' or 'toll' manufacturers and 'commissionnaire' sales entities or 'simple' distributors. The business would also be supported by 'shared service centres' to take care of back-office functions. These models were very successful, changing the landscape for competitors, and accelerating the rate of change towards centralised business models. Today, most multinationals don't derive a significant proportion of their profits from the physical act of making products but rather from the ideas they generate which lead to those products, wherever products are made. It makes commercial sense to centralise the development, ownership and control of their intellectual property.

8.6   Business restructurings create, by their very nature, an enormous strain on a MNE so they are not undertaken lightly and certainly not purely for tax reasons. However, the most important factors in judging business performance and success remain the ability to drive up top-line growth and to drive down costs to maximise shareholder value. As these factors are now measured at the after-tax line, business taxes have to be taken into account when deciding where the more valuable activities should be located; this will have an impact on these decisions.

8.7   Governments understand that businesses must include the potential tax burden in their deliberations about where to invest. The sovereign nature of countries means that governments are free to set tax rates that are appropriate to their country and population, and with the increasing globalisation of business, tax rates are therefore a very effective tool that governments use to influence investment decisions. This leads to tax competition amongst nations but, in the view of some, it has also led to 'unfair' tax competition (see 'Harmful Tax Competition: An Emerging Global Issue' (OECD 1998)). There is now a strong political will to refresh the international tax framework and this has extensive political interest in many countries. Some territories (including the UK and Australia through their Diverted Profits Tax regimes) have already begun to adopt laws that change the balance of international taxation. However, if every country acted unilaterally there is a significant risk that double taxation would be unavoidable, which (together with uncertainty as to what tax burdens an enterprise would face) could lead to a reluctance to invest; that, in turn, could lead to a slowing of global GDP. To minimise these risks, the OECD began its BEPS project which is intended to establish international coherence in corporate income taxation ('Action Plan on Base Erosion and Profit Shifting' (OECD, 2013), p 15). Though the BEPS project has finished the OECD continues to look at the further changes that are still needed to modernise international tax law; however, the international tax compliance landscape has already seen some significant changes that aim to better align tax rules with modern business models and practices. For example, the definition of Permanent Establishment has been widened in the Model Tax Treaty to capture the activities of *commissionnaires* and agents. In addition, information available to tax authorities has been improved through the introduction of 'Country by Country reporting' (a BEPS minimum standard).

8.8   Lower tax rates do affect the investment decisions of multinational companies. In 1981, Ireland introduced a 10% tax rate for financial service companies with the express aim of encouraging inward investment. This 'special' tax rate was accepted by the EC (what is now the EU) as not amounting to 'State aid' because of the investment stimulus needed by Ireland; indeed, in 1988, the EC approved the extension of the 10% tax rate band to 'special trading houses', designed to market the products of companies employing fewer than 200 people (EC Press Release IP/88/59). This tax policy is credited by some as one of the reasons for the tremendous Irish growth and it was very effective ('Low-tax policies created the Tiger' *Irish Independent*, 24 October 2004). For example, in the three years to 2000, this small country of 3.8 million people attracted more foreign direct inward investment than either Japan or Italy (See United Nations, *World Investment Report 2001* (New York: United Nations Conference on Trade and Development [UNCTAD], 2001), p 291). When the EU thought that Ireland no longer needed dispensation from competition rules, and therefore should remove the special 10% tax rate, the Irish government settled on a business tax rate of 12.5% for all trading companies which was, and still is, 'low' compared to many other EU Member States; but things are changing.

8.9   Whilst Ireland's 12.5% remains one of the lowest business tax rate within the EU, the rate of UK corporation tax has seen a gradual decline in recent years, as part of the UK government's long-term objective of creating the most competitive corporate tax system in the G20. The UK is not alone in looking to reduce the burden of taxes on business to become, or remain, a competitive place in which to invest; but, following the public vote in June 2016 to leave the EU (so-called 'Brexit'), the UK Chancellor has lowered UK corporation tax rates even further, to ensure the attractiveness of investing in the UK.

8.10   When a business restructuring takes place, the rate of business tax is one of the factors taken into account when deciding where investment should be directed. In most reorganisations, a country with a high tax rate will not be chosen as the location for the principal value-creating elements of the business (if more than one choice is available) because, when everything is taken into account, the after-tax return is not greatest for the MNE. As the number of businesses that adopt a centralised model increases, this means that there are clear 'winners' in terms of attracting inward investment; but wherever there are 'winners' other territories see themselves as losing out. Countries that see an outflow of business activity, business profits and taxes, employment and employment taxes are therefore inclined to audit very closely both the conversion event (to ensure that any exit taxes due are identified, assessed and paid) and the transfer pricing of the new business arrangement.

8.11   For many years the OECD Transfer Pricing Guidelines did not provide specific help for MNEs and tax authorities to understand how a business restructuring should be viewed, priced and audited. In 2010, the OECD introduced a new chapter to the Guidelines, Chapter IX, which deals with the significant transfer pricing questions that arise following a business restructuring.

8.12   Although business restructurings are typically born out of a commercial need for change, it is not unreasonable to imagine that MNEs may need to restructure in response to changes to national tax law and international tax treaties which will happen as a result of the OECD's BEPS project. This is because fundamental revisions to international tax rules brought about by the BEPS project may negate the administrative and commercial benefits of certain supply chain arrangements and encourage some MNEs to alter how they operate to better fit with the new rules.

CHAPTER IX OF THE OECD TRANSFER PRICING GUIDELINES

8.13   The addition of Chapter IX in 2010 was the first fundamental change to the Guidelines since 1965. In fact, the process of developing guidelines for business restructurings had started in 2005, finally coming to fruition at the end of 2010 so the process was long and thorough. UK transfer pricing legislation, when it was originally enacted, required that our law be interpreted as best secures consistency with the Guidelines (see *Taxation (International and Other Provisions) Act 2010 (TIOPA 2010), s 164(4)*), but as Chapter IX did not exist at the time, it took a specific provision in *Finance Act 2011, s 58(1)* to bring the July 2010 version of the Guidelines into consideration. Hence, Chapter IX is arguably relevant to the interpretation of UK transfer pricing legislation only for company accounting periods beginning after 1 April 2011.

In July 2017 the OECD released a new version of the Guidelines to reflect a consolidation of changes resulting from the BEPS project. Chapter IX was not substantially updated as part of the BEPS project, but other parts of the Guidelines, particularly Chapter I (Guidance for Applying the Arm's Length Principle) and Chapter VI (Intangibles), which often both underpin Chapter IX analyses, have been updated and therefore should be taken into consideration when reviewing business changes. In most cases, these updates are regarded as being a clearer articulation of existing transfer pricing principles, not a 'new approach' and, as such, they need to be considered when analysing business restructurings from the date when Chapter IX came into UK law.

8.14   After a short introduction, there are two parts to Chapter IX and they deal with the following topics:

● Arm's-length compensation for the restructuring itself.

● Remuneration of post-restructuring controlled transactions.

Introduction

8.15   The following useful points are made in the introduction to Chapter IX.

8.16   There is no definition of what constitutes a 'business restructuring', but the chapter is concerned with the cross-border reorganisation of the commercial or financial relations between associated enterprises, including the termination or substantial renegotiation of existing arrangements. Therefore the chapter does not deal with the organic extension of a business or, indeed, the sale or disposal of a business.

8.17   The scope of Chapter IX extends to the application of the arm's-length principle in a restructuring, in the context of Article 9 of the Model OECD Double Tax Treaty. Critically, this means that Chapter IX should be considered to be explanatory material assisting the application of the arm's-length principle, as explained in Chapters I, II and III, in a restructuring event. That means that all of the concepts that we understand (and apply) – such as the reference to what happens between unconnected persons – also apply in Chapter IX. Chapter IX applies to transactions involving more than one entity, but not to the allocation of profit within one entity, between a head office and one or more branches, which is covered by Article 7 of the Model OECD Double Tax Treaty. Neither does Chapter IX cover 'domestic' anti-abuse rules that deal with issues such as controlled foreign companies (CFCs) and, in some countries, mandate how, in some circumstances, an 'exit charge' is to be calculated (such rules exist in Germany, for example).

The arm's-length principle does not, and should not, apply differently to a restructuring transaction or to related-party transactions after the restructuring compared to related-party transactions that have remained unchanged or to a business which is created in the same form as the restructured business. The question remains whether the actual transactions undertaken between related parties differ from those that would have happened if the parties were not related.

Part I: Arm's Length compensation for the restructuring itself

Understanding the restructuring, risks and 'options realistically available'

Risk

8.18 As noted, the substance of Chapter IX in the July 2017 version of the Guidelines has not changed significantly from the 2010 version. There has been some movement of commentary in that the explanation as to how to analyse risk in the context of transfer pricing has been moved to Chapter I (Section D.1.2.1) where it has been expanded upon. However, the identification of business risks and how they are allocated before and after any business restructuring remains fundamental to understanding the transfer pricing of the restructuring and the post-restructuring business model and therefore this section in Chapter I remains crucial to the transfer pricing analysis of restructurings.

Non-recognition and options realistically available

8.19 The starting point on this subject is paragraphs 1.119 to 1.128 in Chapter I of the revised OECD Guidelines. Paragraph 1.122 is of such importance that it is worth reminding ourselves here:

'This section sets out circumstances in which the transaction between the parties as accurately delineated can be disregarded for transfer pricing purposes. Because non-recognition can be contentious and a source of double taxation, every effort should be made to determine the actual nature of the transaction and apply arm's length pricing to the accurately delineated transaction, and to ensure that non-recognition is not used simply because determining an arm's length price is difficult. Where the same transaction can be seen between independent parties in comparable circumstances (i.e. where all economically relevant characteristics are the same as those under which the tested transaction occurs other than that the parties are associated enterprises) non-recognition would not apply. Importantly, the mere fact that the transaction may not be seen between independent parties does not mean that it should not be recognised. Associated enterprises may have the ability to enter into a much greater variety of arrangements than can independent enterprises, and may conclude transactions of a specific nature that are not encountered, or are only very rarely encountered, between independent parties, and may do so for sound business reasons. The transaction as accurately delineated may be disregarded, and if

166

appropriate, replaced by an alternative transaction, where the arrangements made in relation to the transaction, viewed in their totality, differ from those which would have been adopted by independent enterprises behaving in a commercially rational manner in comparable circumstances, thereby preventing determination of a price that would be acceptable to both of the parties taking into account their respective perspectives and the options realistically available to each of them at the time of entering into the transaction. It is also a relevant pointer to consider whether the MNE group as a whole is left worse off on a pre-tax basis since this may be an indicator that the transaction viewed in its entirety lacks the commercial rationality of arrangements between unrelated parties.'

Assuming that the economic substance and the legal form of the business arrangements are in harmony, there is no authority in the OECD Guidelines to ignore the actual transaction, and to price instead a fictitious transaction that did not happen, unless the actual transaction lacks commercial rationality.

8.20   That being said, it might be possible to look at a different transaction to assist in the task of discerning the arm's-length price for the transaction that did take place. This is referred to as 'options realistically available' in Chapter IX of the Guidelines. The theoretical basis of this approach cannot be faulted; in its most simple terms it is referred to by economists as the 'make or buy' decision. If an entity has more than one option then it will compare the advantages and disadvantages of these options to decide which path to take. Therefore, if the cost of 'making' software is £1 million, the sales lost during software build time are £0.7 million and the net present value (NPV) of licensing existing software from another party is £1.9 million, it is very likely that management would choose to build the software rather than license it in. If, due to group pressure, the software is licensed, then the cost of the alternative build option available might set a limit for the NPV of the licence payment that the entity would be prepared to make. This is not a re-characterisation of the transaction, but rather a method of determining the price that an independent company would be prepared to pay for the licence rather than building the software itself.

8.21   A clear difficulty in applying this concept to business restructuring is that there have to be other options that were realistically available. The key point here is 'realistically'. It is not open to any party to simply assert that 'they would not have gone along with the restructuring'. It is incumbent on the party suggesting that this approach could be applied to explain and support the option that they propose. For example, a distribution licensee on whom notice of termination of the licence has been served does not have a 'realistic option' of simply continuing its current business; that would mean, perhaps, trading in 'counterfeit' goods and laying itself open to considerable costs for breach of contract.

8.22   Anyone considering a restructuring of their business would be well advised to consider, from the viewpoint of each affected entity, what options that entity might have. Consideration of these options to see if any of them are 'realistic' will then direct thoughts to pricing that option and considering what, if any, impact it has on the transfer pricing of the restructuring. Equally, identification of why options are not realistic will provide valuable material to defend the transfer pricing of the restructuring using other transfer pricing methods.

8.23 Where a realistic option is identified it is important to identify all of the costs and benefits of that option so that the pricing calculation is robust. For example, it might be argued that locally-owned intangibles relating to goods that account for a small fraction of trading would mean that there is an option for those goods to remain outside the restructuring and to be dealt with locally. Is that realistic? It might be that the ERP environment of the MNC is adapted to the new business model, and this system does not allow for locally traded products. In that case the cost of the option would include a separate, stand-alone ERP system to deal with locally traded goods. Suppose the price of that system is £20 million; the option no longer looks to be 'realistic' as the profitability of that option will be low (or negative) due to the cost of the standalone ERP system, so the option of licensing or selling local intangibles looks to be more attractive.

8.24 Furthermore, the revised 2017 Guidelines have introduced new documentation requirements for restructurings, with a particular emphasis on documenting risk transfers. Taxpayers must describe restructuring transactions that have occurred during the relevant fiscal year in the master file, and where relevant in the local file.

Transfer of something of value

8.25 The restructuring event gives rise to transfer pricing questions concerning the potential right of an entity to compensation for the impact of the restructuring, and for the costs of restructuring. There are three circumstances in which compensation might be due and three types of cost to consider.

The three circumstances in which compensation might be due for the restructuring are:

● where assets belonging to the entity are transferred;

● where local law or the contract provides a legal right to compensation; or

● where the cooperation required of the entity is such that an unrelated party would most likely negotiate payment for that cooperation.

8.26 The three types of cost that we need to consider are:

● Expenditure in the period prior to termination of the old business model – is this expenditure arm's length in the light of the decision to terminate?

● Expenditure incurred to get out of the old business model – should this fall on the entity or on someone else?

- Expenditure incurred to get into the new business model – who should bear that cost?

We will look first at the question of compensation and then turn to consider costs.

8.27   Before going any further on the topic of compensation, it is important to note that there is no automatic right to compensation simply because there has been a restructuring, or because a restructuring results in a reduction in the profitability of an entity (see para 9.39 of the OECD Guidelines). This might appear to be an obvious statement but, between unrelated parties, similar claims have been made and litigated in the UK, with the same result. The UK Court of Appeal decision in *Baird Textile Holdings Limited v Marks & Spencer plc* [2001] EWCA Civ 274 is instructive in this matter, as the business of the claimant was intertwined with Marks & Spencer to a degree that would not be unfamiliar within an MNC group. However, compensation would be due if, as between unrelated parties, compensation would be paid, so we must consider why unconnected parties might conclude that compensation should be due.

Assets transferred

8.28   The most obvious reason for payment to be made to the restructured entity is that it has transferred an asset that it owns to someone else. This might relate to the whole business, or to an asset of the business depending on the circumstances of the parties and the way in which the restructuring is effected. Transfers of particular assets are easier to recognise and price. A full functional analysis of the business pre- and post-restructuring is one of the best ways to identify assets that have been transferred. As part of the functional analyses, care should be taken when defining any transferred intangible assets, applying the language in the new Chapter VI of the OECD Guidelines; if an intangible is not capable of being 'owned or controlled' (eg if a product goes off-patent), there may be no requirement for compensation on transfer. See **8.43** for an illustration of this point.

In addition, when calculating the arm's length price of an asset that has been transferred, predicted future cash flows are not always indicative of an asset's value. A recent case, *Denmark v Water Utility Companies (Case No 27/2018 and 208/2018)*, warned against assuming that an asset has minimal value because the group at present does not charge for it. By analogy, in a business restructuring context, where a group has not been charging for the use of an asset, it does not mean that the asset has no value on any transfer.

8.29   Intangible assets, particularly marketing intangibles such as goodwill, often cause the most disagreement, but reference to the position of independent parties should provide the answer. Intellectual property is 'property' and can be transferred only by contract; members of a sales force in a distributor will always interact with customers and will generate 'goodwill'. The sales force that remains can exploit 'existing' goodwill while serving a new master without transferring it, even if they do not build 'new' goodwill (which is the case for an entity moving, say, from being a distributor to being an agent).

8.30   Whilst this book does not cover the creation of permanent establishments (PEs), it is worth noting that one of the changes brought about by the OECD's BEPS project has led to a revision of the definition of a PE under the model double tax treaty. One example concerns *commissionnaires* and similar undisclosed agency arrangements (see Chapter 4), which are now regarded as giving rise to agency PEs of the principal company under the redraft of Article 5.5 of the OECD Model Tax Treaty. This has encouraged businesses to convert from *commissionnaire* or undisclosed agent business models to local buy/sell distributors, to mitigate the additional compliance exposure. *Commissionnaires* and undisclosed agents are generally not regarded as creating marketing intangibles in their own right (all goodwill accruing to the principal), and therefore it would not be right to consider there to be a transfer of goodwill *by* the *commissionnaire* or undisclosed agent in the course of becoming a buy/sell entity. This demonstrates the need to carefully consider and identify any intangible assets in advance of any restructuring, to ensure they are treated appropriately.

8.31   A related point to be mindful of relates to the new sales and distribution contract which would be agreed between the principal and the newly converted distributor (formerly *commissionnaire* or undisclosed agent). It should be made clear that the distributor does not acquire 'goodwill' in the product or service, or the trademarks associated with those products or services, which it distributes. Any pre-existing marketing intangibles belonging to the principal are retained by the principal and made available to the distributor to use only in relation to the business of the principal. Going forward, the distributor will generate its own 'parallel' goodwill within the customer base; customers interact with the local entity, and hence the sales force will create an impression with customers. That 'local goodwill' is different from the goodwill in the goods, services and associated marketing intangibles of the principal. As all distributors have this 'local goodwill', it will be an integral part of the value contributed, and return earned, by the unrelated party distributors selected as comparables, and so there is no additional value to be considered over and above that arm's-length reward.

8.32   It is worth noting that disclosed agents (which usually fall within the scope of the EU's Commercial Agents Directive – see **8.47** below) could also give rise to new agency PEs under the new Article 5 definition. Where it is intended to change from a disclosed agent relationship to something else, the Directive should be considered. Under the Directive, the cessation of a commercial agent relationship will, in almost all circumstances, trigger a right to compensation that would be a taxable event.

8.33   When considering what might be an arm's-length price for a transfer of an intangible asset, it is important to be aware of new commentary included within the revised Chapter VI of the OECD Guidelines (paras 6.186 to 6.195) concerning 'hard-to-value intangible' assets (HTVIs – see Chapter 6).

This states that, where there are significant differences between the anticipated, or *ex ante*, projections used to determine a transfer price and the pricing subsequently suggested by the actual, or *ex post*, outcomes, and these differences arise from reasons other than unforeseeable events, a tax administration may be entitled to use the *ex post* outcomes to adjust the *ex ante* pricing. This differs from the standard transfer pricing approach of respecting *ex ante* projections in most instances. Thus, where an HTVI is involved in a business restructuring, it is important to fully assess the pricing of any such intangible asset when it is transferred, by using robust forecasts and considering in full the possible future events that may affect pricing, in order to reduce the risk of subsequent adjustments that could lead to additional tax being payable.

8.34   Where an entity has all that it needs to execute its business (profitably or not) and it 'voluntarily' (or on instruction from its shareholder) relinquishes that business to another MNC then it is arguable that this is little different than selling the business outright. In that case compensation would be due based on the value of the whole business.

8.35   Sometimes it is argued that due to increasing costs or competition, the entity would face a future of declining profitability and that this should negate arguments about a 'disposal' of its business; it does not. Declining future profitability affects the price of the disposal, not the question of whether there has been a disposal.

8.36   It is sometimes argued that the value of any disposal is reduced by the value of the new business arrangement. This can be the case if the restructuring has been organised in such a way that there is a disposal of elements of the old business while others have been retained. This point must be considered carefully, however, as it may be that the whole business has been disposed of and a new business contract has been created. In that case the old business may have been disposed of in full and payment may have been made partly in kind, in the form of the new business contract. If that is the correct analysis then the disposal value would be charged to tax in full, subject to any tax rules that allow any part of the disposal proceeds or taxable gain to be rolled, or held, over against the acquisition price (if any) of the new contract.

8.37   Suppose, though, that the unrestructured business is reliant upon another member of the MNC for its existence (eg the rights to manufacture the product and use the trademark by which it is known are held by an overseas parent and used by the business under the terms of a contract). In that case one should still consider whether the restructuring has taken place by way of a disposal of that contract to another party; if it has, then the value of that contract should be taken into account when calculating the compensation due to the entity. If there has not been a disposal of that contract by the entity, but the contract has been lost (ie not renewed or terminated), the Court of Appeal decision in *Baird*, cited above, is applicable and there is no automatic right to compensation for the loss of that contract, no matter how valuable it has been in the past. However, that is not the end of the matter, as compensation might still be due as a matter of contract law or statute (if the circumstances demand), or there might be payment for the services rendered by the entity in supporting the restructuring.

Contract provision

8.38   There are several aspects of the contract that could lead to a claim for compensation.

8.39   If the contract that regulates the old business model provides for compensation to be paid on termination of the business arrangement then, provided that these terms are 'arm's length', they must be honoured. The value of compensation is then the contracted amount.

8.40   Compensation would also be due under the terms of the contract if it provides for a notice period for termination without cause and this period is not respected or if the contract has a period left to run and there is no right to terminate the contract without cause at an earlier time. In that case, compensation would relate to the profit lost in the notice period or the period remaining on the contract that was improperly terminated. This compensation for inadequate notice of termination would be separate from any consideration of compensation for the loss of the contract or business itself.

8.41   If the termination notice period has been respected, that is not necessarily the end of the matter. The termination provisions must themselves be arm's length in nature; if they are not, then they might be ignored and the conditions that would have arisen between unrelated parties might prevail. The commercial courts in a number of countries have considered how long a period of notice is required before it is 'reasonable' The Australian case of *Crawford Fitting Co v Sydney Valve and Fitting Pty Ltd* (1988) (unreported, NSWCA) is not binding outside Australia, but it provides a very useful summary of the main principles that will be applied by a court in deciding whether a notice period between unconnected parties is reasonable. The main purpose of a notice period is to enable the parties to end their relationship in an orderly way, so that they have a reasonable opportunity to enter into alternative arrangements and wind up matters arising from the old relationship. The court considered that expenditure in the initial stages of the agreement provides a ground for implying a term that the business is to continue for a reasonable period (citing *Jack's Cookie Co v Brooks* (1955) 227 F 2d 935 at 938–939). Extraordinary expenditure at any stage of the agreement is also a factor that must be taken into account and the appropriate weight to be given to this will vary between cases and the particular circumstances. This does not apply for *ordinary* expenditure – inability to reap the benefits of ordinary expenditure or effort incurred during the course of the agreement may be regarded as a business risk an enterprise takes when it enters into an agreement that is terminable at any time. It was also noted in the case that if the nature of the business produces a lapse of time between effort or expenditure and earning, a certain amount of that effort or expenditure will go unrewarded regardless of the period of notice given. Critically, the court concluded that the prospect of obtaining profits in the future is *not* a relevant factor to be taken into account, except insofar as it is consequential on the incurring of extraordinary expenditure or effort within the scope of the agreement. Similarly, the Irish case of *Hennigan v Roadstone Wood Ltd* [2015] IEHC 326 demonstrated that a notice period can effectively be extended beyond the actual term based on the conduct of the parties; in this situation, the plaintiff bought a piece of equipment on the reasonable expectation of five years' paid work to fund it, but the contract was terminated shortly after the purchase. The court awarded compensation based on the lost five years' earnings.

In the case of *Ward Equipment Limited v Preston [2017] NZCA 444*, the court found that a clause specifying termination at reasonable notice is not necessarily a characteristic of an arm's length contract and that there is 'no evidence to suggest that licensing contracts are customarily understood to be terminable on reasonable notice'. The court also found that 'where a contract already contains comprehensive terms for termination it will be difficult to construe it as allowing termination on reasonable notice if that right is not included in the clauses dealing with termination'. Therefore, in a situation where a contract does not specifically mention termination at reasonable notice, such a clause may not necessarily be imputed and compensation is due upon cancellation even when this was done with reasonable notice.

8.42　　In summary, a business must be given reasonable time to make a return on its investment. The longer the agreement has run, the more profitable the agreement has been in any year; and the less investment that has been made, the shorter the notice period might be.

8.43　　In contrast, contracts are sometimes argued to continue to run long after they would have ended, had the actual contract been between unconnected parties, effectively continuing beyond what would be considered to be a reasonable amount of time, based on the facts. In *Kimble v Marvel Entertainment LLC* No 13-720 (US, 22 June 2015), it was found that royalties were no longer payable in respect of a patent after it has expired, despite the contract having no expiry date. This case echoes the revised OECD definition of an intangible, being something that is capable of being owned or controlled; for example, if a product goes off-patent, it is typically no longer possible to exert control, and third parties would not be willing to 'use the patent idea'. As a result of this decision, under US law it is not possible to demand a royalty for use of an expired patent, even if the parties contract to do so; the US Supreme Court decided that such an agreement was not allowed, even if the parties wished it to be so, because this ran counter to the purpose of enacting a patent law in the US. Similarly, in *Leslie Klinger v Conan Doyle Estate Ltd* No 14-1128 (US 7th Cir, 2014), it was held that characters introduced in books on which US copyright had expired were now in the public domain, notwithstanding that these characters were further developed in subsequent books that were still within copyright. Thus, no royalties were due where legal protection had expired, even though such protection remained in force in respect of character traits developed in later books which were still subject to copyright protection. These cases both demonstrate that, under US law, when legal protection on an asset expires, that asset is then open to others to exploit. Contracts drawn under US law that are dependent on that protection are therefore much reduced in value or cease to have value altogether once the legal protection expires, meaning that compensation may not be payable on termination of such contracts.

8.44   When considering whether the terms of a contract entitle one of the parties to compensation, it is also worth noting that a contract may be found to be in existence, even where no written contract exists. The case of *Vancouver Canucks Limited Partnership v Canon Canada Inc*, 2015 BCCA 144 (CanLII) illustrates this point. In this case, it was found that a contract was in existence, even though no signed agreement had been executed; the contract was created purely because of the conduct of the parties. The court paid particular attention to emails between the parties, and considered (i) whether the parties intended to be bound, (ii) whether the agreement was subject to execution of a formal contract, and (iii) whether the essential terms had been agreed. It was found that the essential terms of a contract had been set out in emails between the parties, and that the parties had intended to be bound and in fact had begun to act in line with the terms. Furthermore, there was nothing in the emails that suggested that the contract had to be formally executed. Accordingly, compensation was due for breach of that contract, even though there was no written, signed document.

Statutory notice periods

8.45   In some countries, but not the UK, there is a legally specified minimum notice period for termination of a business contract without cause. For example, some US states apply the so-called 'Missouri rule' under which a dealer relationship cannot be terminated until the dealer has a reasonable opportunity to recover its investment. Some US states also have special termination rules for dealers of certain types of goods, such as motor vehicles or farm implements. Under certain state franchise laws, a dealer relationship can even be considered to be a 'franchise' despite neither the seller nor the dealer intending it to be a franchise. An 'inadvertent franchise' means that the dealer may be entitled to special protection which significantly limits the seller's ability to terminate the relationship (eg a minimum notice period before termination, a requirement that the seller repurchase the dealer's inventory or even a prohibition on termination without cause). Other countries also have laws determining the minimum notice period. For example, at the time of writing, Belgian law requires that 'reasonable' notice is given, and Turkey requires a minimum of three months' notice (but longer in certain circumstances). As ever, it is wise to check the laws under which the parties operate and the law under which the contract is drawn, if different.

Statute law

8.46   Statutory compensation for termination of a business arrangement itself is less common, but it can happen. If the law of a country provides that compensation would be due on termination of a business arrangement, as between unconnected parties then, in related-party transactions, that rule should be observed for transfer pricing purposes.

8.47 For example, if the current business model involves a commercial agent within the EU, then local law to implement Council Directive 86/653, the Commercial Agents Directive, will mandate the payment of compensation on termination of the commercial agent arrangement. The right to statutory compensation is not given by an EU-wide law, but by the enactment of laws in each Member State and it is not possible to apply the law of one Member State to a termination in another, for obvious reasons. The rights of a commercial agent will therefore differ by territory, as each country 'interprets' the EU Directive into national law; for example, in the UK, only an agent dealing in goods, not services, will potentially qualify for compensation, because of the definition of 'commercial agent' (*Commercial Agents (Council Directive) Regulations 1993, SI 1993/3053, reg 2.1*); whereas, in France, services activity can also qualify.

8.48 Some countries, such as Germany (but not others, such as the UK) have extended this agent's right to compensation, by analogy, to certain distributor or franchise relationships. The right to commercial compensation for a commercial agent in Germany is based on *section 89b* of the *German Commercial Code*. It has been confirmed by the highest German civil court (ie the Federal Court of Justice) that, by analogy, the right to compensation given to agents by *section 89b* can be extended to sales or distribution relationships if certain prerequisites are met (see *Zeitschrift für Wirtschaftsrecht*, BGH ZIP 2000). In short, these are that the distributor is integrated into the sales organisation of the superior company in the way that an agent would be integrated, and is contractually obliged to transfer the customer base to the superior company on termination of the contract. This second condition is essential because the fundamental basis for statutory compensation for an agent relates to the goodwill of the customer base. A distributor builds a customer base for itself and it may continue to sell to that customer base after termination of the current distributor agreement, unless contractually obliged not to do so. By contrast, an agent builds a customer base for the principal and it is lost on termination of the agency relationship. An agent may not use that customer base to its advantage, other than as a consequence of acting for the benefit of the principal. The statutory compensation given to the agent is in recompense for the value created in the customer base which it cannot continue to access and derive benefit from. Therefore, a sales entity or a distributor who is not an agent has suffered no loss unless, on termination, it is required to transfer the benefit of the customer base and not to exploit it for its own use.

Economic factors

8.49 It is possible that the trading relationship between a licensor and licensee might lead to the licensee having a simultaneous right to enjoy the value created by an intangible even if ownership of the intangible remains with the licensor. This would be the case where the licensee contributes to the development, enhancement, maintenance, protection and/or exploitation of the intangible (see Chapter 6). Disputes between unrelated parties that have been heard by the UK commercial court (and the courts of other countries) illustrate activities of a licensee which go beyond a 'bright line' and create a right to enjoy income from the intangible. This 'bright line' test has echoes in some tax cases, notably the Indian case of *Maruti Suzuki India Ltd v Additional Commissioner of Income Tax Transfer Pricing Officer New Delhi* WP (C) 6876/2008 (High Court of Delhi at New Delhi, 2010) and the US case of *DHL Corp* (TC Memo 1998–461, RIA TC Memo). What is clear is that the party who is entitled to the income is the party to which a court would award the income if the parties were to dispute that point before a competent court. The primary rule is that this will be the party that holds legal title to the intellectual property and that rule will be set aside only if there are circumstances so special that a so-called 'bright line' is crossed, in which case the parties can become simultaneously jointly entitled to enjoy the value that IP can create. The background to this is covered in more detail in Chapter 6, dealing with intangibles, but the point is of importance here as, where such rights exist, termination of the licence should be of sufficient notice that the licensee can extract its profit from this asset or compensation might be due if that is not possible.

Costs of restructuring

8.50   One must also consider how the decision to restructure the business impacts the operating costs incurred in the final period of trading and the costs of getting out of the old business model and into the new business model. Should these be the costs of the local entity? If they are, is there a service being provided that should be charged for? If not, who should bear these costs?

Operating costs in the final period of trading

8.51   Ordinary operating costs of the entity that is being restructured should not ordinarily be considered to be passed on to another business. However, that is not to say that parties acting at arm's length would continue to incur the same level of operating costs after the termination notice was given. For example, unless the entity is contractually obliged to do so, investment in new plant, training new staff and marketing initiatives would not be commenced if the pay-back period for that investment was longer than the time remaining in the contract. As the giving of notice of termination to an unrelated party would cause them to consider the financial implications of any investment not mandated by their contractual relationships it should also cause us to consider the transfer pricing implications of such expenditure in related-party situations.

8.52   Sometimes, as between unrelated parties, the contractual relationship does require the entity to continue to promote the business and to 'leave it in good health'. If such terms are present in related-party contracts these should be respected. What, then, if there are no such terms?

8.53   Suppose, for example, that the impact of an advertising campaign for a licensed distributor A is to create additional sales that lead to profits 2.5 times the advertising spend, spread over a 36-month period with 50% of that value generated in the first six months and with zero time lag between spend and initial impact. Modelling the impact of advertising might show (for example) that the break-even point for the advertising spend of distributor A is reached seven months after the advertising spend. If distributor A, as licensee, is given 12 months' notice of termination of their distributorship, why would they continue with advertising spend four or five months later? Sometimes, in arrangements between unconnected parties, the contract requires the distributor to continue spending on advertising during the notice period, and sometimes it does not; there could be a case to consider if the licensor should reimburse some or all of distributor A's expenditure during the final months of the notice period.

8.54   The value of advertising spend within 36 months prior to termination (in our example above) will generate some benefit for the next distributor of that product, B, but if distributor A ran the advertisement for its own profit, then this benefit is 'incidental' to the purpose of the expenditure and so does not create any transfer pricing issues. However, once the break-even point is reached, the 'purpose' of distributor A making further voluntary investments does not relate to the business of distributor A and raises the question of whether the licensor should reimburse some or all of this expenditure.

8.55   There is a clear potential for investment expenditure in a termination notice period to impact both the question of who should bear the cost and whether the expenditure influences the arm's-length period of notice and/or creates an exit gain that should be charged. The overlap is not complete, as 'normal' operational expenditure can create issues for cost allocation but not for notice periods or asset creation, and expenditure beyond a 'bright line' from periods up to three years ago can create issues for ascertaining the arm's-length notice period and the creation of assets subject to exit charges. That said, care is needed to ensure that costs that are eliminated from the outgoing distributor's accounts by transfer-pricing reallocation to the licensor are not then also taken into account as if they were expenses of the distributor in justifying a claim to compensation based on a notice period extension or asset transfer.

Costs of exiting the old business model

8.56   All businesses carry one inescapable risk (they carry many others, but this risk is important here); one day they are going to go out of business. Going out of business is costly – staff who are laid-off are entitled to redundancy payments, the plant has shut-down costs, premises must be vacated, environmental damage might have to be reinstated – the list is not endless, but it is certainly much longer than this.

8.57   Any business that trades only with unrelated parties has no source of income from which to meet the costs of going out of business other than its retained profits from trading activity. In other words, when we use comparable data to set transfer prices, that comparable data already contains the reward due to a business for carrying the risk of going out of business. As such, any funds from which the costs of shutting down must be met are the ordinary revenues of the business whilst it continued.

8.58   Let's apply this concept to business restructuring in which the local entity either terminates all business, or terminates one contract but continues to perform some business functions under another. Under the arm's-length principle there is no basis to argue that the cost of getting out of a business should be passed on to another entity as a matter of course. A contribution towards the cost should be inferred only if one could be sought by unrelated parties in the same circumstances.

8.59   Typically a contribution towards the cost of getting out of a business arrangement would be made only if the restructured party either provides a service (eg assists in a smooth transition, helps the new licence holder to become 'expert', etc) or has options other than to go along with the restructuring that were realistically available to them and this contribution towards exit costs would 'tip the balance' in favour of accepting the restructuring. The concept of 'options realistically available' will be discussed later, but for now it is sufficient to say that it is rare to find that any 'realistic' alternative to the restructuring is available. Where the restructured party does not go out of business completely, any value they provide by assisting in a smooth transition would also need to be weighed against the value they receive by being invited to enter into the new contract; it may be that these two values offset and cancel each other out.

Costs of entering the new business model

8.60   Just like the cost of getting out of a business arrangement, costs will arise when preparing to trade in a new business arrangement. Entities that trade only with unrelated parties will not normally have a source of income from which to meet these costs other than the future income stream from ongoing trading.

8.61   Accordingly, the reward for this risk/expenditure is contained in the income and profits of the comparable data used to set arm's-length pricing once the business has begun. Other than in specific circumstances, pushing those costs away from the local entity to another part of the MNC is not 'arm's-length' behaviour and will result in double reward for future services (as the arm's-length range would otherwise have to be reduced with respect to this change in functional comparability).

8.62   'Special circumstances' can arise in a restructuring, and do sometimes arise between unrelated parties, and so it can be arm's-length for some element of the costs of getting into a new business arrangement to fall on another party.

The list below is not exhaustive, and the question is very fact specific, but some examples would be:

- If the ERP system that the local entity is required to use (by the shareholder) to assist in consolidated reporting obligations of the group is far more sophisticated, and expensive, than is justified by the local business activity, a case might be made for the shareholder to meet part of the expense.

- If a contract manufacturing arrangement requires significant expenditure on new equipment, the principal might contribute towards the cost of that equipment. If it does, the cost base applicable for testing the arm's-length nature of the reward for contract manufacturing services would need to exclude any costs met by the 'customer' (eg depreciation of the cost of machinery). For example, it is common for the moulds used to make glass bottles to be paid for by, and belong to, the brand owner and be supplied to the glass company contracted to produce the bottles.

- Where new ways of working require extensive training or retraining of staff, the principal might wish to take part in that process to ensure that the end result meets its requirements. Here, the costs not carried by the local entity will not form part of the cost base applicable for testing the arm's-length nature of the reward for contract entity for the service provided.

Who bears recharged costs?

8.63   As part of the exercise to ascertain whether there are costs associated with the restructuring that should not remain with the local entity, it should be apparent which entity will actually benefit from the spend. However, care is needed here, as the following example will illustrate.

8.64   A Ltd is a UK-licensed distributor of product. The licensor is B Plc, who intends to end the relationship and instead to licence Co Y, who might appoint A Ltd to assist in the local UK market. After receiving notice of termination of the distributor relationship from B Plc, A Ltd continued to spend on advertising. A review of the facts, including contractual obligations, showed that relationships with unrelated parties did not include a contractual obligation to continue to spend on marketing during the notice period, which led to the conclusion that A Ltd, acting independently, would have ceased making any advertising investment when only four months of the contract remained. A disallowance of £0.5 million of advertising spending is proposed under UK transfer pricing rules, and it is clear that the beneficiary of the goodwill generated by this expenditure will be Co Y, who took over the market. However, the additional advertising expenditure should not be charged to Co Y, but to B Plc. The reason for this is that A Ltd's UK contract was not assigned to Co Y but came to an end. Co Y entered into a new contract with B Plc, and B Plc is offering the opportunity to license this successful brand. The expenditure will further reinforce the brand value, so B Plc, as the owner, should bear the cost. The value of marketing expenditure undertaken by B Plc during this time is also a relevant factor to take into account in establishing the arm's-length licence fee to be paid by Co Y to B Plc.

Part II: Remuneration of post-restructuring controlled transactions

8.65 One must also consider how the post-restructuring transfer pricing should be structured. The transfer pricing position of two MNEs with the same functional analysis must be the same, regardless of how each came to be in the current business model: built this way from the start, or restructured from an earlier, pre-existing business. Therefore, it is not an appropriate approach to start with the 'old' business model and transfer pricing, assuming that it is correctly priced, and then try to adapt the transfer pricing result for the things that have changed. The new business model is very unlikely to be appropriately priced by looking to the transfer pricing model which applied to an earlier, more complicated business. In addition, the new business model is likely to generate considerable commercial savings, compared to the old arrangement and the benefit of these savings would not flow to the appropriate party unless the transfer pricing was approached correctly. Therefore the transfer pricing post-restructuring should be approached as a new exercise.

8.66 The key question for the country tax auditor looking at a restructured business is 'What level of substance is required to show that this new business model is acceptable?' OECD and tax authorities accept that a centralised business model holds a clear attraction for multinationals, but tax authorities remain concerned that sometimes a multinational seeks the tax benefits of adopting the business model without actually adopting the business model in terms of the way it is resourced and operated. The tax auditor will therefore be rightly suspicious of all reorganisations until they can see, amongst other things, that real commercial change has taken place.

8.67 The term 'substance' has come to be used by both business and tax authorities alike to describe the levels of activity and responsibility located in the central entity, which drives the change in profit recognition reported by the group. With adequate substance, the tax audit will concentrate on matters such as potential exit charges on moving IP and on the correct transfer pricing of the new business model. Without adequate substance the tax auditor will instead contend that 'nothing has changed' and thereby refute the profit shift entirely.

8.68 Multinationals considering a business reorganisation can find differing approaches to tax rules and tax audits to be a significant potential barrier to restructuring. On the one hand the disruption and commercial risk involved in the change may mean that it is preferable to evolve into the new business model over time. On the other hand, the potentially negative and aggressive response of tax authorities to the restructuring means it is important to have good substance from the outset. This leads many to ask what the minimum substance requirement will be, such that they can aim to meet or exceed this and then build the remaining elements over time. Though this is a natural reaction, it is perhaps reversing the true question.

8.69   In reality, the substance that is 'right' for the commercial operations of the business will drive the transfer pricing analysis which, in turn, results in the profit recognised by each legal entity. That said, for the purpose of modelling the business restructuring and thereby creating an actionable change strategy and plan it is instructive to look at the level of profit shift that differing levels of substance will support. There are three simple rules to keep in mind:

- the level of substance and the degree of profit shift are directly related, though not in a linear fashion;

- there is a continuum of impact, not a series of discreet answers; and

- the degree of substance required to support the profit shift is the activity, responsibility or asset ownership that is needed commercially to execute the business model that results in the profit shift.

The final rule may not sound helpful – it could be paraphrased as 'you need exactly what you need to do the things that you say you are doing' – but, in practice, this common-sense check is perhaps the most useful of all. Transfer pricing is an output of the business model, as described by the functional analysis, not the other way around.

Transfer pricing documentation

INTRODUCTION

9.1   In transfer pricing, the term 'documentation' is often used broadly to describe any support for the arm's-length pricing of a particular inter-company transaction. A company selling products will have lots of documentation to support its sales, such as sales contracts and agreements with customers and suppliers, price lists, picking and packing lists, invoices, customs declarations and perhaps much more. Although this documentation is indeed relevant to support its transactions with related parties, the term 'transfer pricing documentation' is generally used to describe the specific records and evidence that tax law and tax authorities require a business to have, to demonstrate that the results of transactions with related parties for a particular financial year are in line with the arm's-length principle. Some of the items listed will form part of that evidence but there will be some items that are created only to satisfy the documentation requirements of transfer pricing.

9.2   Tax law may require, or a tax authority may request, a number of different classes of records/evidence, such as:

(i)   primary accounting records of transactions entered into the company's systems;

(ii)   tax adjustment records identifying adjustments to, say, transaction values to arrive at an arm's-length result;

(iii)   identification of parties and transactions that are subject to the transfer pricing rules; and

(iv)   evidence to demonstrate the arm's-length result.

Detail for items (i) and (ii) will often be required for other purposes, eg to produce the company's statutory accounts. For the purposes of this chapter, we use the term 'transfer pricing documentation' as being specifically in relation to items (iii) and (iv). We have also focused only on requirements where the transactions between related parties are cross-border, ie between entities in different countries; this has traditionally been the focus of tax authorities, although some have also introduced the same or similar rules for domestic transactions, either generally or in respect of specified circumstances.

9.3   While the exact format of transfer pricing documentation required does vary from country to country, due to the documentation requirement being a function of national laws and practice, the broad structure is likely to require:

- identification of the related parties;

- a description of the business;

- identification of the related-party transactions;

- a comparability and functional analysis of the parties to those transactions to show how entities add value to the transactions; this will draw out the information relevant to pricing the inter-company transactions (including the characteristics of the property or services provided or received, the contractual terms between the parties, the business strategies adopted by the entity, a functional analysis which outlines the functions performed, the risks assumed and the assets used by the entity and the underlying economic circumstances which may include an analysis of the industry in which the entity operates); and

- the application of an economic analysis to support the pricing applied.

9.4 Transfer pricing documentation should generally be 'look back' in nature. That is, it is a document to test an actual result of an arrangement with a related party, and whether it is in accordance with the arm's-length principle. This can be contrasted with a policy document which describes beforehand the rationale for setting a pricing policy for the arrangement. Multinationals often try to trade at arm's-length prices because they wish to have arm's-length prices reflected in their statutory accounts, as this reduces the risk of either suffering double taxation or incurring additional costs to deal with double taxation when it arises. In practice, however, all of the work performed for a policy document can be very useful in preparing documentation for a particular financial year, requiring only that the actual financial results and the underlying facts and circumstances of the year are incorporated into the 'policy' material to update (or replace, if needed) the material. This step is vital because the arm's-length standard is not met simply by setting a target margin based on the budget for the year; we are expected to test the actual results of the year, and not just the intention. Where the actual results depart from the intended policy, the documentation will then also include an explanation of facts, circumstances or events that brought this about. The objective of this is to identify the party that should take ownership of the variance, according to the application of the arm's-length principle.

9.5 With increasing levels of documentation requirements introduced in different countries and the implementation of proposals under BEPS, as we are already seeing, there is likely to be an increasing focus on the form and content of any documentation. But firstly we will examine in more detail the purpose of preparing documentation.

THE PURPOSE OF TRANSFER PRICING DOCUMENTATION

9.6   The OECD, in its revised wording for Chapter V of the Guidelines, gives three objectives for producing documentation (see paragraph 5 of Chapter V):

(i)   'To ensure taxpayers give appropriate consideration … in establishing prices … between associated enterprises and in reporting the income derived from such transactions in their tax returns';

(ii)   'To provide tax administrations with the information necessary to conduct an informed … risk assessment'; and

(iii)   'To provide tax administrations with useful information to employ in conducting an appropriately thorough audit … although it may be necessary to supplement the documentation with additional information as the audit progresses'.

9.7   While the form, content and sometimes even the preparation of transfer pricing documentation is not mandated in all countries, having comprehensive, contemporaneous transfer pricing documentation allows the taxpayer to be on the front foot when supporting its tax return, particularly in the case of an audit by a tax authority. By having a position documented, the company is in a better position to push the burden of proof back onto the tax authority to show that the position taken is incorrect.

THE CURRENT STANDARD – A LOCAL APPROACH

9.8   The number of countries that have effective documentation requirements is significant. However, currently there is quite a lot of variation in the requirement to prepare documentation, the information required to be presented within the documentation, the timing of when such documentation is required to be prepared, whether or not the documentation (or some other form of information) is required to be submitted to the tax authority along with the tax return, and the penalties imposed for non-compliance.

9.9   While there are many standard components that would be considered necessary to include within transfer pricing documentation, the specific requirements vary from country to country. Some countries provide a list of what information is required to be presented in the transfer pricing documentation before it can qualify for penalty protection purposes. While some countries will accept an OECD-style transfer pricing report, it is not unusual for local requirements to be more prescriptive and require additional information to that suggested in the OECD Guidelines, Chapter V. For example, in Australia, transfer pricing legislation requires a comprehensive analysis of local reconstruction provisions before the transfer pricing documentation can qualify for penalty protection.

9.10 The timing requirement for preparation of transfer pricing documentation also varies by country. It is often the case that tax authorities require transfer pricing documentation to be 'contemporaneous', by which they mean 'prepared by the time the tax return is lodged for a particular year'; however, as explained above, in most (but not all) cases, the documentation is usually only required to be submitted upon request by the tax authority. Once requested, the taxpayer may be required to respond and submit their documentation immediately (eg Japan), or they may be set a deadline to provide it; that time frame also varies by country, with examples of one week (eg Poland) and two months (eg Germany). Both the UK and the US allow 30 days for documentation to be produced, once a request has been made. While generally uncommon, some countries (including Colombia, Ecuador and Peru) require certain companies to submit transfer pricing documentation along with the tax return in certain circumstances. There is also a selection of countries that require the Master file to be submitted (eg India, Japan and Taiwan) although again this is generally uncommon.

9.11 In other countries (such as France, Australia and India), tax administrations require certain disclosures in a transfer pricing schedule that is lodged in conjunction with, or within a certain period of lodging, the tax return. If such disclosures are required, they aid the tax administration in performing a risk assessment as part of the process of audit selection, even though the information in the schedule would only provide transactional and financial data and may not provide sufficient context of the transactions relative to the worldwide operations of the group.

9.12 The OECD recommends that, in complying with the arm's length principle, a company should not be required to incur costs and burdens that are disproportionate to the circumstances. As such, it recommends that the tax authorities have regard to the materiality and level of risk for each transaction when assessing the quality of the transfer pricing documentation for penalty purposes. In practice, however, the preparation of documentation can be a time-consuming process, with some tax administrations (eg Italy) imposing penalties even if immaterial transactions are not documented. In many cases, penalties for lack of, or incomplete, documentation are linked to adjustments (eg up to 30% of the adjustment in Finland) or under-assessed tax (eg up to 100% of the tax increase in the UK and Malaysia, and 200% in India), and can be even higher where the tax authority can prove negligence or criminal intent. With interest charged on top, such penalties can be considerable.

THE MOVE TO A NEW GLOBAL STANDARD

9.13 As the volume (and complexity) of international intra-group trade has grown significantly, the goal of the tax administration – to obtain all the necessary information from a company's returns and documentation to conduct an informed transfer pricing risk assessment or audit – has been made ever harder. Despite this, up to now, the tax authority approach to transfer pricing has been a local one (as we saw above), with each jurisdiction imposing its own laws and rules.

9.14 In light of this, the OECD created Action 13 as part of the OECD's Base Erosion and Profit Shifting (BEPS) initiative. The goals of Action 13 were to develop

> 'rules regarding transfer pricing documentation to enhance transparency for tax administration, taking into consideration the compliance costs for business. The rules to be developed will include a requirement that MNEs provide all relevant government with needed information on their global allocation of the income, economic activity and taxes paid among countries according to a common template.' (OECD *Action Plan on BEPS*, Action 13 at page 23)

The rules developed under this initiative have now been incorporated into the OECD Transfer Pricing Guidelines for Multinational Enterprises and Tax Administrations (2017).

THE FUTURE STANDARD – THE BEPS APPROACH

9.15 In response to the aims proposed by the OECD's *BEPS Action Plan*, Action 13 was completed and the final report issued late in 2015. This resulted in the deletion of the original Chapter V of the OECD Transfer Pricing Guidelines in its entirety and replacing it with a new Chapter V setting out transfer pricing documentation guidance based on a three tiered approach – the 'Master File', 'Local File', and 'Country-by-Country report' in the 2017 guidelines.

9.16 The purpose of the Master File is to provide tax authorities with a high-level overview of the global business and transfer pricing policies, and to provide context as to the related-party transactions within the group. This is an interesting change. In the past, tax authorities have often looked at transactions in isolation and just from a local perspective, since they have found it difficult to find broader information relating to other parties in the group. However, now, there is a push to understand the whole business, its value chain and how the local operations fit in with that business. This will allow them to ask the question: if profits from an activity are not being taxed locally, then where are they being generated?

9.17 The Local File is more akin to the traditional country-specific transfer pricing documentation with which we are more familiar. This includes details of the local business, details of material related-party transactions and, for each transaction, a comparability analysis and an economic analysis which applies the most appropriate transfer pricing method(s). The Local File is meant to be reviewed in conjunction with the Master File so that the tax authority gains a broader picture on what drives profits in the business.

9.18 Finally, the Country-by-Country report (which the OECD suggests should apply to large multinational enterprises (MNEs) with global revenues over €750 million) collects financial and other quantitative information for each jurisdiction where the MNE does business, allowing tax authorities to run ratio analyses to quickly identify where there may be a risk of BEPS.

Together with the Master and Local Files, the package is intended to put a tax administration in a much better position to assess what aspects create value, where the related functions and assets are situated, and how that affects the spread of profits in the group.

9.19 The countries participating in the BEPS project agreed on the core elements of the three-tiered structure and, while consistency was one of the key focuses of Action 13, in practice transfer pricing documentation requirements have been legislated at a national level. There remains the issue that, despite the approach being integrated into the 2017 transfer pricing guidelines, not all countries have implemented it in the same way, with some countries requiring additional information to that outlined in the Guidelines for Master File / Local File material, and other countries that are yet to implement the recommendations at all. However, there does appear to be consistency as to the content of the Country-by-Country report throughout the majority of territories.

9.20 Further details of recommended contents, in accordance with Chapter V of the OECD Guidelines, for the Master File, the Local File and the Country-by-Country report are provided below.

Master File

9.21 While the Master File should be prepared on a global basis for the overall MNE, the guidance allows for it to be organised by product or business line if the facts support this, which may be appropriate for a large MNE consisting of multiple business lines that operate autonomously.

9.22 The information which OECD suggests should be presented in the Master File can be grouped in five categories and includes the following information:

Category	Information required
Organisational structure	● Legal ownership structure chart
	● Geographies of each jurisdiction
Description of the MNE's business	● Drivers of profit for the business
	● Overview of the supply chain for the five largest products/services (or any products/services that account for over 5% of global turnover)
	● Important service arrangements (excluding R&D) including locations, capabilities, cost allocations and pricing
	● Main geographic markets

Category	Information required
	• Brief functional analysis showing principal contributions to value creation
	• Details of important business restructurings, acquisitions and divestitures during the year.
Intangibles	• Description of strategy for developing, owning and exploiting intangibles
	• Location of principal R&D facilities and R&D management
	• List of important intangibles (perhaps grouped) showing legal ownership
	• List of intangibles-related intragroup agreements, such as cost contribution agreements, license research service agreements,
	• Related transfer pricing policies
	• Details of intragroup transfers of intangibles during the year.
Intercompany financial activities	• Overall explanation of how group is financed (including financing arrangements with third parties)
	• Group financing companies, their location
	• Transfer pricing policies with respect to related party financing arrangements.
Financial and Tax position	• Annual consolidated financial statements
	• List and brief description of unilateral advance pricing agreements (APAs) and other tax rulings relating to allocation of income among countries.

(OECD *Transfer Pricing Guidelines for Multinational Enterprises and Tax Administrations (2017)* Annex I to Chapter V, page 501.)

9.23   The OECD recommends that the Master File should be finalised by the filing date for the tax return of the group parent company, and that it is delivered (in conjunction with the Local File) directly to local tax administrations, when requested, by each member of the MNE group. Some countries require local submission of the Masterfile regardless of where the group parent company is located (eg India and Mexico).

Local File

9.24 Unlike the Master File, the Local File is intended to provide specific details relating to inter-company transactions between a local company and a related party, to demonstrate that the local taxpayer has complied with the arm's length principle.

9.25 The Local File, when read in conjunction with the Master File, is meant to allow a tax authority to undertake a risk assessment to assess whether the related-party transactions entered into by the local entity are consistent with the arm's length principle, and therefore to decide whether to start a transfer pricing audit.

9.26 The information suggested by the OECD to be presented in the Local File is described in the table below:

Category	Information required
Local entity	• Management structure and local organisational chart
	• Description of the business and business strategy
	• Key competitors
Controlled transactions	For each material category of controlled transactions:
	• Description of the transactions and context
	• Amount of intra-group payments and receipts
	• Identification of related parties and relationship
	• Copy of material intercompany agreements
	• Comparability and functional analysis of taxpayer and related party
	• Selection of most appropriate transfer pricing method and reasons for selection
	• Selection of tested party and reasons for selection
	• Important assumptions made in applying the selected method
	• Reasons for performing a multi-year analysis
	• Description of selected comparable uncontrolled transactions, if any, financial indicators for independent enterprises used in the transfer pricing analysis and search strategy
	• Explanation of any comparability adjustments performed
	• Rationale for concluding on arm's-length pricing

Category	Information required
	• Summary of financial information used
	• Copy of existing APAs or other tax rulings related to the transactions (where local entity is not a party)
Financial information	• Local audited financial statements if available, or else existing unaudited statements
	• Reconciliation between financial data used in applying the transfer pricing method to the financial statements
	• Summary of financial data for comparables and source of data

(OECD *Transfer Pricing Guidelines for Multinational Enterprises and Tax Administrations (2017)* Annex II to Chapter V, page 505.)

9.27   The OECD recommends that the Local File is reviewed annually, to ensure that the facts are appropriately updated, and that the analysis remains relevant. If the business has not materially changed, the OECD notes, in its revised guidance, that it should be unnecessary to undertake a benchmarking study annually. It is suggested that a benchmarking search is refreshed once every three years, although financial data relating to parties chosen as comparables should be updated each year, to reflect the latest position.

9.28   As the documentation should present the most reliable information available, the revised guidance notes that it is often (but not always) the case that local comparables should be used instead of regional comparables, if available. The guidance states that, where transfer pricing documentation is prepared for various countries in the same geographic region, this may be a situation where it is appropriate to conduct a regional benchmarking study. It is also noted that, while there are clear benefits in reducing the number of benchmarking studies required (such as lower time investment and professional fees), we are warned that 'trying to simplify compliance processes should not undermine compliance with the requirement to use the most reliable information' (OECD *BEPS Action 13: 2015 Final Report*, para 46). In practice, for many countries it is difficult to obtain local comparables in sufficient quantities, and so the reality is that many multinationals use regional comparables.

Country-by-Country report

9.29   The third tier of the transfer pricing documentation proposed by Action 13 and incorporated in to the Transfer Pricing Guidelines is the Country-by-Country report. The guidance suggests that MNEs, with group consolidated turnover that exceeds €750 million in the previous year, should be required to submit a Country-by-Country report at the ultimate parent level, to the tax authority of the parent's jurisdiction, within 12 months of the group's financial year end. The first year of Country-by-Country reporting was recommended to commence on 1 January 2016 although some countries are still yet to implement measures in local legislation (eg the Philippines) which presents some issues around where to file and whether a surrogate filing is needed (see below).

9.30   The Country-by-Country report is made up of two main parts: the first part sets out requirements for financial data for the MNE by country in a prescribed template; and the second part requires a list of all the constituent entities (including any permanent establishments) per country and their main activities.

9.31   The financial data to be included in the report (on an aggregated basis, by country) is:

- turnover (split between related-party and third-party sales, but excluding dividends received);

- profit before tax;

- cash tax paid (including withholding taxes paid in other jurisdictions);

- current year tax accrual;

- stated capital;

- accumulated earnings;

- number of full-time equivalent employees; and

- net book value of tangible assets, excluding cash and cash equivalents.

9.32   While many countries have implemented the Country-by-Country report recommendations, there are cases where certain jurisdictions have not brought Country-by-Country reporting into their local legislation. If the ultimate parent is not required to file a Country-by-Country report, or its jurisdiction has not signed up to the relevant information exchange agreements or has systematically failed or suspended its agreement to exchange information, the OECD recommends that the group should nominate a 'surrogate parent entity' which will file the Country-by-Country report.

9.33   Once filed with the tax authority in the country of the parent (or selected surrogate), the Country-by-Country report will then be exchanged with all other relevant tax authorities, automatically and confidentially, through international agreements or a multilateral instrument between participating countries. At the time of writing, the following 87 countries have signed up to the Multilateral Competent Authority Agreement to facilitate this exchange process: Andorra, Argentina, Armenia, Australia, Austria, Barbados, Belgium, Belize, Bulgaria, Burkina Faso, Cameroon, Canada, Chile, China, Colombia, Costa Rica, Côte d'Ivoire, Croatia, Curaçao, Cyprus, Czech Republic, Denmark, Egypt, Estonia, Fiji, Finland, France, Gabon, Georgia, Germany, Greece, Guernsey, Hong Kong, Hungary, Iceland, India, Indonesia, Ireland, Isle of Man, Israel, Italy, Jamaica, Japan, Jersey, Kazakhstan, Korea, Kuwait, Latvia, Liechtenstein, Lithuania, Luxembourg, Malaysia, Malta, Mauritius, Mexico, Monaco, Netherlands, New Zealand, Nigeria, Norway, Pakistan,

Panama, Papua New Guinea, Peru, Poland, Portugal, Qatar, Romania, Russia, San Marino, Saudi Arabia, Senegal, Serbia, Seychelles, Singapore, Slovak Republic, Slovenia, South Africa, Spain, Sweden, Switzerland, Tunisia, Turkey, Ukraine, United Arab Emirates, United Kingdom and Uruguay. As a result, the tax authority of each country in which the MNE group has a presence will have access to the group-wide information listed in **9.31** above. This detail is to be used for risk assessment purposes only (ie not as the sole reason to raise a tax adjustment during audit on one of the members of the group). The OECD have released the Country-by-Country Reporting Handbook on Effective Tax Risk Management. This practical guide details the expectation of how tax authorities will use this information.

PRACTICAL CONSIDERATIONS

9.34   While the OECD has recommended this three-tiered approach, it is up to each individual country to implement these requirements at a local level. As discussed above, there are currently significant differences in the way that different countries approach transfer pricing documentation. As such, while the recommendations in the OECD transfer pricing guidelines (2017) do provide a good starting point, it must be noted that some countries will likely impose additional requirements, some may accept the OECD guidelines recommendations without modification, and other countries may only adopt certain aspects.

9.35   For example, Spain is one country that was quick to legislate transfer pricing documentation following the three-tiered approach, with an extended version of the Master File. By contrast, countries such as the UK will not implement the Master File / Local File structure and content for documentation (although, clearly, if a UK-headquartered multinational has a subsidiary in one of the countries that requires a Master File, the group will need to prepare a Master File and, typically, this will be best completed at the centre – ie in the UK). Additional material not required in the report – such as details of the five largest product groups – can, in any case, be requested under audit, if this information is considered to be relevant.

9.36   Businesses will likely find it necessary to prepare or coordinate their transfer pricing documentation centrally, to ensure that the Master File, Local Files and Country-by-Country report all provide consistent information about a group's global and local operations, and their transfer pricing policies. This will be particularly important in the event that information is shared between tax authorities, and any inconsistency in description or analysis leads to, at best, confusion over the underlying facts and, at worst, double taxation due to conflicting positions taken on audit.

Master and Local Files

9.37   Even if a MNE group is headquartered in a country that does not adopt the full raft of Chapter V recommendations, it may still be required to comply with the revised guidance if it operates in countries that have legislated for the Master File / Local File approach. Consider a practical example of a MNE group which is headquartered in the UK, with subsidiaries around the world, including in Spain, and which has global turnover of £1 billion. While the MNE group will be required to prepare a Country-by-Country report in the UK (which will be shared with the Spanish tax authority), the UK itself does not require a Master File to be prepared. However, in Spain, tax authorities will expect to see a Master File submitted alongside the Local File and, as this contains information for the group as a whole, it would still make sense for this to be prepared centrally, where the information required will generally be available. In other words, while the UK may not require a Master File, it is likely that a Master File will still be required to be prepared for assessment in other tax jurisdictions.

9.38   It is important to ensure that MNE groups keep up to date with local rules on content and deadlines in this ever-changing landscape. It is therefore recommended to use a diary system to monitor progress in advance of their various relevant completion and filing dates.

9.39   Another practical question is how to pull together this structure of documentation in a cost-effective manner? The best management of compliance costs comes from a rigorous process:

Phase 1	Strategy & design	In order to manage their increased compliance costs, businesses may find it helpful to implement an upfront rigorous design and direction-setting procedure at the commencement of the documentation project. This phase can help a group to co-ordinate the approach to documentation, maintain consistency, utilise existing documentation, agree upfront which countries and transactions to cover, and obtain a suitable level of compliance whilst avoiding inefficient duplication. Preparing a strategy at this early stage can save significant time and resource further along down the process.
Phase 2	Information gathering	All relevant qualitative and quantitative data is now collected. Financial and other data can be collected from various internal and external sources, and key people are interviewed. The objective is to obtain the appropriate information for the established documentation strategy.

Phase 3	Review and analysis	The information is assessed to ensure that the key value drivers are identified, and comparability and economic analyses are performed in order to characterise the counter-parties to the various transactions and test the result against the arm's length range
Phase 4	Document	This stage involves creating a report in the form of a local file which meets the needs of a local tax authority and/or taxpayer
Phase 5	Finalise and respond	Finally, the local documentation is finalised, stored and – to the extent required – shared with other stakeholders eg group management, statutory auditors and tax auditors. An approach should be discussed and agreed at group level, again to ensure that there is consistency in information being shared and approach. Decisions here might involve collating and sharing data that is above what is required strictly by local legislation, particularly in the case of an audit. This may be particularly important in relation to analysis that is subjective.

Of course, for larger and more complex businesses, the upfront process of designing the documentation structure will be critical when it comes to creating efficiencies in the documentation process itself. One such approach may be to consider a modular approach, which separates the data to be included in the report from the actual reports – in much the same way that an enterprise resource planning (ERP) system holds data and produces reports rather than holding the report itself. Various modules might then be prepared centrally, for particular transactions or businesses within the group that are similar in nature, and are incorporated in the Master File or relevant Local Files. This method will be especially useful when there is a high degree of standardisation or commonality of transaction or business types between different entities within the group. Notwithstanding the intention of OECD to standardise the process, though, it is still likely that some countries will require documentation customised to their specific rules, with no overlap to other territories. Some degree of local adaptation may be more cost-effective and it should not be ruled out without thought.

Country-by-Country reporting

9.40   Another practical concern for MNEs is how they gather data to compile their Country-by-Country report. Given these concerns, the OECD has provided considerable flexibility for businesses to use the best available sources for providing the data, be it consolidated reporting packages, separate entity statutory financial statements, regulatory financial statements or internal management accounts. While the source of the data is not mandated, the OECD stresses that it is important to ensure consistency of treatment across each entity within the group, and from year to year. Multinationals need to work out the most appropriate data to present, based on ease of gathering and the consistency with business operations.

9.41 By accessing the information provided in the Country-by-Country report, tax authorities are able to analyse various ratios, to determine whether there is a risk of BEPS. For example, where there is significant revenue and profit in a jurisdiction with a very low number of employees, this may suggest to a curious tax Inspector that profits might be diverted to somewhere where there is little substance. Another example of how the data from the Country-by-Country report could be used by tax authorities is to compare the level of profit achieved by different countries with the same or similar operations. While these ratios are certainly not definitive as to this risk of base erosion or profit shifting, it does provide the tax authorities with some base information to allow them to decide whether to include a business in their tax audit examination process. As mentioned previously, the OECD have released the Country-by-Country Reporting Handbook on Effective Tax Risk Management, which provides further information on the expectation of how tax authorities will use the Country by Country report, and is therefore a good reference point.

9.42 A final intricacy in relation to the Country-by-Country report relates to process, specifically a requirement by most tax authorities to have a notification submitted in advance of the filing deadline, which details which entity will be submitting the report (see **9.29**). All taxpayers need to be able to monitor deadlines and format for such notifications as these vary by country and this is an annual requirement.

Conclusion

9.43 The overall environment for transfer pricing is getting harder for MNEs to comply with, and this is certainly the case in the sphere of documentation. The increase in requirements, the collection of transparent data for the Country-by-Country report, the greater need for global consistency of reporting, and the need for transfer pricing policies to reflect the underlying substance of the transaction are likely to increase the compliance burden for taxpayers in the next few years.

9.44 Businesses will therefore want to anticipate what impact this will have on their workloads and how the new formats and data provision will affect the stance taken by their tax authorities, and have a plan to cope with these new requirements in as consistent and cost-effective manner as possible. As always, the time spent in upfront planning and thought will be hugely beneficial in the long run.

Chapter 10

Operational transfer pricing

INTRODUCTION

10.1   In summary, the point to keep in mind is that tax authorities audit the outcome of the implementation and application of a transfer pricing policy on the tax return, not simply the policy itself.

10.2   Tax authorities focus their audit resources on whether the tax returns which the multinational enterprise (MNE) submits reflect arm's-length pricing. In many countries, those tax returns are based on the accounting profit shown in the commercial accounts, drawn according to accountancy principles and practices, and it is common to find that MNEs try to actually trade on an arm's-length basis. The benefits of doing so are clear: transfer pricing rules in most countries demand an upward adjustment to reflect the arm's-length profit but do not allow for a downward adjustment, and so profits over the arm's-length amount will be doubly taxed once the other end of the transaction is adjusted to arm's-length pricing. This necessitates a claim under a double taxation treaty (where one exists) for 'mutual assistance' to eliminate double taxation (see Chapter 11 for further details). Transacting at arm's-length prices will reduce the incidence of adjustment to taxable profits, and both time and costs are saved by avoiding 'mutual assistance' claims. Notwithstanding that the MNE has an acceptable transfer pricing policy and appropriate margins for transactions, a failure to actually apply that policy and margin through the year will still lead to a non-arm's-length result in the financial accounts and, without adjustment, in the tax return. If that failure is discovered only during tax audit, it brings substantial risk of adjustment and, potentially, of penalties followed by a claim to 'mutual assistance'.

During the OECD Base Erosion and Profit Shifting (BEPS) initiative, both tax authorities and the general public have focused on whether, in their view, multinational groups are paying the right amount of taxes in every country in which they operate. The outcome of this initiative has been reflected among others in the implementation of annual Country-by-Country reporting across many tax jurisdictions, allowing tax authorities to compare the quantum of tax paid by the MNE in their jurisdiction and other counties on a global basis. Consequently, it is more important than ever that transfer pricing policies, designed in line with the arm's-length standard, are actually implemented in the transactions of the company and correctly recorded in its financial records and its accounts.

10.3 Bridging the gap, from a chosen arm's-length transfer pricing policy to a set of systems, processes and controls that reliably deliver tax returns consistent with that policy, can present a significant challenge. This is because implementing and operating transfer pricing policies as intended requires the identification of people with the skill, and access to information necessary, to implement the transfer pricing policy into the business systems. Those people will need to understand the right transfer pricing processes and controls and be supported by the right technology. These processes, controls and technology should contribute to enhanced operational transfer pricing efficiency whilst at the same time reducing tax risk and increase audit transparency.

10.4 The next paragraphs examine what is meant by operational transfer pricing, look at a holistic approach to tackling operational transfer pricing and highlight other areas which need attention to both minimise risk and comply with the arm's-length standard.

WHAT IS OPERATIONAL TRANSFER PRICING?

10.5 'Operational transfer pricing' refers to the activities that an organisation undertakes to ensure that its chosen arm's-length transfer-pricing policies are ultimately correctly reflected in its books and statutory accounts, and thereby in its tax returns.

The objectives of implementing a transfer pricing policy will include:

- Accuracy – in pricing reported in each legal entity, in line with the assumptions made in the transfer pricing policies.

- Efficient processes – for budgeting, calculating and monitoring transfer prices that create minimum disruption to the business, with a view to documenting and defending the transfer pricing position of each group entity and their intercompany transactions.

- Risk reduction – of non-compliance through a robust controls and governance framework and audit transparency.

A HOLISTIC APPROACH

10.6 Figure 10.1 contains a possible framework for tackling the challenges in correctly implementing transfer pricing policies. This framework is based on three pillars: people, processes and technology. This approach is intended to help businesses through the process, starting with a robust, supportable policy, moving on to its practical implementation, the filing and defending of tax returns, and creating an ongoing system for internal and external monitoring. This framework can help businesses to implement or to audit and (if necessary) correct the implementation of their transfer pricing policies.

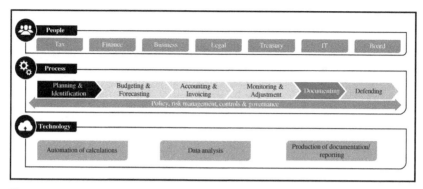

Figure 10.1 – Operational transfer pricing framework

Each of the three pillars of the operational transfer pricing framework is discussed in the paragraphs below, and further illustrated through various examples of operational transfer pricing challenges that organisations face in practice.

People

10.7   A lack of clarity as to responsibility is one of the biggest contributors to any failure to achieve an arm's-length result from arm's-length pricing policies.

Businesses should assign clear roles and responsibilities so that someone has ownership for each key stage in the process, including (but not limited to): extracting, formatting, calculating and processing financial data in the accounting system; booking inter-company transactions; and monitoring progress through the year, comparing that to the intended result and determining if adjustments should be made to the transfer prices. Although the person chosen will often be from the tax or finance departments, the objectives cannot be achieved without the support and involvement of other departments.

10.8   Coordination between various internal functions is, therefore, a critical matter. Table 10.1 illustrates potential allocation of responsibilities between departments relevant for successful implementation of transfer pricing policies.

Table 10.1 – Role of departments in operational transfer pricing

Department	Role in operational transfer pricing
Finance/Tax	• Identification of, extracting and gathering relevant data and formatting the data (putting the data into the needed format) for calculating the transfer pricing position
	• Segmenting and filtering the data in line with the documented transfer pricing calculation algorithm
	• Checking the transfer price calculations

Table 10.1 – *(Continued)*

Department	Role in operational transfer pricing
	• Calculating and monitoring the actual level of prices, margins and mark-ups against the specifics of the transfer pricing policies
	• Finance and tax teams also play the key role in identifying the organisation's needs for automating transfer pricing calculations and improving related data extracting and gathering processes. Input provided by these teams in this respect to other relevant stakeholders (eg to IT, Board of Directors) constitutes a key prerequisite towards designing the appropriate and efficient transfer pricing systems
Business	• Information on new, and changes to existing, intercompany transactions (eg changes to the functional and risk profile of entities, changes to market conditions affecting inter-company pricing, changes to transaction pathways)
	• Information on business strategies that may have an effect on the level of transfer prices (eg temporary decrease of prices to support new market entries)
	• Provision of calculation data not available from the finance department (eg information on time spent by individuals on provision of services to related parties)
	• Support for finance and tax teams in getting understanding of commercial and business viability of particular transfer pricing policies (eg does a given policy support internal KPIs and promote operational efficiency?)
Legal	• Information on new contracts and changes to existing ones
	• Identification of regulatory requirements that may affect the level of pricing (eg potential limitations to availability of year-end discounts in certain industries)
	• Comments on consistency between transfer pricing policies and contracts
Treasury	• Information on finance arrangements within the group requiring the implementation of transfer pricing policies (eg cash pooling, short and long term lending, guarantees etc.)
	• Information on foreign exchange and its impact on intercompany pricing

Table 10.1 – *(Continued)*

Department	Role in operational transfer pricing
IT	• Updating financial systems in line with the transfer pricing requirements reported by other stakeholders, in particular by the tax and finance teams.
	• Identifying and reporting potential showstoppers in the current systems or infrastructure that may affect the successful implementation of a new policy or modification of an existing one (eg related to introducing a new entity to the supply chain, re-routing transactional flows etc)
Others	• There will be other areas, depending on the specifics of the business. For example:
	– HR providing certain data and information for calculating transfer prices (eg salary data, information on length of employment, or incentive plans), and supporting internal communication of key operational aspects or recruiting the right people resources
	– Procurement providing specification of potential technology available in the market, or comparable market data for products purchased from related parties

10.9   Additionally, a key role is played by the Board of Directors. The primary purpose of the Board is to ensure the company's prosperity by collectively directing the company's affairs to meet the appropriate interests of its shareholders and stakeholders; hence the Board needs insight into the company's tax matters. In particular, the Board should be aware of key transfer pricing policies and related challenges in order to direct, delegate and approve actions needed to mitigate transfer pricing risks and address implementation challenges.

Processes

10.10   The second pillar of an operational transfer pricing framework is 'processes', ie the steps performed from budgeting, through calculating transfer prices, filing correct tax returns, to defending (if necessary) at audit the company's transfer pricing position.

10.11   Thought should be given upfront to questions such as:

•   What will the complete process for each intercompany transaction look like with people responsibilities for each stage?

•   How will the data be collected and put into the format needed for calculations?

- What and how many sources will the data be obtained from?

- Who will review and control the calculations and supporting data?

- How will an audit trail be created such that the application of transfer pricing policies is transparent?

10.12 Robust operational transfer pricing processes should address the steps set out in Figure 10.1. Table 10.2 illustrates potential processes relevant for successful implementation of transfer pricing policies.

Table 10.2 – An overview of process steps within an operational transfer pricing framework

Process steps	Transfer pricing process
Planning and Identification	Identification of a new or a change in intercompany transactions and transfer pricing environment, which will require a transfer pricing policy to be designed or amended and applied.
Budgeting and Forecasting	Determination of standard unit transfer prices for input into an enterprise resource planning (ERP) system based on budgets or forecasts.
Accounting and Invoicing	Computation of transfer prices and production of intercompany invoicing at a transactional level. This will be more challenging for policies not based on unit prices (eg profit split charges, cost allocations etc), where thought will be needed in designing the process to gather the necessary data. The accounting record must be capable of transparently showing the application of transfer pricing policies and of supporting the analysis needed to monitor and defend them.
Monitoring and Adjustment	Review and adjustment (true-up) of transfer prices to the arm's-length level, where forecasts have proved inaccurate or items such as foreign entity or local GAAP adjustments have caused variations, including multi-entity/country true-ups.
Documenting	Production of transfer pricing compliance documentation and country-by-county reporting, including testing the final transfer pricing position. A robust transfer pricing system should also allow for producing underlying calculations or replicating the calculations of historical transfer prices upon request.
Defending	Respond to enquiries from tax authorities on a timely basis including protocols about how to manage the enquiry.

10.13   These process steps are further explained and illustrated, through examples of operational transfer pricing challenges (discussed in **10.19–10.28** below).

Technology

10.14   Alongside people and processes, the third pillar of operating transfer pricing is technology.

10.15   Automating key processes presents an opportunity to reduce both the risk of human error and the time commitment / cost, freeing up time for review and interpretation of the results of the policy and other transfer pricing activities that can deliver value. The degree of automation will depend on the nature and scale of the intercompany transactions, on system capability and alignment across the organisation and on the willingness to invest in system development.

The use of enhanced technology to automate or further automate the implementation of transfer pricing policies can bring significant rewards. In considering how technology can best enhance the transfer pricing implementation process it is necessary to evaluate the operational transfer pricing solutions based on the specific requirements of the group and the transfer pricing model, considering functionality, user experience, ease of implementing changes to the solution, fit with current IT architecture and scope beyond the immediate requirements. In addition the cost to implement and maintain must be taken into consideration alongside the benefits that such technology would bring.

When a technology solution has been selected, it is helpful to allow for sufficient flexibility to be designed at the outset that will facilitate future developments/ enhancements in a cost-efficient manner. In short, the technology architecture must take into account the long-term business and IT strategies. If not designed effectively, automation can present a risk as it creates a false sense of security. Periodic monitoring of performance is essential, and poor design can become a blocker of future change/improvement because the costs to overhaul an inflexible system are prohibitive.

10.16   Another advantage of using technology is the possibility to automate the production of transfer pricing documentation, country-by-country reporting, and to analyse sets of segmented data. The latter allows the taxpayer to analyse its transfer pricing position in detail for risk assessment and monitoring purposes, and produce evidence documenting calculation steps undertaken to arrive at arm's-length prices in line with the assumed pricing policies.

10.17   There are four primary options to consider in evaluating the technology solutions, these are set out in Table 10.3. New options are starting to be considered and it is likely that these will increase in the future, these include the Cloud, process robotics, cognitive computing and blockchain.

Table 10.3 – Routes to developing the technology supporting operational transfer pricing

Solution overview	Summary
ERP provider solutions	Processes to calculate, book and invoice transfer prices form part of the ERP system.
Embedded third-party transfer pricing solutions	Solutions specifically designed to manage transfer pricing have been developed and can be 'bolted on' to a business' ERP system.
Bespoke solutions	A bespoke solution is designed and built to meet the exact requirements of the users.
Microsoft Excel	Calculating transfer prices in spreadsheets outside the system is still the most widely used approach. This approach is easy to use and familiar to users but clearly can be time consuming and presents high risk of user-introduced errors. There are many enhancements that can be made to typical Excel schedules that can improve their functionality and robustness. Lower technology costs are at the expense of higher people costs and increased risk.

10.18   Key functions that an IT system should provide include data extraction, supporting pricing calculations, reporting intercompany payments, adjusting terms and flagging issues such as underpayment and overpayment, producing in-year and year-end analytics and providing an audit trail of the process and decisions made on pricing and adjustments, where appropriate. Ideally, the systems should also support the production of transfer pricing documentation and country-by-country reporting, eg through delivering data necessary for production of the global documentation in a timely and consistent way. Additionally, systems should support producing underlying calculations or replicating the calculations of historical transfer prices upon request (eg to further evidence for purposes of a transfer pricing enquiry that a transfer policy was implemented correctly).

Finance and tax teams should work with their IT departments to determine the most effective way to implement transfer pricing policies, given any constraints arising from the business' IT systems. The teams should also work collaboratively to design new or improve existing systems in order to enhance the correct implementation and operation of transfer pricing policies. Where transfer pricing policies are not aligned with the accounting system and manual calculations are required, this will result in an increased risk of human error, issues around staff continuity and, potentially, the lack of a clear audit trail. Difficulties can also arise if the information required is collated by the business unit and is not available on a legal entity basis.

WHERE DOES IT GO WRONG?

Typical challenges

10.19 Having discussed the three pillars of building an operational transfer pricing framework, we highlight below a number of common challenges faced during each process step summarised in Table 10.2 above. The examples presented do not constitute an exhaustive list of potential issues that companies may face when operating their transfer pricing policies. They are intended to be illustrative, to explain from a practical perspective why the development of an appropriate transfer pricing operational framework around people, processes and controls and technology plays the key role in implementing transfer pricing policies as intended.

Planning and Identification

10.20   Challenge: Business entities not 'bought in' to the policy

Issues will arise if local entities neither understand nor agree with the transfer pricing policy. This is more common where employee incentive structures are tied to business metrics affected by the transfer pricing policy (eg entity revenue generation, cost savings, profitability etc); it is vital to consider the impact of the transfer pricing policy on employee incentives or other local issues. It is 'best practice' to have an open line of communication between finance/tax and management/HR teams to keep aligned the goals of employees' and the company's transfer pricing policy, and to address quickly any potential conflict between the two.

10.21   Challenge: Communicating changes

Often the finance/tax departments do not have sufficient visibility into all business lines and entities to identify changes in transactions, markets, strategy or activities that impact the transfer pricing policy. Therefore, it is important to implement processes that flag the inclusion of the finance/tax departments (and other stakeholders, where relevant) in business decisions so that they may design and execute any necessary changes to transfer pricing policies and their implementation. Regular updates from the business to the finance/tax departments will help to ensure that transfer pricing policies reflect changes to the business and new transactions on a contemporaneous basis.

Budgeting and forecasting; monitoring and adjustment

10.22   Challenge: Use of budgets without subsequent review

Transfer pricing implementation starts with budgeted revenues and costs to determine pricing that will achieve the objectives of the transfer pricing policy. Without monitoring the actual revenues and costs and making adjustments to pricing during the year, the final result may not reflect arm's-length pricing.

Performance against budget should be monitored throughout the course of the financial year through ordinary operational review. Any variance from budget should, in turn, be considered to assess whether there is a need to update transfer prices, or make pricing adjustments, to align the policy with business strategy, or to alter the application of the policy in pricing to achieve the policy aims. Where pricing adjustments are made (ie amended futures prices, additional charges or rebates, rather than tax return adjustments), the wider implications should also be considered. For example, withholding taxes, indirect taxes and reporting, and customs duty valuations should always be considered.

Ongoing monitoring needs to be considered and designed as a process in itself, considering the same three elements: people, processes (and controls) and technology. On the people side, the key questions are: who is responsible for ongoing monitoring? Is it finance and tax, or does internal audit have a role? On the process and controls side, consider the frequency and scope of reviews, how they will be undertaken, who the results will be reported to, and who will determine what follow-up actions are required? Finally, the technology project needs to consider how the accounting systems can best be used or, if necessary, adapted to support the implementation and monitoring process.

10.23   Challenge: Effective and efficient data collection

In practice, no transfer pricing policy can be operated as intended if there are inadequate procedures for collecting and segmenting relevant calculation data. First, it is important that people who are responsible for operating the policies understand the key assumptions and components so that they are able to identify all relevant calculation data and, in turn, the source(s) from which this can be obtained.

Assuming the data and its sources have been identified correctly, the company should consider the most efficient way of gathering and preparing the data for calculating transfer prices. Procedures in this respect should cover, in particular, the following:

- **Timing** for collecting the data (and performing calculations). People responsible for the calculations need to understand upfront how long it takes to gather and process the data. A lack of a clear timeline often leads to gathering the data at the very last moment (eg just before closing the financial years), with no time for reviewing data quality and for the related calculations which may lead to significant errors.

- **Format** in which the data will be obtained from relevant sources (e.g. from the controlling department, local entities etc). The lack of prescribed format for data gathering significantly increases the time needed to prepare the data for calculations, and may lead to errors and misinterpretation of the data. The right presentation of raw data is key to ensure that the calculation models work correctly. It also aids the tracing of potential errors. All of this is particularly relevant in case of any future transfer pricing enquiries, when the passage of time will otherwise create problems in understanding and defending actions.

- **Form** of the data – budget, actual or a mixture – will impact the timeline for calculations. If the data contains (wholly or partially) budget data, are the processes in place for true-ups against the actual data (see **10.22** above)?

- **Automation** of data retrieval from ERP systems, as opposed to gathering data manually. Understanding the capability of systems to generate data is the key to collecting correct and complete data. When data is collected manually, the information providers need accurate and adequate instruction on data, format and timing to avoid errors of interpretation and delays in data preparation.

- **Segmentation quality** of data for calculations should be considered. For example, if unit prices are to be calculated on a 'cost-plus' basis:

  - Is there a clear definition and understanding of the cost base components?

  - Is there a procedure for allocating indirect costs to the cost base (eg allocation of depreciation, considering the production capacities used)?

  - Are there any pass-through costs that should not be uplifted by a mark-up?

The lack of appropriate data preparation procedures will most likely lead to calculation errors, to a lack of transparency of the calculation process and to delays in finalising the transfer pricing position and the tax return. Subsequently, they will cause significant problems during any future tax audit.

Accounting and Invoicing

10.24   Challenge: Central costs 'overlooked' when calculating charges

Give careful consideration to the cost base when calculating, for example, a service fee charge. Where services are charged on a cost-plus basis, a robust policy, together with appropriate guidance notes and process documentation, should be available to ensure a consistent approach across the group to determine which costs to include in the service fee calculation, and on what basis. Whilst the treatment of employment costs for key individuals providing the services will be clear, treatment of other costs (eg overhead allocations, management cost allocations, pension costs, share scheme costs, redundancy costs, etc) will require more specific thought and instruction. If any of these costs are incurred, at least partly, in connection with the service but then not included, they may be non-deductible in the tax return of the company that incurs them or lead to a transfer pricing adjustment upon being discovered at tax audit.

10.25   Challenge: Lack of care with cost allocations

Although the OECD Guidelines present a pragmatic approach to charging services based on a cost-plus basis, which may rely on the application of an appropriate allocation key, it is still necessary to consider carefully the nature of the services being provided, the need for those services and the benefits being enjoyed by the recipient. In implementing a far-reaching transfer pricing policy, it is important to recognise that not all countries follow OECD principles and, even in those countries that do, they are still subject to interpretation through local law and practice. An understanding of local law and interpretation is critical to preparing appropriate 'in country' approaches. In practice, this may require individuals to track time spent on different types of activities and the retention or preparation of key documents demonstrating the value of the services as part of the transfer pricing documentation. Appropriate processes to collate and share this information need to be designed at the outset.

Documenting[1]

10.26   Challenge: Inadequate intercompany legal agreements

A common issue is that, while there may be transfer pricing policies and some documentation, there are no formal, written legal agreements. Alternatively, the agreements that are in place may not contain adequate third-party terms. Though it is clear in contract law that a contract exists even though it is undocumented (a contract can be written, verbal or implied by the conduct of the parties), or that there are reasons why the terms should be accepted even though they appear to deviate from terms seen in third-party situations, this is not an 'ideal' situation. In many cases, this will undermine the arm's-length nature of the transfer pricing approach as a whole, rather than the specific transaction. As an example, a company may have benchmarked intra-group services to determine an appropriate mark-up on costs and may have documentation, including legal agreements, to demonstrate that the methodologies are appropriate. However, if those legal agreements do not include key terms, their value is diminished. It is not uncommon for intra-group agreements to omit payment terms or, when they include payment terms, the parties do not stick to them and in practice the balance simply builds up on an intercompany account. This arrangement is not at arm's length in totality. Third parties are unlikely to operate in such a way; interest is applied to overdue payments and, ultimately, services are withheld from non-paying clients. Careful consideration should be given to ensure that contracts exist, their terms are arm's length in nature and that the terms are applied in practice. In addition, only individuals with sufficient authority to conclude contracts on behalf of a company should sign legal agreements in line with group internal controls.

---

1   As transfer-pricing documentation, including aspects related to the effective gathering of such documentation, is discussed in detail in Ch 9 of the book, in this section we focus only on challenges related to developing appropriate inter-company agreements.

Defending

10.27   Challenge: Access to evidence and documentation

An important part of operating a transfer pricing process is responding to requests for information by tax authorities as a part of their tax audit. In designing operational transfer pricing it is vital to consider how a transfer pricing audit might progress, what information might be needed, and what analysis might be requested to demonstrate compliance with the arm's-length standard. A structured approach for recovery and submission of documents, data and calculations to tax authorities, and for responding to enquiries, increases efficiency and reduces costs of the audit. This effectiveness is significantly impaired if there is limited access to material that demonstrates the application of transfer pricing policies and processes and provides data to support the achieving of an arm's-length result for the years under tax audit.

Appropriate procedures for comprehensive data and documentation gathering and archiving are critical so that all pricing evidence is easily accessible. This includes aspects like:

- appropriate indexing and naming of the documentation and evidence, so that relevant material can be identified and collated easily;

- centralised storage with appropriate accessibility controls;

- procedures for collecting and collating potentially relevant material; and

- procedures for reviewing and releasing information for the purposes of the tax audits.

10.28   Challenge: Controlling release of information to tax authorities

Another operational challenge related to defending transfer pricing policies is a lack of procedures for collecting and collating potentially relevant material and for its review and release to tax authorities. Providing incomplete, or irrelevant, data or information to tax authorities may extend the length of a tax audit and might negatively affect its outcome. It also may suggest that the taxpayer is not fully aware of their transfer pricing policies and, therefore, is not prepared to defend its application of the arm's-length principle.

For this reason, it is important that companies have an appropriate governance framework in place covering protocols for interacting with tax authorities and the release of information.

SUMMARY

10.29   Transfer pricing is much more than just designing a policy: the policy has to be implemented correctly so that both statutory accounts and tax returns reflect the intended objectives. It is this process that we call 'operational transfer pricing'. Success here requires a thoughtful and well-designed, holistic approach to address each step supported by the right people, processes and controls and technology.

Chapter 11

Tax audits and eliminating double taxation

INTRODUCTION

11.1   One consequence of national sovereignty in tax matters is that, in addition to the pricing of a cross-border transaction being subject to transfer pricing legislation in each territory, it is also subject to a tax audit in both countries. Transfer pricing tax audits can be time consuming affairs that eat up considerable resources of the business under audit, even if little or no adjustment is finally made to the transfer price; but that need not be the case. The first part of this chapter looks at UK transfer pricing tax audits and how to ensure that they proceed as smoothly as possible to conclusion.

11.2   Yet that is only half of the picture. It is important to keep in mind that, when one tax authority decides that the transfer price under-rewards the entity under audit, an adjustment to profits will follow which results in additional tax being paid. With increased collaboration between tax authorities there is potential for joint audits where the multinational enterprise (MNE) will be approached by more than one jurisdiction, or Multilateral Control (MLC) enquiries where multiple jurisdictions will collaborate via automatic exchange of information. In the latter, the MNE may not be aware that an MLC is occurring. In the worst case, and this does sometimes happen, both tax authorities investigate the opposite ends of same transaction without coordinating and both tax authorities conclude that the pricing that has been applied by the MNE is incorrect, each claiming that *their* taxpayer was under-rewarded (eg paying too much/too little for goods or services); as a result of these uncoordinated audits, there will be an increase in the amount of taxes due in both territories. Revisions to the OECD Guidelines contained in Actions 8–10 of the OECD/G20 BEPS project have increased disputes between taxpayers and tax administrations, and also between tax administrations. There is scope not only for disagreement on interpretation of the revised guidance, but also the date from which the revised Guidelines are applicable. The UK tax authority (HMRC), for example, regards the revised Guidelines as being simply a clarification and improvement of the existing Guidelines, rather than anything new; though they are not *precedent* for interpreting UK transfer pricing rules in an earlier period the concepts can be argued from first principle and so HMRC enquiry teams tend to use the revised guidelines in current tax audits which relate to years before the new OECD Guidelines were adopted.

Where one (or more) party to a transaction is subject to a transfer pricing adjustment by a tax authority after the fact, due to the sovereignty of each territory there is no automatic correction of the corresponding value in the tax return of the other transacting party. In many countries there is also no way for the other party to make an opposite adjustment to their tax return themselves, if still in time to amend their tax return, as domestic transfer pricing legislation often only acts to increase taxable profit, not to reduce it. Hence an adjustment by (at least) one tax authority will usually mean that some element of profit is included in the tax return of both parties to the transaction and it will be subject to tax in both countries. This is known as 'double taxation' and it is recognised by both MNEs and governments to be a hindrance to international trade and something that needs to be resolved.

11.3   If, in the main, domestic legislation or actions of the MNE alone cannot resolve double taxation, then another solution is needed. This comes in the form of bilateral or multilateral agreement under which the representatives of the two tax authorities can get together and come to a resolution as to the correct transfer price which they both will apply and respect, and a mechanism for that agreement to be made effective for the taxpaying entities. Bilateral tax treaties between countries usually contain a clause allowing two tax authorities to work together to this end. The Arbitration Convention provides the framework for this within the European Union. Mindful of the scope for increased dispute arising from changes to national tax laws in areas considered in the OECD BEPS project, Action 14 of the BEPS project set out to improve the mechanism for eliminating double taxation within bilateral treaties. The outcome of this work (binding arbitration to eliminate double taxation when the participating states cannot agree themselves how to do so) is now being enacted by some jurisdictions via their 'options selection' in the Multilateral Instrument. These options are covered in the second part of this chapter.

11.4   The work required to create bilateral tax treaties and the negotiation that occurs under them is carried out by people known as *competent authorities* for each country. Competent authorities are officials appointed by their government to undertake inter-jurisdictional dialogue and negotiation on such matters as exchange of information and the resolution of disputes. Sometimes these individuals work directly within the tax authority (as in the UK) and sometimes, they work at some remove from the revenue authority (as in Germany where the competent authorities work in the Ministry of Finance). When international disputes arise, it falls to these officials to do their upmost to resolve matters. Their brief is wider than the resolution of transfer pricing disputes, but this chapter is concerned only with transfer pricing disputes.

11.5   However, it is often far better to avoid double taxation at the outset. This can be achieved only if no transfer pricing adjustments are made to the tax return of either party. It is only possible to be certain that no such adjustment will be made during a tax audit by either tax authority through the obtaining of an advance pricing agreement (an APA). This process has been adopted by many countries and allows tax authorities to agree a position without the need for a tax enquiry and double taxation. APAs are becoming increasingly attractive to taxpayers and will be covered in the third part of this chapter.

UK TRANSFER PRICING TAX AUDIT

11.6 In the years leading up to the publication of this edition, there have been statements by a number of tax authorities around the world to the effect that transfer pricing of multinationals will be audited more closely than it has been in the past. The introduction of a Diverted Profits Tax by the UK (25% rate) and Australia (40% rate) has also increased the focus on transfer pricing and international structures. The volume and value of cross-border intra-group flows in goods, services and intangibles continue to rise and increasingly this is seen by Governments as a potential risk to the raising of business taxes; their reaction is to audit those flows more carefully. The BEPS project is a consequence of the increased political profile of cross-border flows, and the transfer pricing elements of this are intended to give tax administrations improved, or new, tools to challenge arrangements where the transfer pricing outcomes are not in line with what the tax authority understands in terms of 'value creation'. As a result, an audit of the transfer pricing policies and practices of a MNE is increasingly likely. Having a cohesive transfer pricing policy and following the implementation and monitoring steps set out above should provide a sound base from which to explain and support the tax return of the MNE if, and when, the transfer pricing tax audit happens. However, if the audit is to be undertaken effectively and efficiently, it is important to understand how that audit will unfold and where the seeds for delay, confusion and disagreement are most often first sown. What follows is based on a UK transfer pricing tax audit, but the steps are similar to those which occur in many countries and so, with a little adaptation, this process map might be a useful tool in many tax audit situations.

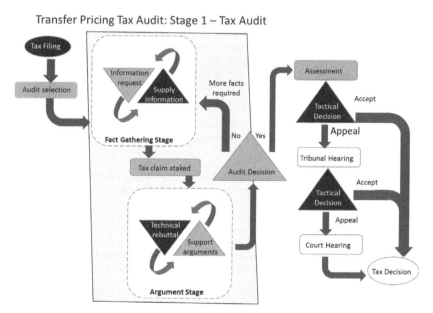

Transfer Pricing Tax Audit: Stage 1 – Tax Audit

Figure 11.1 – Tax audit

11.7 Not all tax filings are subject to a detailed tax audit every year (or in blocks of years) in every country, and that is the case in the UK. Even if a tax audit commences, it might not include a transfer pricing discussion; for example, UK tax audits can be targeted at specific areas of the tax return. The UK tax authority, HMRC, operates a governance process for selecting transfer pricing audits, whose membership includes senior and experienced international tax specialists. This is intended to reduce the overall number of transfer pricing enquiries so that resources can be concentrated on more significant and risky cases. However, once a transfer pricing enquiry is begun, it will usually result in a communication from HMRC requesting information about transfer pricing policies and practices. This represents the start of what is termed the 'fact gathering stage' in Figure 11.1 and is likely to focus on the functionality of entities that are party to the transactions in question. In many cases the tax authority will have limited knowledge of a MNE's transfer pricing policies and the initial fact gathering will often be wide and seemingly unfocused. The adversarial nature of tax audits might lead to an intuitive 'defence' response, but that might not be the best option in all cases.

11.8 If no thought is given to the strategy of a tax audit at the start of the process it is likely that the entity under audit will respond to the specific questions raised by HMRC, gathering and delivering material and information in line with specific questions asked. In many cases these answers do not satisfy the question that is in the mind of the tax inspector (the UK tax auditor) and so that approach often leads to more demands for information. Without care, the fact gathering stage might continue for a considerable time. Eventually, HMRC will express a view, which could be that additional tax is due, and the two sides turn their attention to arguing about that contention. In Figure 11.1, this second phase is called the 'argument stage'. This can continue for several months before the two sides are forced to consider whether they can agree the claim; mostly agreement cannot be reached. At this point HMRC might – and often does – decide (if the case has run as described above) that it requires more information about the business, its transactions and its transfer pricing policies and practices. This is often born out of new points coming to light in the argument stage that require further corroborating facts. The fact gathering stage recommences and a new round of demands for information and responses ensues.

11.9 The cycle above could be avoided if a strategic view of the tax audit is taken at the outset. The critical points in Figure 11.1 are:

- both parties should understand the point(s) at issue, and agree to contain the scope of the enquiry accordingly; in particular, given the increased focus on risk and risk management in the revised OECD Guidelines, it is important that the inspector understands at an early stage the key business risks and how, where and by whom those risks are managed;

- the MNE under audit should provide information to address the point(s) at issue, rather than simply responding to the questions asked. In addition to the information requested, the MNE should supply voluntarily any other information that will deepen the tax authorities' understanding of relevant facts concerning its market, business, transactions under audit and transfer pricing policies and practice;

- any movement from the fact gathering to the argument phase should not happen until both sides confirm that they have the full facts; and

- agreed facts makes the argument stage efficient and prevents a reversion to fact gathering. In turn, this facilitates a movement towards an audit decision.

11.10   When the first audit letter is received, it is possible that the inspector assigned to the case does not have a detailed understanding of what the business is and how it operates. Beyond the information contained in the country-by-country report, the UK has no filing requirements in relation to transfer pricing so the only additional information HMRC will have obtained will be via the Business Risk Review (BRR) or equivalent risk assessment process. Without that clear understanding, the questions asked and the information requested may not be focused on the point at issue; it may even be that the wrong point is being raised. It is therefore preferable, if possible, to ensure that the inspector gains a deeper understanding of the business, the commercial risks it assumes and about the intra-group transactions and the transfer pricing policies as quickly as possible in their audit. In that process it is possible to check, to the satisfaction of both parties, that the correct point is being enquired into and that everyone understands what the point of the enquiry is. Only when both sides have agreed this point is it possible to appreciate what information might be available to provide insight into the matters that concern the tax authorities and, when supplied, to allow the enquiry to move forward.

11.11   This process has a second benefit; with an in-depth understanding of the business, the intra-group transactions and the transfer pricing policies and practices, the inspector will be able to agree the precise scope of the enquiry. Early engagement with a tax authority on this basis will pay dividends in terms of mitigating unnecessary compliance costs and the overall time of the audit.

11.12   Typically an approach of this kind will be welcomed by the inspector. In practice, responding to the first enquiry letter by asking the inspector to attend a meeting at which the business risks and risk management policy and practice are explained, together with the intra-group transactions and the transfer pricing policies and practices, can be a very useful way to increase knowledge for the inspector, and thereby save time in the audit. This is also a good opportunity to explore the risk areas that prompted the enquiry notice and gain a better understanding of HMRC's concerns. At that meeting, material might also be made available, either of a general nature (such as a transfer pricing report) or more specifically if the scope of the enquiry already allows that. It may be possible to revisit any initial information requests made by HMRC and agree amendments to ensure that only relevant documents and information are being pursued. This last point is important because without a discussion about the business, how it works and what data is created and kept, it might be impossible to comply with the information request issued by

HMRC. Without this knowledge the information request might include items that do not exist, or the information request might be made in such general terms that it is arguable that no matter how much material is supplied, further data might be outstanding and so the request has not been complied with.

Over recent years, there has been a noticeable increase in the investigative nature of transfer pricing enquiries and requests for prime records such as emails and internal correspondence is becoming more common. A MNE is likely to see information requests such as 'all correspondence, notes of meetings, telephone notes, internal records and briefing papers relating to [insert transaction]'. This can often be frustrating for the MNE when the reason for the request is not explained by HMRC and can create long delays in both collating the information and HMRC reviewing it. In this situation it is important for a MNE to agree a strategy with HMRC which may include key word searches for relevant documents and restricting the period over which documents are provided. It is likely that an initial request will require documents for a full year when in reality a period of say one month would be equally valuable in evidencing the risk management functions of an entity. Maintaining a continuous dialogue with the tax authority will ensure that the MNE does not receive a seemingly endless demand for documents and information.

11.13 Assuming that the specific transfer pricing point(s) at issue were established at the outset and that good data demand and flow has now been secured, it is important to complete the fact gathering stage before moving on to any technical disagreements in the next phase. Moving too early into argument brings with it the risk of reversion into more fact gathering as the argument phase illustrates this hole in the knowledge base.

11.14 When agreement is reached between the Inspector and the MNE, HMRC is required to present the settlement to the appropriate governance panel who will authorise the settlement. It is vital at this stage that the MNE understands whether the Inspector is minded to recommend the settlement in the governance process. Although it is possible for a settlement to be considered to be acceptable in the governance process when it is not recommended by the Inspector the chances of it being approved are reduced.

Once approval is achieved the transfer pricing enquiry is completed and HMRC will close by either accepting the tax return as submitted or propose adjustments. In cases where the MNE and HMRC agree the process of settling the enquiry is that HMRC will write to the MNE confirming the finalised position and the MNE then has a period of 30 days in which they can resile from the agreement. If no such action is taken, HMRC will formally conclude the enquiry at the conclusion of the 30-day period and issue an assessment aligned with the agreement as set out. Assuming that there is an adjustment to the tax return, this may be the end of HMRC's enquiry, but it is not the end of the process for the taxpayer. At this point the taxpayer must make the decision either to accept the additional assessment and move on to deal with the double taxation that results, or to appeal the assessment. A detailed discussion of the UK tax appeals process is not within the scope of this book.

MUTUAL AGREEMENT PROCEDURE

11.15   Once a domestic audit is concluded, any adjustments agreed will result in (a) the same element of profit being recognised as belonging to two different entities within the MNE, and (b) to double taxation. It is open to the MNE to try to resolve the double taxation via the Mutual Agreement Procedure (MAP), where there is a bilateral tax treaty in place between the relevant countries, and that treaty includes a MAP article. This section will consider further the mechanism for requesting MAP assistance, the current OECD developments and arbitration. Figure 11.2 shows how the process operates. Other instruments may give access to a similar procedure, for instance the EU Arbitration Convention (*Convention 90/436/EEC*), along with the Revised Code of Conduct (*2009/C 322/01*), or the EU Dispute Resolution Directive (*Council Directive (EU) 2017/1852*).

Transfer Pricing Tax Audit: Stage 2 – Relief from Double Taxation

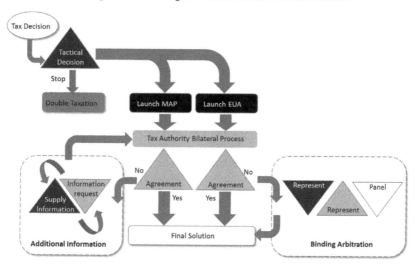

Figure 11.2 – Relief from double taxation

OECD FRAMEWORK FOR BILATERAL TREATIES

11.16   The competent authorities of two states can engage in discussion with each other if they are authorised to do so by the provisions of a double taxation agreement between their two states. A double taxation agreement is a bilateral treaty, the chief purposes of which are to address areas where the two states' domestic codes might tax the same income and to counter avoidance and evasion. A huge number of such treaties have now been signed – and the UK alone is party to more than 100. The UK's treaties, in common with those signed by other OECD members, are based on the OECD Model Treaty which is, if you like, an OECD approved template for double taxation agreements.

This template comes complete with model clauses and a commentary on how those clauses are to be interpreted.

11.17 Article 25 of the OECD Model Treaty sets out the MAP provisions. That is the procedure under which tax authorities can (through their designated competent authorities) resolve double taxation disputes. Most double taxation agreements provide for the competent authorities of the two states to consult each other when a taxpayer claims that it is being taxed 'otherwise than in accordance with the convention' (see below), as a result of the actions of one or both of the tax authorities.

11.18 A taxpayer who is on the 'other end' of a transaction that has been adjusted by a tax authority may start the process by making a claim to the competent authority for the country of which it is a resident). A claim should specify the year(s) concerned, the nature of the action giving rise to taxation not in accordance with the convention and the full names and addresses of the parties to which the procedure relates. The taxpayer who has been audited may also start the process in his country.

'Taxation not in accordance with the convention' effectively means double taxation, since as noted already, one of the chief purposes of the Treaty (Convention) is to eliminate double taxation.

11.19 If the application for MAP is successfully made, the competent authority to whom the claim is made will try to resolve the problem and, normally, will discuss the matter with the competent authority in the other country with a view to reaching a mutual agreement under which the double taxation is eliminated. In theory, double taxation should thus never arise on the total profits arising from cross-border transactions between two countries with appropriate tax treaties but not all cases can be resolved. In such cases, the only option for a MNE to relieve double taxation is arbitration, if it is provided for in the treaty.

OECD DEVELOPMENT ON MAP

11.20 MAP was specifically considered in BEPS Action 14. The aim of this action point was to deliver greater certainty and predictability for MNEs, and this would be delivered by improving the effectiveness of MAP. The output of Action 14 sought to ensure that barriers to entering the MAP process were removed, that negotiations are in good faith and that cases are resolved. In addition to the outputs of Action 14, it was recognised that many of the changes proposed would require amendments to existing treaties, of which there are in excess of 3,000. To address the administrative burden and time delay of renegotiating every treaty, Action 15 proposed the Multilateral Convention to Implement Tax Treaty Related Measures to Prevent Base Erosion and Profit Shifting (Multilateral Instrument or MLI). This was a unique way to allow countries to sign-up to all the BEPS actions and give effect to the changes in the treaty without renegotiating individual treaties. The key changes from a MAP perspective are now considered.

11.21   The first important aspect is time limits. Most modern treaties that follow the OECD Model Treaty requires a MNE to make the necessary application for MAP within three years from the action that creates double taxation. For the UK this is normally the closure notice issued following resolution of the transfer pricing audit. Many older treaties do not necessarily state a time limit for accessing MAP. In the UK this means the time limit is six years from the end of the accounting period for which the double taxation occurs. The MLI proposes to update older treaties so that they consistently contain the three-year time limit.

11.22   To demonstrate the risk of a MNE being double taxed where a treaty does not contain the three-year time limit we can consider a UK audit commenced in 2016, focussing on the accounting year ended 31 December 2014, and resolved in 2018. Due to the UK provision to make discovery assessments it may be that the audit makes adjustments as far back as 31 December 2010. If the treaty has a three-year time limit, the MNE would have access to MAP for all periods as long as the MAP application was made by 2021. However, if the treaty did not state a time limit, the six-year rule would apply resulting in the MNE being out of time to make a MAP claim for the accounting years ended 31 December 2010 and 2011 by the time the audit was concluded in 2018. It is vital that MNEs under a tax audit understands the time limits imposed by the relevant treaty and whether the jurisdictions in question has signed up to the MLI. If in doubt it is recommended that protective claims are made to maintain rights under the relevant tax treaty.

11.23   The MLI addresses two points related to a MNEs rights to access MAP, where the lack of certain clauses in the treaty have caused issues. The first is where the existing treaty does not include an Article 9(2) clause. Article 9(2) considers whether or not to make an 'appropriate adjustment', normally referred to as a corresponding adjustment ie an adjustment by one tax authority that corresponds to a transfer pricing adjustment made by the other. Not every treaty includes an Article 9(2) but where it does contain an Article 25 (mutual agreement procedure) it is the view of most Member States that Article 25 can be used to resolve transfer pricing disputes. However, some countries take the position that in the absence of an Article 9(2), there is no obligation to either grant access to MAP or make a corresponding adjustment. The MLI seeks to adopt Article 9(2) into all signatories' treaties and therefore avoid any dispute on the ability to relieve double taxation.

11.24   The second is cases where a MNE makes a self-assessed transfer pricing adjustment in one jurisdiction and then seeks double taxation relief via MAP. This has been refused by certain tax authorities due to the wording of Article 25 which states: 'Where a person considers that the actions of one or both of the Contracting States result or will result for him in taxation not in accordance with the provisions of this Convention ...'. As a self-assessed transfer pricing adjustment does not require an 'action' by either state, it has been viewed by some tax jurisdictions that such adjustments are precluded from the treaty. This is not an issue if the treaty includes the wording from Article 25(3) as this authorises discussions of cases that do not otherwise come within the scope of the treaty, but taking the UK as an example this only features in one third of treaties. Action 14 recommends that the MLI introduces the wording of Article 25(3) to ensure that the treaty accommodates the resolution of double taxation as a result of a self-assessed transfer pricing adjustment.

11.25   The final aspect of the MLI discussed here is that the MLI allows for jurisdictions to commit to mandatory binding arbitration, which would allow a MNE to gain relief for double taxation in situations where the competent authorities cannot reach agreement. Arbitration is considered later in this chapter.

The MLI came into effect on 1 July 2018 following the ratification of the instrument by the minimum five signatories required. For individual articles in tax treaties to be modified, both treaty partners must be a signatory to the MLI, must have accepted the same modifications and must have ratified the instrument in domestic legislation. Until both treaty partners have ratified, the MLI does not have any effect on that particular treaty. Therefore, the date the MLI comes into force for MAP and binding arbitration will vary between treaty partners.

Not all countries have signed up to the MLI and many countries have taken the option to opt out of certain aspects, meaning there is still a significant amount of work before there is global consistency and certainty for MNEs. Although the MLI is an important step forward, MNEs must consider the same risks of double taxation and the difficulties associated with a MAP application, which are discussed further in the next section.

MAP IN PRACTICE

11.26   The competent authorities have considerable discretion to determine whether relief will be granted. The wording of a typical treaty provision is '… if the objection appears to it to be justified …'. Added to this, the competent authorities are obliged only to 'endeavour' to reach agreement. They must try to, but they do not have to. They are obliged to consider the technical merits of each case and, if they hold genuinely contrary views as to what is the correct arm's-length result, they might simply agree to disagree, leaving behind them a measure of double taxation. So, in short, the taxpayer's right in most bilateral treaties is to ask the tax authority to consider its case, but nothing more.

In practice most MAP cases are resolved with the elimination of double taxation. But how effective the procedure is can vary depending on what countries are involved and for a number of often practical reasons. The United Kingdom, for example, has a good track record (with one or two high-profile exceptions) in achieving the elimination of double taxation, so it is very likely, statistically speaking, that a claim involving the UK would result in the elimination of double taxation.

Certain tax authorities may not agree to revise their own adjustments in a subsequent MAP if they have finalised their tax audit in a particular manner in their own country. Under these circumstances, the competent authority will only enter into MAP to persuade the second country to give relief but will resile from their audit adjustment. In the United Kingdom there is a specific statute (*Taxation (International and Other Provisions) Act 2010 (TIOPA 2010), s 124*) giving HMRC the authority to implement mutual agreements 'despite anything in any enactment' which certainly means that the HMRC competent authority can reduce HMRC's own assessments to resolve double taxation.

11.27   An important point to remember in reaching a settlement on an audit is that some tax authorities may attempt to restrict access to MAP as part of the conclusion of an audit. This may be presented in a manner seemingly beneficial to the MNE, such as a reduction in penalties or greater mitigation of the tax under dispute but remember agreeing to this would affect a MNEs ability to relieve double taxation created as a result of the audit settlement.

11.28   Two other big issues repeatedly arise in relation to competent authority procedures. First, the length of time that claims resolution often takes. Again, the OECD's Guidelines offer some recommendations; these range from urging the delegation of certain aspects of the procedure to encouraging the use of the telephone instead of formal written exchanges. Secondly, that the taxpayer and their advisor are, to a large extent, excluded from the process in that they are not involved directly in the negotiations between the two competent authorities.

In addressing these issues many jurisdictions, including HMRC, will consider an application to suspend the tax collectable as a result of the audit as part of the application from assistance under MAP. This means that the tax will only be collected when the competent authorities have resolved the matter, or the MAP process is concluded by alternative means. This can be of great benefit in terms of managing cash flows resulting from double taxation.

11.29   At the conclusion of the MAP negotiations, if the competent authorities can reach agreement, then they will inform the entities affected setting out the finalised position. If the MNE accepts the conclusion, the double taxation will be relieved in the appropriate jurisdiction (or in some cases and element of the relief in each jurisdiction). Some tax authorities at this stage will require that the cash position of the entities is adjusted to accord with the arm's-length position as stated by the MAP conclusion. This is often done via a payment between the entities or an imputed (and interest bearing) loan being put in place. This aligns the commercial position with the arm's-length position and is known as a secondary adjustment. Although HMRC does not currently require a secondary adjustment either at the conclusion of the MAP or audit process, they will often cooperate if the other tax authority requires it. HMRC has also recently proposed secondary adjustment legislation which has undergone extensive consultation. At the time of writing, such legislation has not been introduced.

ARBITRATION

11.30   In cases where the competent authorities are not able to resolve the double taxation by negotiation, the MNE may have the opportunity to seek resolution via arbitration. This allows for an independent body to consider a claim and reach a final conclusion, which is binding to the jurisdictions in question. This is often done on a 'last best offer' basis whereby each respective jurisdiction makes a final offer and an arbitrator selects one of them. As already noted the MLI proposes that each jurisdiction signs up to mandatory binding arbitration which will provide better certainty for MNEs but with the ability for tax authorities to opt-out, it is unknown at this time how commonplace arbitration will become as a mechanism to relieve double taxation. Arbitration though is not a new concept, and the EU Arbitration Convention has been in place for a number of years now acting as the ultimate arbiter of intra-European transfer pricing.

WHAT IS THE EU ARBITRATION CONVENTION?

11.31 The EU Arbitration Convention, in its original format, came into force on 1 January 1995 following ratification by the 12 older EU Member States. It was first extended to 31 December 2004, with automatic five-year extensions thereafter unless the signatory states decide otherwise. New Conventions, which have the effect of extending the original Arbitration Convention, were then created and entered into force as new countries acceded to the European Union over the years, and have since been ratified by all Member States. The current Convention applies in all 27 EU Member States. The scope of the Convention is limited to transfer pricing. The wording is similar to that in many double tax treaties based on the OECD model. In particular, the Convention:

- identifies which taxes are subject to the procedure;

- identifies who can claim relief under the Convention;

- establishes that taxable income is to be determined using arm's-length pricing principles; and

- establishes a 'competent authority' (or mutual agreement) procedure where a taxpayer considers that an adjustment to taxable income in one country would give rise to double taxation unless there were some form of related adjustment in another country.

Whilst the wording of the Convention is similar to the provisions of many double tax treaties, it is necessary to cover those matters because not every member of the EU has a double tax treaty with every other member. However, nothing in the multilateral Convention affects the terms of any bilateral treaty which may establish wider obligations regarding the elimination of double taxation.

11.32 The unique element of the Convention, at the time, was the introduction of an arbitration procedure and the establishment of deadlines and time limits for completing each step, some of which will extend those set out in the domestic legislation of certain countries.

11.33 The starting point for the arbitration procedure is the submission of a 'competent authority' application. Once a tax authority has notified a taxpayer that it is making a transfer pricing adjustment to taxable income (eg in the UK by raising an assessment), a taxpayer has three years in which to present his case to the relevant competent authority. If the case is well founded, the competent authority has two years in which to agree action to remove the resultant double taxation, usually in conjunction with the competent authorities of other relevant countries. If, however, the taxpayer has recourse to domestic law and the case is submitted to a court or tribunal, the two-year period does not start to run until the judgment of the final (domestic) court of appeal has been given.

11.34 If no such agreement is reached within two years of the taxpayer submitting his application for action, or, if later, within two years after the decision of the final court considering the matter under domestic law, the matter must be submitted to an independent 'advisory commission', which will be provided with relevant facts and documentation by the competent authority. The taxpayers concerned will be able to submit to the commission any information, evidence or documents that they believe are likely to be of use to the advisory commission in reaching a decision. They can also ask to appear before the commission.

11.35 The advisory commission is required to deliver its opinion within six months of the date on which the case was referred to it.

11.36 Once the advisory commission has delivered its opinion, the relevant competent authorities have a further six months in which to come up with their own method of eliminating double taxation. In the event that no such alternative is forthcoming, the competent authorities must act in accordance with the commission's opinion. In the United Kingdom there is specific legislation obliging the UK tax authorities to follow any agreement or decision made under the Convention by HMRC and any other competent authority or an opinion of the advisory commission.

11.37 The Convention itself defines, in broad terms, only two acceptable means for eliminating double taxation:

- if profits are increased in one Member State, there should be a corresponding reduction in another Member State; or

- any increase in tax payable in one Member State should be matched by an equal reduction in taxes payable in another Member State.

It is important to note that the Convention applies to EU Member States only. It does not encompass dealings between those states and non-members.

11.38 The Convention permits the competent authorities to publish advisory commission decisions if they so wish and provided that the taxpayers concerned give their consent.

HOW DO THE MEMBER STATES INTERPRET THE ARBITRATION CONVENTION?

11.39   Below is a summary of a typical Member State's interpretation of the Convention. The typical state in question is the United Kingdom; we understand that the UK government have discussed this interpretation with other EU states and believe it to be representative of members' views generally.

11.40   A case can only be considered under the provisions of the Convention if it is validly presented while the Convention is in force. Such a case can be considered under the Convention provisions even though the action that results, or is likely to result, in double taxation took place before 1 January 1995. The Convention provides for independent arbitration to ensure the elimination of double taxation that could result from a transfer pricing adjustment made in one of the contracting states. For the purposes of the Convention, transfer pricing adjustments must relate to profits of enterprises in contracting states.

11.41   The first stage of action under the Convention is a mutual agreement procedure, not unlike that contained in the MAP article of typical double taxation agreements, but with one notable difference: the Convention contains deadlines by which the relevant tax authorities must complete certain stages of their review and reach agreement if they are going to.

11.42   Under the Arbitration Convention, an agreement reached will be implemented irrespective of any time limits prescribed by the domestic laws of the contracting states. It is to be noted that claims under the mutual agreement procedure of the relevant double taxation agreement are constrained by the six-year UK domestic time limit. As a result, enterprises are required to state clearly whether the Arbitration Convention is being invoked when presenting cases to the competent authority.

11.43   The submission of a case to independent arbitration would take place within three years of the first notification of the action that results or is likely to result in double taxation. There is no provision for extending this time limit.

11.44   If the competent authorities cannot eliminate the double taxation by mutual agreement within two years of the date on which the enterprise presented its case, then the Arbitration Convention provides for a second stage, in which the case goes to an advisory commission. This two-year time limit is extended where the case is still under appeal through domestic procedures in one of the contracting states, and can also be extended by mutual agreement between the competent authorities and the enterprises.

11.45   The advisory commission, before which the enterprise may appear, must deliver within six months a decision that will eliminate the double taxation. The competent authorities must then act within six months in accordance with the decision, unless they agree to eliminate the double taxation by some other means. Under the Convention, neither of the two stages, mutual agreement or advisory commission, will be initiated where one of the enterprises is liable to a serious penalty.

EU DIRECTIVE ON TAX DISPUTE RESOLUTION

11.46   The objective of the EU Directive was to develop the work already established through the Convention but address some shortfalls and provide for better tax certainty for MNEs. The Directive is much wider than the Convention and can address non-transfer pricing issues.

At the time of writing, the UK is still a member of the EU and the future of the UK is unknown in terms of how leaving the EU (if/when it happens) will affect the country. The access of UK group companies to the EU Arbitration and Directive is unknown at this time.

The proposal of the EU Directive will ensure that all Member States that cannot reach agreement on a dispute within two years will be required to set up an Advisory Commission to arbitrate, and if they fail do so, the MNE can request the national court to do so. An Advisory Commission will be made up of three independent members and representatives for each of the relevant competent authorities. It is envisaged that over time the use of arbitration to resolve MAP issues will become more common and both the EU and the OECD are promoting this as a dispute resolution tool.

ADVANCE PRICING AGREEMENT DEFINITION

11.47   Advance pricing agreements (APAs) are the flipside of transfer pricing audits and MAPs. With the increased number of transfer pricing audits and therefore MAPs but still considerable uncertainty as to how the improved MAP rules, MLI and arbitration instruments will operate, APAs will remain a viable consideration for MNEs looking to prevent transfer pricing disputes from arising in the first instance.

11.48   The definition of an 'advance pricing agreement' (see para 4.134 of the OECD Guidelines) is as follows:

> 'An advance pricing agreement ("APA") is an arrangement that determines, in advance of controlled transactions, an appropriate set of criteria (eg method, comparables and appropriate adjustments thereto, critical assumptions as to future events) for the determination of the transfer pricing for those transactions over a fixed period of time. An APA is formally initiated by a taxpayer and requires negotiations between the taxpayer, one or more associated enterprises, and one or more tax administrations.'

An APA can be seen as the primary way of ending an international dispute before it even begins and creating tax certainty for the MNE. At least, a bilateral APA might be. Broadly, a bilateral APA is a forward agreement made between associated parties (usually two members of the same MNE) in two separate countries and the tax authorities in those countries. This means that in relation to the transactions considered by the APA ('the covered transactions'), both tax authorities and confirming their agreement to the transfer price. There are variants on this, for example multilateral agreements covering numerous group countries and territories; or agreements involving only one company which happens to do business in several territories through permanent establishments; but the bilateral model is the most common. The content of the agreement depends to a large extent on the attitude of the tax authorities involved. They will only agree to things that can be predicted with some safety and some are bolder than others. By and large, an APA is likely to cover the application and appropriateness of a particular transfer pricing methodology, and the specific pricing or level of profitability.

11.49   APAs are available in a large and increasing number of jurisdictions. The process is initiated at the request of the taxpayer. When might a MNE make such a request? The pros and cons of the APA option are discussed in more detail at paragraphs **11.62** and **11.63** below; suffice it to say here that a MNE will seek an APA in situations where forward certainty in respect of particularly difficult or sensitive pricing arrangements is worth more to it than the upfront cost of inviting tax authority scrutiny in advance. These situations could include the following:

- when there is a genuine lack of publicly available comparable data;

- when the taxpayer has a unique method of operating that may result in differing attributes to comparables for which no adjustments can be made;

- when the taxpayer's existing pricing arrangements are constantly under examination from different tax authorities; and

- at the end of a transfer pricing audit, an APA may be considered alongside a MAP application if the facts and circumstances in future periods are sufficiently comparable to those in the audit period.

In cases such as these, the MNE is likely to be devoting significant resources and management time anyway to assessing and defending its intercompany pricing arrangements to any number of tax authorities. One of the most effective ways for the taxpayer to obtain certainty and clarity with regard to its intercompany pricing method may be to negotiate one or more bilateral APAs.

THE SPREAD OF APAS

11.50   As with so many aspects of the modern transfer pricing age, the United States led the way, instituting a formal APA programme in February 1991. Through the 1990s the OECD debated at length on the subject: Were they a good idea? Should Member States be encouraged to offer them? Where Member States had no domestic rules permitting APAs could the MAP article of a particular bilateral treaty be used as a convenient back door into the process in specified instances? The 2010 Transfer Pricing Guidelines contain two sections on APAs: Chapter IV (Administrative Approaches) introduces the idea in general terms, while the penultimate Annex of the Guidelines covers the conduct of APAs under MAP.

11.51 During the 1990s a number of countries, including the United Kingdom, started to enter into APAs using the MAP article. The particular trigger was the growing incidence of global financial trading, which was considered abnormally problematic primarily because value-added functions were split across numerous jurisdictions and the book was open in all those territories round the clock, giving real-time pricing issues on a truly global basis. The UK, along with other countries, took the view that it was no great stretch of the provisions and purpose of Article 25 to seek to resolve international disputes ahead of time instead of retrospectively, and so began a lively business in APA negotiation even though it had no separate domestic statutory mandate to do so.

11.52 Inexorably, the lure of a real APA programme grew. At the very end of the 1990s the United Kingdom, Belgium and France all introduced their own regimes, all to a large extent inspired by and modelled on the Annex to the 1995 Transfer Pricing Guidelines. At the time of writing it is more common to find that a country with transfer pricing regulations also has an APA programme, than not. More details can be found in Appendix B to this book.

DOCUMENTATION REQUIREMENTS

11.53 The documentation requirements to support an APA application can vary from a prescriptive list, as is the case in the US, to more general guidelines. However, in all jurisdictions the applicant is required to provide sufficient documentation to demonstrate that the proposed transfer pricing methodology satisfies the arm's-length principle. Annex II to Chapter IV of the 2017 OECD Guidelines sets out at paragraph 39 the kind of information that should typically be provided. The requirement runs modestly from a) to k) and in summary covers anything the tax authority might think of while explicitly saying that it is neither exhaustive nor prescriptive. However, the 2017 Guidelines at paragraph 4.166 state that:

> 'Tax administrations should ... seek to ensure that APA procedures are not unnecessarily cumbersome and that they do not make more demand of taxpayers than are strictly required by the scope of the APA application.'

WHAT CAN BE COVERED IN AN APA?

11.54 It is usually possible for MNEs to confine the scope of an APA to issues they pick out for themselves. Most modern regimes will admit applications in respect of particular transactions or product lines or group members, and will not insist on blanket and total coverage of all possible issues. Many will move beyond mainstream transfer pricing and accept applications concerning the allocation of profit to permanent establishments. It is fair to say, though, that MNEs can expect some resistance to requests to evaluate transactions in isolation, for example where a number of transactions are highly interrelated but the request does not cover them all, or where the presence of intentional set-offs or some other factor necessitates the evaluation of a particular business relationship as a whole.

11.55   It is worth noting that the absolute size of the transactions involved is often not regarded as a relevant factor for the acceptance of an APA request. In some countries (eg Australia and the United States) special expedited APA programmes exist for smaller taxpayers. The purpose of such programmes is to enable small businesses to achieve compliance certainty at a cost that is reasonable, relative to the size and complexity of the transactions involved.

11.56   There is no such programme in the United Kingdom. The UK will only admit issues that it regards as 'complex', where there is a high risk of double taxation, or where the transfer pricing approach has been highly tailored to a taxpayer's own circumstances. A complex issue is defined as one to which there is doubt over how OECD methodology can be applied, and in respect of which there are no publicly available comparables. The UK tax authorities apply these criteria both to direct UK applications and to applications for bilateral APAs made to other tax authorities in respect of transactions to which the counterparty is in the United Kingdom. In other words, an application in respect of UK-Japanese transactions accepted by the Japanese tax authorities might not be accepted by the UK tax authorities if the UK does not see the issue as a 'complex' one. This can have the unfortunate effect of limiting an MNE to a unilateral APA even though both the MNE and OECD would much prefer a bilateral agreement.

11.57   There is also an important interaction between the UK APA programme and diverted profits tax (DPT). This tax is said by HMRC to be domestic anti-avoidance legislation and thus not subject to treaty protection. There is also no mechanism for giving advance clearances on DPT, although HMRC have indicated that they are prepared to provide certain assurances, as part of the APA process, that the risk of DPT applying to the covered transactions is low. Alternatively though if a transaction is perceived by HMRC to have a higher risk of DPT applying, there may be reluctance by the tax authority to enter into APA discussions with a MNE. In the UK, a DPT review is mandatory as part of an application for an APA.

UNILATERAL, BILATERAL AND MULTILATERAL APAS

11.58   A unilateral APA is an agreement between a taxpayer and a single tax authority, usually the taxpayer's own home authority. A bilateral or multilateral agreement is one into which two or more tax authorities enter with the MNE.

11.59   The overwhelming preference of the OECD is for bilateral or multilateral agreements, and indeed, some countries do not offer unilateral agreements. The reason for this preference is that a successful bilateral or multilateral agreement will eliminate the risk of double taxation in respect of the transactions covered, whereas a unilateral agreement will not. First, a unilateral agreement will not have been scrutinised by the tax authority dealing with the counterparty; that tax authority simply might not agree that the deal done satisfies the arm's-length principle. An investigation begun by this authority may well result in double taxation or the unwinding of part or all of the unilateral APA, thereby undermining its purpose at least as perceived by the MNE. Second, to put it crudely, a tax authority offering a unilateral agreement might well give agreement once it is satisfied that it is not receiving less than an arm's-length share of the profit. That is not the same as agreeing that its share is arm's length. Once again, there may well be problems when the counterparty's tax authority comes to look at the same transaction from its perspective.

From an MNE's perspective, a unilateral APA may have certain attractions particularly where the entity in question is a sales hub (or similar) with multiple local distributors. Entering into individual bilateral agreements with each local distributor would be timely and expensive for a MNE and not necessarily cost effective. In this situation although a unilateral APA does not give full tax certainty, having the pricing of the central hub agreed with the home jurisdiction may still be worthwhile.

As part of the Directive on Administrative Cooperation, particularly DAC 3, tax administrations are required to automatically exchange all clearances including APAs. Unilateral APAs, such as described above, are likely to be scrutinised by other tax authorities which could lead to a greater risk of tax audits in other territories. And in the territory where a unilateral APA is being sought, the process can in itself resemble an audit.

11.60   Strictly, the outcome of discussions involving three or more tax authorities is not a multilateral APA, but a series of bilateral agreements. So a deal signed up to by the United Kingdom, the United States and Canada would not be a trilateral agreement signed by all at once, but a set of bilaterals, (eg between Canada and the UK and Canada and the US). In such a case there might also be an agreement between the United Kingdom and the United States, but then again, there might not: if the MNE is headed up by a Canadian corporation, the group may well want to avoid a situation in which discussions take place to which the Canadian tax authority is not a party.

UPSIDES AND DOWNSIDES – SHOULD YOU OR SHOULDN'T YOU?

11.61   MNEs need to bear a number of possible downsides in mind when considering an APA application. For instance:

- APAs require a substantial commitment on the part of taxpayers in terms of management time and resource. This is most likely not a greater burden than would arise during a tax audit of the same point, but the upfront burden has to be carried nonetheless.

- The outcome will almost certainly be a compromise between the two tax authorities involved, so an APA is not recommended where the taxpayer is wedded to a particular position, especially where that position could be regarded as aggressive.

- Where complex transactions and more than two tax authorities are involved, negotiations can be lengthy and it may take a number of years to successfully conclude agreements. There used to be an old joke that the first real benefit you get from the APA process is the renewal. Not terribly funny but, unfortunately in the past it was also not completely untrue. Things are better now, and APAs are being concluded in as little as nine months (for simple cases) with the majority of APAs being concluded between the UK and the US, for example, in two years or less. Many regimes offer a renewal at the end of the original term, and where material facts and circumstances have not changed significantly, it should be possible to roll the agreement on for another term with only a fraction of the investment required first time around.

- In requesting an APA, a MNE is effectively consenting to a thorough examination of its current and historical transfer prices on that particular transaction. However, this can be advantageous as if something is discovered that needs to be addressed the involvement of both tax authorities means that it is usually possible to deal with past problems using 'roll-back', in which the tax authorities agree to apply the final APA position to other 'problem' years. In effect this means that MAP relief is built into the adjustment process. This is discussed in more detail below.

- Additionally, taxpayers should appreciate that documentation concerning trade secrets and other sensitive information is likely to be forwarded to the other tax authorities involved in the APA process.

11.62 On the other hand, in the right circumstances an APA offers distinct advantages:

- An advance agreement will allow the taxpayer more certainty in computing future tax liabilities in the countries covered by the APA.

- In certain circumstances, for example in the United States or the United Kingdom, APAs can be used as a way to bring about the resolution of a complicated and protracted audit. Where an audit is brought to a successful conclusion (from the taxpayer's perspective), it might be desirable to enter into an APA to make certain of the benefits of the agreement for a few more years.

- The APA process offers more certainty than taking a chance on filing, being audited, and having to go through the mutual agreement procedure. MAP is not prospective and so cannot offer assurance for future years. In addition, MAP comes at the end of an audit conducted at the behest of a tax authority and is primarily a government to government affair; the APA process is, by contrast, a proactive and forward-looking one in which the taxpayer is able to propose their own solution to particular problems and to take the lead in discussions with the tax authorities.

- Once an agreement has been reached between the parties involved, and as long as the taxpayer adheres to the principles set out in the agreement, then the only compliance work involved is likely to be an annual report confirming that the company has applied the agreed method in a correct manner.

- Costly and time-consuming transfer pricing audits will be avoided.

- APA negotiations are generally conducted in a spirit of cooperation amongst the various parties. This contrasts with the adversarial manner in which audit negotiations often take place.

The certainty that an APA offers, combined with the process and administrative advantages of taking control of the timetable (rather than facing an audit at HMRC's initiative) can make an APA attractive.

11.63   The US, UK and many other countries anticipate an increase in applications for the APA program, as a result of the changes in transfer pricing and permanent establishments proposed in BEPS Actions 7–13, and are marshalling resources accordingly.

Chapter 12

UK transfer pricing legislation

INTRODUCTION

12.1   OECD transfer pricing principles, for testing the arm's-length nature of transfer pricing applied by multinational enterprises (MNEs), are not in themselves 'law' by which taxpayers and tax authorities in any country are governed. The OECD guidance on transfer pricing principles has its roots in Article 9 (the associated enterprises article) of the Model Tax Treaty and so guidance issued by the OECD is relevant where a bilateral tax treaty, based on the OECD model, has been entered into and covers the two countries concerned in an intra-group transaction. However, even in this case, as tax treaties cannot generate a charge to tax – they can only give relief from tax – a country cannot defend its tax base with bilateral tax treaties alone. If transfer pricing principles are to be used, as they are, to increase the profits subject to tax in any country, then transfer pricing rules must be brought into domestic law in each and every country that wishes to use them. This is rather a long way of saying that each country has to have its own domestic legislation governing transfer pricing.

12.2   If we consider any one example of a bilateral treaty, based on the OECD model, it is often possible to see areas where the two countries concerned have departed from the model and agreed something (slightly) different. It will not be a surprise to learn that the potential for different views is much greater once one moves away from bilateral treaties and into the field of domestic legislation. For this reason, although the OECD principles and Guidelines are important for transfer pricing, it is critical to understand the domestic transfer pricing legislation that gives the force of law to transfer pricing practice in a particular country and the relationship that the Guidelines have with that domestic legislation. It is with that legislation – and not the OECD Guidelines per-se – with which a taxpayer must comply.

12.3   In the case of the United Kingdom, transfer pricing legislative history first began in 1915, though it was a short-lived episode and the idea died only nine months later. The UK returned to the legislative forum in 1952 to enact rules that were 'anti-avoidance' in nature, in that they only applied if the UK tax authorities gave notice that they should – such notice was not issued lightly. As a result, there was not a great deal of transfer pricing activity in the UK, and such activity that there was involved the largest of taxpayers/amounts of tax in dispute and were handled by specialist Inspectors from either the International Division or the Oil Taxation Office. These rules and this practice continued to apply, for many years, through consolidation Acts (which bring together individual items of legislation enacted into law by each Finance Act) and these transfer pricing rules became *s 770* of the *Income and Corporation*

12.3 UK transfer pricing legislation

Taxes Act 1988 (ICTA 1988). Before going on to what happened in 1999, and subsequently, it is worth sketching out a legislative timeline from 1952 through to today.

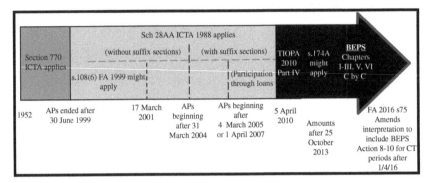

Figure 12.1 – UK legislative timeline

12.4   *Section 108* of the *Finance Act 1998* created what was to become *Sch 28AA* to *ICTA 1988* and it changed UK transfer pricing law and practice significantly. This was no consolidation Act; it ended the role of transfer pricing as an anti-avoidance weapon available to the tax authority and made it into an everyday compliance responsibility for all MNEs. It also changed many aspects of UK transfer pricing law and practice, notably the parties to which the legislation applied, and it brought UK rules into line with OECD thinking on transfer pricing. The UK transfer pricing law that companies must apply today has been further refined through the mechanism of various Finance Acts, as illustrated in Figure 12.1 above, and then finally consolidated in *Taxation (International and Other Provisions) Act 2010 (TIOPA 2010)* which reordered and reworded the law. UK transfer pricing rules are today contained in *TIOPA 2010, Pt 4*. However, as *TIOPA 2010* was a consolidation Act, it did not set out to change, nor should it be understood to have changed in any material way, the rules that existed prior to consolidation. Hence, transfer pricing practitioners are (mainly) concerned today with UK legislation written in the *Finance Act 1998* and subsequent legislation.

12.5   It is not the aim of this book to cover the detailed history of each legislative change. The timeline above is useful, however, because of the time delay between the close of a tax accounting period, the submission of a tax return, the selection for enquiry and the closing of an enquiry. If one is unfortunate enough to be considering transfer pricing in relation to an accounting period that ended on 30 April 2004, then the timeline above shows that legislation dealing with participation through loans and the 'suffix' sections of *Sch 28AA* (eg dealing with guarantees) would not be applicable. It is therefore important to understand how tax law changes with time, and to use the law that applies to the year under enquiry. Similarly, as the requirement to interpret UK transfer pricing rules in a way that best ensures consistency with OECD Guidance (*TIOPA 2010, s 164*) adopts (or not) OECD transfer pricing reports as they arise, the interpretive aids to understanding

234

UK transfer pricing legislation are different in some years. In addition, the history of how legislation is created can also be important in interpreting the legislation, as will become clear.

TIOPA 2010, PART 4

12.6   Before launching into the detail, it is worth recalling that reading tax legislation in an Act of Parliament is more akin to being in a library than simply reading a book. Different parts of a library serve different purposes, so it is important to understand where you are in the library if you are to make sense of the material that you are reading. For example:

> 'Suppose that you have guests coming to dinner this weekend. You want a really great recipe so that you might prepare an unforgettable meal. You go to the library to seek inspiration, but if you select something from the "True Crime" section of the library in a book entitled "*Poisoners Through History*" then there is a significant risk that your dinner party might be "unforgettable" for all the wrong reasons.'

So it is with tax legislation. *Part 4* of *TIOPA 2010* is just like a room in a library, and the sections and headings must be understood so that the legislation can be interpreted correctly.

12.7   The construction of *TIOPA 2010, Pt 4* is set out below. It is divided into chapters which have the following headings:

Chapter	Heading	Sections
1	Basic transfer pricing rule	146–148
2	Key interpretive provisions	149–164
3	Exemptions from basic rule	165–173
4	Position, if only one affected person potentially advantaged, of other affected person	174–190
5	Position of guarantor of affected person's liabilities under a security issued by the person	191–194
6	Balancing payments	195–204
7	Oil-related ring-fence trades	205–206A
8	Supplementary provisions and interpretation of part	207–217

12.8   Even at this level, the importance of understanding the construction of the legislation is clear. The transfer pricing rule is contained in *Chapter 1*, but one must consider other chapters to be able to apply the rule. In particular, some of the explanation as to what the legislation means is actually contained in the final chapter. When trying to interpret transfer pricing legislation, it is therefore important to consider *TIOPA 2010, Pt 4* as a whole, rather than coming to a conclusion after having looked only at a specific section or chapter.

It would be far too dry to adopt this 'Chapter' approach and to consider each one separately. Instead, a subject-orientated approach will be adopted:

- How wide is the scope of UK transfer pricing legislation?

- What are the basic rules and the pre-conditions for the rules to apply?

- If required, how big should the adjustment be under the rule?

- Does UK law allow re-characterisation of a transaction?

- What about compensating adjustments and balancing payments?

- Small and medium-sized enterprises.

12.9 One final point. As the aim of this book is to consider the application of OECD transfer pricing principles, this chapter, dealing with UK transfer pricing law, is not the central purpose of the book. There are other matters concerning UK transfer pricing rules that must be omitted for the sake of brevity. For example, UK transfer pricing rules have been written with corporate entities in mind, but transfer pricing law also applies to partnerships and there are particular issues with other legal structures, such as trusts. This book sticks to 'corporate' relationships, and readers should consult other works for detailed reference to partnerships, individuals, trusts and the like.

12.10 All legislative references in this chapter are to *TIOPA 2010* unless otherwise stated.

HOW WIDE IS THE SCOPE OF UK TRANSFER PRICING LEGISLATION?

12.11 Before embarking on any exercise in transfer pricing under UK tax law, it is instructive to consider how wide-ranging the transfer pricing legislation actually is. Are there, for example, any limitations on the interpretation of *Pt 4* of *TIOPA 2010*? As, to be frank, if not, then it is very widely drawn indeed.

12.12 It is absolutely clear that the basic UK transfer pricing rules go much further than is permitted in the OECD Transfer Pricing Guidelines and Article 9 of the OECD Model Tax Convention. If UK rules were to be applied in this fashion then double taxation could arise when the other tax authority concerned with the transaction follows the OECD Guidelines to the letter. That could lead to a claim under a bilateral tax treaty for the treaty rule to override UK law, which it would.

12.13 In considering this apparent problem, history is again our ally. When the *Finance (No 2) Act 1998* came to be debated in Standing Committee E on its way to becoming law, Mr Geoffrey Robinson, speaking for the government in defending the proposed legislation, explained why this cannot actually be a problem. UK legislation should not be interpreted as going further than Article 9 of the OECD Model Tax Treaty. He said:

> '... Our provisions are in line with the OECD guidelines. We have consulted fully and have changed several of the undertaking in the

published guidance, but the legislation will not go wide of the OECD formulation.' (For the original text, see Hansard, Standing Committee E, Tuesday 9 June 1998 (Afternoon) Part II, available at www.publications. parliament.uk/pa/cm199798/cmstand/e/st980609/pm/pt2/80609s01.htm.)

12.14   This statement could be made because specific provision was made in (what is now) *s 164* of *TIOPA 2010* to require *Pt 4* of *TIOPA* to be interpreted in such a manner as 'best secures consistency' between the UK rules and the OECD model treaty as informed by the Transfer Pricing Guidelines. However, as we shall see, there are limitations to this statement.

WHAT ARE THE BASIC RULES AND THE PRE-CONDITIONS FOR THE RULES TO APPLY?

12.15   The basic rule is contained in *ss 146–148* of *TIOPA 2010, Pt 4*. The first step is to ask, 'Is this source of income subject to these rules at all?'. This is a very important step that is sometimes overlooked; if the rules do not apply, it is senseless to waste time and energy debating what impact the rules might have, for the answer is clearly 'none at all, the rules do not apply'.

12.16   At the very beginning of *TIOPA 2010, Pt 4*, it is stated, with encouraging clarity, that UK transfer pricing rules apply to both income tax and corporation tax. As this is an exclusive definition, the conclusion from that is that UK transfer pricing rules do not apply to any other UK taxes – *unless* the rules governing those other taxes specifically provide for *Pt 4* of *TIOPA 2010* to be applied. Therefore, without a contrary instruction, these transfer pricing rules do not apply in considering customs duties, or inheritance tax, or stamp duty, or any other tax, unless that other tax specifically brings them into consideration. As noted earlier, it might be necessary to go the very end of *Pt 4* to ensure that there is a clear definition, and that is good advice in this case as there are still further restrictions on the application of UK transfer pricing rules. Specific restrictions to applying an adjustment to any tax return are laid out in *s 147(6)*, which states that an adjustment can be made only subject to:

- *s 165* (the exemption for certain dormant companies);

- *s 166* (an exemption for small and medium-sized companies);

- *s 213* (generally no adjustment to capital allowances);

- *s 214* (generally no adjustment to capital gains);

- *Corporation Tax Act 2009* (*CTA 2009*), *s 447(5)* and *(6)* (the calculation of exchange gains or losses from loan relationships are generally outside the scope of *TIOPA 2010, Pt 4*);

- *CTA 2009, s 694(8)* and *(9)* (the calculation of exchange gains or losses from derivative contracts are generally outside the scope of *TIOPA 2010, Pt 4*); and

- *Corporation Tax Act 2010 (CTA 2010), s 938N* (relating to the application of *Pt 21B* of *CTA 2010*, which deals with group mismatch schemes).

12.17 Once satisfied that the source of income is within the scope of income tax or corporation tax AND it has not been excluded by one of the restrictions, we can then consider the second question, 'Have the preconditions for applying *Pt 4* of *TIOPA 2010* been met?'.

12.18 If the pre-conditions are not met, then *Pt 4* of *TIOPA 2010* cannot be applied. The pre-conditions can be extracted from *ss 147* and *164*, though some readers might be forgiven for thinking that a valid attempt has been made to make this a confusing exercise. In summary, there are six pre-conditions, detailed below. If all of these conditions are satisfied, the 'provision' can be amended to the 'arm's-length provision':

(a) '**provision**' has been made or imposed;

(b) that provision has been made or imposed **between any two persons, one of whom is either a partnership or a corporate entity**;

(c) that provision has been made or imposed between those two persons, **acting as enterprises, by means of a transaction or a series of transactions**;

(d) the **participation condition** is satisfied;

(e) the **actual provision is different from the arm's-length provision**; and

(f) **a UK tax advantage** would accrue to at least one party.

12.19 In dealing with (a) and (c) above, the best advice of all is to consider these terms to have the widest possible meaning. If doubts exist about this advice, take a look at the arguments and decision of the Special Commissioners in *(1) DSG Retail Ltd (2) Mastercare Coverplan Service Agreements Ltd (3) Mastercare Service and Distribution Ltd* [2009] TC 00001 (commonly referred to in the UK as the '*DSG Retail case*'), or consider the 2018 Upper Tribunal, Case No 0316 (TCC), in which the bonus issue of shares was confirmed to amount to Provision. 'Provision' is likely to have been made or imposed between two parties if advantage or benefit has been conferred by one for the other, no matter how that has arisen. The act of giving that benefit will constitute the transaction, or series of transactions. There is no need for a more obvious transaction – such as a contract – to exist between the party giving the advantage and the party that enjoys the advantage. It is therefore very difficult to think of circumstances in which one party has gained any form of advantage from, or with the help of, another party that could not be said to satisfy the preconditions listed in (a) and (c) above.

12.20 Similarly, when dealing with (e) and (f) there is little to dispute, but there is also a little to understand. Condition (e) requires us to consider what the transaction would have been had the parties been unconnected. That is not to say that we should always take the transaction that has occurred and look for a comparable price; sometimes, such as an interest-free loan to a thinly capitalised group company, the arm's-length transaction would have been 'no loan at all'. That is important when one gets to condition (f), as 'no loan at all' would have generated no interest income; an interest-free loan generates no interest income, hence there is no UK tax advantage and transfer pricing rules are not applicable. (This transaction is one to which we will return when considering the question of whether UK transfer pricing law allows re-characterisation – a question that was addressed in two UK cases, *Abbey National Treasury Services* and *Altus v Baker Tilley*.) It is important to remember that condition (f) requires transfer pricing specialists to perform two calculations of UK taxable profit – one without any adjustment and one with the proposed adjustment – to show that there is a UK tax advantage to at least one of the parties and so show that transfer pricing rules should be applied. Suppose, for example, that a UK-based MNE overpays another group member for providing client entertaining. Transfer pricing logic suggests that this overpayment should be denied as the arm's-length payment would have been smaller. However, as UK tax legislation denies a deduction for all client or customer entertaining expenditure (with no reference to arm's-length amounts) the calculation of UK taxable profit both with and without the proposed transfer pricing adjustment will be the same; therefore the transfer pricing rules will not apply as condition (f) is not met. Interestingly, in the arena of costs and expenses, this primacy of other tax legislation over transfer pricing adjustments will mean that where adjustments are possible under other tax legislation the disallowance will not create the possibility of a Mutual Assistance claim under a relevant bilateral tax treaty (see OECD Model Tax Treaty Article 25). Early in this section, it was noted that consideration of these preconditions is sometimes skipped by transfer pricing practitioners. These examples provide evidence of why it is important not to shortcut the analysis in this way.

The participation condition

12.21   *The participation condition* is set out in *s 148* of *TIOPA 2010* in two parts: one that deals with financing arrangements, and the other relating to all other kinds of transactions. The two parts are identical, except that, for finance transactions, the test of participation applies not only at the time of the transaction but also within six months following the date of the transaction. In both cases the participation condition is applied to the two persons between whom provision has been made; one must be directly or indirectly participating in the management, control, or capital of the other, or the same person or persons must be directly or indirectly participating in the management, control or capital of both of them. *Sections 157* to *163* of *TIOPA 2010* provide further help in understanding what this means.

12.22   Before so doing, it is important to understand the definition of the term 'control'. *Section 217(1)* sets out that this is the definition given in *s 1124* of the *CTA 2010*. (For partnerships, the definition is quite clear: it means the right to a share of more than half the assets, or of more than half the income, of the partnership, although, as noted earlier, the transfer pricing of partnerships will not be considered in detail in this book.) For corporates, the definition can lead to complications, discussed shortly. It reads:

'(2) In relation to a body corporate ('company A'), 'control' means the power of a person ('P') to secure–

(a) by means of the holding of shares or the possession of voting power in relation to that or any other body corporate, or

(b) as a result of any powers conferred by the articles of association or other document regulating that or any other body corporate,

that the affairs of company A are conducted in accordance with P's wishes.'

This might sound straightforward, but it gives rise to a number of areas for interpretation.

Now, the participation condition

12.23 *Direct participation* means that the person controlled is a corporate entity or a partnership (the other party(ies) might also be a corporate entity or a partnership, but do not need to be. One of the parties to the transaction must have control of the other (ie the corporate entity or partnership), or that one person (any person, not just a corporate entity or partnership) has control of both of the tested parties (*TIOPA 2010, s 157*).

12.24 *Indirect participation* means one of two things: either that the person would be directly participating if one were to attribute to them certain rights and powers that are actually held by certain other persons, or by themselves at different times; or they are one of several potential major participants. Looking to the first test, attributed rights and powers, one must consider in relation to person 'P' (*TIOPA 2010, s 159*):

(a) rights and powers which P is entitled to acquire at a future date;

(b) rights and powers that P will, at a future date, become entitled to acquire;

(c) rights and powers held by another person who might be required to use them on behalf of P, as directed by P, or for the benefit of P (including rights and powers that they are entitled to acquire at a future date, or will become entitled to acquire at a later date); and

(d) rights and powers that are held by connected persons, or rights and powers that can be directed to be applied by, or for the benefit of, that connected person (including rights and powers that they are entitled to acquire at a future date, or will become entitled to acquire at a later date).

12.25 The legislation is clear that one must consider rights and powers that people are entitled to acquire at a future date or will, at some future date, become entitled to acquire. This does not require us to hypothesise what might happen in the future, but to address things that are already going to happen – in other words things that will happen without any further condition outside of the parties' control being satisfied as a precondition. For example, if person P sells to person Q the ordinary share capital of a business A under a contract drawn today, but which contains a clause saying that control of the shares passes to Q only in 12 months' time, then at a future date Q is entitled to acquire the rights and powers of those shares. In this example we would attribute control of those shares to Q from the date of the contract and not wait until the future date on which Q actually gains control of those shares. If the same transaction contained an additional clause based on something outside of the powers of Q, such as 'if the share price has risen above £x' then it cannot be said that Q is entitled to acquire, or 'will become' entitled to acquire those shares; we simply do not know as there is a condition precedent for the transaction to happen.

12.26 It's also necessary to consider the rights and powers of someone with whom a person is connected. This term is defined in *s 163* of *TIOPA 2010*, to mean a spouse or civil partner, a relative of either of them, or the spouse or civil partner of such a relative. 'Relative' is defined in *s 163(4)* to mean brother, sister, ancestor or lineal descendant. So, you are connected to your spouse or civil partner and to their brothers and sisters (your in-laws), and to the spouses or civil partners of your in-laws. You are connected to your children, to their spouses or civil partners, and to your parents and grandparents, etc. However, you are not connected to your second cousin, twice removed, and so there are limits to this attribution process.

12.27 *Major participant* is dealt with in *s 160* of *TIOPA*. To paraphrase, it says that where one party has at least 40% control, at least one other person has at least 40% control, and together they control the entity, then the major participation condition is satisfied. In that case there is 'indirect participation' and the participation condition is satisfied. In a simple case, this all seems to make sense, but in **12.29** we will find that things are perhaps not as clear as they might appear.

Practical difficulties in testing 'control'

12.28 We will now cover just two areas of potential disagreement over the definition of 'control', terms used in UK transfer pricing legislation. First, what is the meaning of the word 'persons' in *s 148(2)(b)* and *(3)(b)*? After that, we will consider *s 160(3)(b)(i)* of *TIOPA*; what does it mean to be taken together to have control?

The meaning of 'persons'

12.29 Suppose that the share capital and voting rights in Blazer Ltd and Jacket Ltd are owned by three unrelated individuals Alfred, Bertie and Charlie. Alfred holds 34%, Bertie holds 33% and Charlie holds 33% in each of the companies. Although the same three shareholders hold the same rights and powers in two companies, no one person has control of either company and the three individuals are not connected with each other by way of family or blood ties. Are Blazer Ltd and Jacket Ltd 'controlled by the same person or persons' such that any transaction between Blazer Ltd and Jacket Ltd is subject to UK transfer pricing legislation? Is that view supported by legislation?

12.30 The relevant test is contained in *s 148(2)* of *TIOPA 2010*:

'... at the time of the making or imposition of the ... provision ....

(i) One of the affected persons was directly or indirectly participating in the management, control or capital of the other; or

(ii) The same person or persons was or were directly or indirectly participating in the management, control or capital of each of the affected persons.'

Neither Blazer Ltd nor Jacket Ltd control each other which removes (i) from contention and the key control issue is whether the same person or persons has control of both Blazer Ltd and Jacket Ltd. Direct participation only exists where there is 'control', which is defined by *s 1124* of *CTA 2010*. No one 'person' controls both companies and the test for indirect participation requires either that rights and powers of one participant can be attributed to another, or that major participants control both; these are excluded from contention in the facts given. There is no requirement to aggregate the shareholdings of persons who do not have control when taken separately and who are not otherwise connected with each other.

12.31 As *TIOPA 2010* is a consolidation Act it does not change the legislation that previously existed and this provides further clarity that the term 'persons' does not allow the amalgamation of rights and powers of otherwise unconnected persons.

'who, taken together, control the subordinate'

12.32 This phrase is used in relation to the 'major participant' test. Control over a corporation or partnership exists if a three-part test is satisfied. The detail of this can be found in *s 160(3)* and *(4)* of *TIOPA 2010*. Paraphrasing the three-part test in *s 160(4)*:

(1) The tested party (A) must have at least 40% interests in the rights and/or powers that control an entity.

(2) Another person (B) must also have at least 40% interest in those rights and/or powers.

(3) Taken together, these two parties control the entity.

Imagine a situation (commonly found in practice) where two 50% shareholders in a joint venture company act together to control the entity with neither having a casting vote. In the absence of any specific provisions for joint ventures, UK transfer pricing rules based on 'control' would not apply. When the UK transfer pricing legislation was modernised in 1998 this problem was addressed, and the trigger-point for 'major participant' was set at 40% in order to be sufficiently low to prevent avoidance (the idea being that commercial pressures to not give away value would prevent any further mischief).

12.33 So, where two companies each own 40% of an entity 'in respect of which the pair of them fall to be taken as controlling the subordinate' transactions between the subordinate and each of the two 40% owners will be subject to UK transfer pricing requirements on the basis that the control test is met. (Transactions between the shareholder companies are not within the ambit of UK transfer pricing rules unless, independently, one controls the other or they are both under common control.)

12.34 A question that sometimes arises relates to situations where the shareholding situation is as follows:

- Company A owns 45% of Company C

- Company B owns 55% of Company C

- Company A and Company B are not related.

In this situation, are transactions between Company A and Company C within the scope of the UK transfer pricing legislation? The answer depends on the third element of the control test: 'who, taken together, control the subordinate'. Assuming that there are no complex arrangements or documents giving different rights and powers, in this example the answer is 'no'. Company B controls Company C. Company A and Company B do not need to be 'taken together' in order to determine control.

12.35 The Explanatory Note to *s 160* of *TIOPA 2010* is helpful here.

'For the 40% test to be met two conditions must apply. The first condition is that the person, along with another person, must between them control the body or firm. Then, looking at the holdings, rights and powers that give the pair control of the body or firm, the second condition is that each of the pair must have at least a 40% share of all holdings, rights and powers of the kinds that give them that control.'

In this example, Company A and Company B do not 'between them' control Company C. Company B alone controls Company C. As a result, Company A is not within the scope of the UK transfer pricing rules.

12.36 The UK tax authorities' view on this point is not so clear – for example, as set out in their International Tax Manual (INTM 412060):

'The control rules in TIOPA10/S160 contain an important feature. This is the inclusion of a provision deeming a 40% participant in a joint venture to control that joint venture where there is one other participant who owns at least 40% of the venture.'

The UK rules on the application of transfer pricing to joint ventures have been in place for 14 years, and the point has not been tested before the UK courts. This may be because, in reality, the independent relationship between Company A and Company B in this example is enough to discourage non-arm's-length behaviour.

IF REQUIRED, HOW BIG SHOULD THE ADJUSTMENT BE UNDER THE RULE?

12.37 When non-arm's-length pricing has been used in a transaction or series of transactions between related parties and a UK tax advantage arises, UK transfer pricing legislation requires the taxpayer to adjust their tax return before submission to calculate tax instead on the profit that would have arisen from the 'arm's-length provision'. If the taxpayer does not do this, UK transfer pricing legislation allows HMRC to impose an adjustment to achieve that position, and general tax provisions allow for penalties to be imposed, in appropriate cases, because the taxpayer submitted an incorrect tax return. However, transfer pricing methodologies rarely offer a single price for a transaction. It is more usual for there to be a range of possibilities, all of which are 'arm's-length'. HMRC set this out clearly in their International Tax Manual in relation to settling tax enquiries:

> 'INTM 483070: There is rarely a single 'right' answer as to what is the arm's-length price. There may be different ways of arriving at a reasonable assessment of how the transactions would have been priced had they been carried out between independents. There will often be a range of possible figures (narrowed as far as possible before a resolution report is made). The case team's recommendations should usually identify parameters for the arm's-length price rather than a single target figure.'

In addition, UK transfer pricing legislation does not specify a particular point in the range to which a price should be adjusted if UK transfer pricing rules require an adjustment to be made.

12.38 UK transfer pricing legislation should be interpreted 'as best secures consistency' with the OECD Guidelines (*TIOPA 2010, s 164*), and the Guidelines provide an insight into two areas. First, paragraphs 3.55 to 3.59 recognise the likelihood of there being an arm's-length range, in most cases, of prices or margins that unrelated parties would use to price a transaction. This mirrors the guidance in HMRC's manuals noted above.

12.39 Paragraphs 3.60 to 3.63 then deal with the question of where, within the range, a price should be set. The first – and key – comment (see 3.60) is that when a transaction has been priced by the parties at a level that falls within the range of arm's-length prices (note: not the inter-quartile range unless this statistical tool is required to be used to account for comparability defects, see 3.57) there should be no adjustment made at all. If the need for an adjustment is accepted by both the tax administration and the taxpayer, then all points within the agreed arm's-length range have equal validity. If, as will mostly be the case, the comparable data used to identify the arm's-length range is not assured to be free of comparability defects such that it would be appropriate to make use of statistical tools like the inter-quartile range (see 3.57), then paragraph 3.62 of the Guidelines sets out that:

> '... it may be appropriate to use measures of central tendency to determine this point (for instance the median, the mean or weighted averages, etc.,

depending on the specific characteristics of the data set), in order to minimise the risk of error due to unknown or unquantifiable remaining comparability defects.'

12.40   Where comparability defects cannot be ruled out of the comparable data and statistical tools have been used to ascertain the arm's-length range, one reason for not adopting a centralised point for the purpose of adjustment might be that all points of the range are not of equal validity with respect to the controlled transaction. For example, suppose that the tested party is a distributor that has been stripped of some of the functions and risks that will normally be carried by other distributors. It may not be possible to undertake comparability adjustments for all of the differences between the tested party and the comparable data, such that it might be reasonable to expect the arm's-length price for the tested party to fall below the centralised (mean, median, average, etc) area of the range. Equally, there might be factors that could push the price for the tested party above the centralised area of the range, such as the possession of valuable intangibles.

12.41   In all cases care must be taken to ensure that comparability of the tested party to the comparable data is maximised and to identify qualitatively, and if possible quantitatively, such differences that remain and cannot be eliminated and adjusted for in the data that sets the arm's-length range.

DOES UK LAW ALLOW RE-CHARACTERISATION OF A TRANSACTION?

12.42   The basic principle of arm's-length transfer pricing is that the value of a transaction between connected parties should be set at a level which unconnected parties would have agreed. But what if unconnected parties would not have completed that actual transaction? Paragraph 1.121 of the OECD Guidelines gives clear guidance that the actual transaction undertaken, as it has been structured, should be respected. Restructuring of the actual transaction into something else is recognised to be a somewhat arbitrary exercise. Non-recognition of the actual transaction can be contentious and a source of double taxation, therefore '… every effort should be made to determine the actual nature of the transaction and apply arm's length pricing to the accurately delineated transaction, and to ensure that non-recognition is not used simply because determining an arm's length price is difficult.' Certainly the inequity of recharacterisation could be compounded by double taxation created where the other administration does not share the same views as to how the transaction should be restructured. The Guidelines specifically state that where the same transaction can be seen between unconnected parties it should not be recharacterised, and also note that the mere absence of similar transactions between unconnected parties is not a reason for recharacterisation. Paragraph 122 of the 2017 Guidelines states that:

'The transaction as accurately delineated may be disregarded, and if appropriate, replaced by an alternative transaction, where the arrangements made in relation to the transaction, viewed in their totality, differ from those which would have been adopted by independent enterprises behaving in a commercially rational manner in comparable circumstances, thereby preventing determination of a price that would be acceptable to both of the parties taking into account their respective perspectives and the options realistically available to each of them at the time of entering into the transaction.'

This is a significant change from the 2010 Guidelines as in para 1.65 it suggests that there are two situations in which the actual transaction can be ignored and something put in its place: (1) where the form and the substance of the transaction are not the same; or (2) where the transaction is not one which unconnected parties would undertake and the actual transaction impedes the setting of an appropriate price. Would the same circumstances allow re-characterisation under UK transfer pricing legislation before and after the adoption of the 2017 Guidelines? The answer is 'No' as the rule for recharacterisation has been significantly relaxed.

12.43 Even before the 2017 Guidelines HMRC took the view that, in appropriate circumstances, re-characterisation is allowed. The requirement to construe UK transfer pricing legislation, so as to best ensure consistency with OECD Guidelines (*TIOPA 2010, s 164*), is cited as authority. This has not, at the time of writing, been challenged before a UK tax tribunal, but it was reviewed by the UK court in a non-tax case heard in the Chancery (commercial) Division of the High Court in a case concerning a claim for compensation for negligent tax advice (*Altus Group (UK) Ltd v Baker Tilley Tax and Advisory Services* [2015] EWHC 12 (Ch)). Because this was not a tax hearing, and HMRC were not represented, it is not possible to cite this case as precedent, but the arguments raised could also be raised before a tax court for periods before the adoption of the 2017 Guidelines.

12.44 It was accepted by both sides in *Altus v Baker Tilley* that UK tax legislation, absent consideration of the OECD Guidelines, would not allow for re-characterisation. *Section 147(1)(a)* deals separately with 'provision' made between two associated persons and the 'transaction or series of transactions' through which that provision is made. *Section 147(3)* then allows, in appropriate cases, for the actual provision to be replaced by the arm's-length provision in the calculation of taxable profit. There is nothing in *s 147(3)* to allow for replacement of the actual 'transaction' or 'series of transactions' with something else. The question then is whether the interpretation of *s 147*, which by reason of *s 164* should be as best secures consistency with the meaning of OECD Guidelines, should be taken as to create that extension of the impact of *s 147(3)* to include the 'transaction' or 'series of transactions', or to include the 'transaction' or 'series of transactions' within the 'provision'. The arguments against these steps would be:

- *Section 147(1)(a)* clearly separates the concepts of 'provision' from the 'transaction' or 'series of transactions' under which the provision is given. *Section 147(3)* clearly allows the replacement of the 'provision' only. If it is argued that the intention was to allow for replacement of the 'transaction' or 'series of transactions', that was open to the draftsmen to say, but they did not. It is not the place of the UK courts in interpreting legislation to 'repair' errors of drafting; that is a matter for Parliament.

- It is not correct to interpret the phrase 'provision' in *s 147(3)* to include the 'transaction' or 'series of transactions' under which the provision is made, due to the separation of these concepts (*s 147(1)(a)*). To do so would require two different interpretations of the same word within a single paragraph of the Act.

12.45 The strength of the arguments against re-characterisation of the actual transaction under UK transfer pricing law prior to adoption of the 2017 Guidelines have not, at the time of writing, been tested before a tax tribunal. However strong these arguments might appear, they are contrary to the view of HMRC and it is likely that they would be resisted. In addition, as the UK government has adopted the revised OECD Guidelines which have been developed in the course of the BEPS process. The criteria for re-characterisation have been relaxed somewhat, and these are dealt with in more detail in Chapter 2. The arguments above remain valid for earlier years, however, and transfer pricing practitioners must remain vigilant to apply the correct test either side of the change.

WHAT ABOUT COMPENSATING ADJUSTMENTS AND BALANCING PAYMENTS?

12.46 Where a transfer pricing adjustment is made to a UK tax return the initial impact, in addition to achieving a correct tax payment for the enterprise is to create double taxation. This is because the entity with whom they transacted has over-stated the profits to the extent of the proposed adjustment. Where the counter-party to the transaction is overseas, the solution to double taxation is to lodge a claim under the appropriate bilateral or multilateral treaty (if there is one). For detailed discussion on this topic, see Chapter 11. Where the counterparty to the transaction is a UK-resident entity (ie both companies are resident in the UK) the opportunity to remove double taxation is presented by *TIOPA 2010, Pt 4, Ch 4* (if the claim is to be made by the counterparty) or *Ch 5* (if the claim is to be made by a guarantor). There are a small number of conditions that need to be met for a claim to be valid and there are time limits within which a claim must be made. However, these are relatively straightforward and can be found either by looking at the relevant legislation or by referring to the HMRC manuals (INTM 412130 for claims by the counterparty and INTM 413160 for claims by guarantors).

12.47 However, there is a further complication where one of the connected parties is a company subject to corporation tax whilst the other is not a company and is subject to income tax. Where the potentially advantaged person (on whom a transfer pricing adjustment has been made) is a company, but the other party to the transaction is not a company and is subject to income tax, then *s 174A* acts to deny the person any claim under *s 174*. This measure was introduced by *s 75(3)* of the *Finance Act 2014* in respect of amounts arising after 25 October 2013.

12.48   Where a transfer pricing adjustment is made to a UK tax return and the UK counterparty has made a successful claim for a compensating adjustment there might be one remaining problem: the cash and accounting profit associated with the actual transaction and the transaction for tax purposes are different, and might need to be corrected. UK tax legislation provides a mechanism for payments to be made between the two transacting parties, or in some cases a guarantor, in *TIOPA 2010, Pt 4 Ch 6*. These rules allow a payment to be made to correct the imbalance caused by a transfer pricing adjustment and compensating adjustment claim, with no further UK tax consequences arising. The amount of the payment is at the discretion of the taxpayers, up to a maximum of the value of the adjustment (ie payment is not limited to the value of tax on that adjustment). (This is similar to the UK rules for payment for group relief.) As with compensating adjustments there are a small number of conditions that need to be met in respect of the balancing payment; these can be found either by looking at the relevant legislation or by referring to the HMRC manuals (INTM 412140).

12.49   Both compensating adjustments and balancing payments are relatively easy to understand and to use. In practice, businesses often attempt to transact at arm's-length prices so that no adjustment, compensating adjustment or balancing payment is needed, as this will avoid the additional administrative effort. However, sometimes there are circumstances in which the effect of transacting at arm's-length prices, as opposed to transacting at non-arm's-length prices and then making suitable claims to eliminate double taxation, or the effect of making claims either to compensating adjustments and/or balancing payments following a transfer pricing adjustment, might have other consequences. Three such situations are considered below but they are illustrative in nature, rather than representing an exhaustive list, and so care should always be taken to think through all of the consequences of any decision:

- Interaction with personal taxation for employees

- Interaction with VAT

- Partnerships and subsidiary companies.

Interaction with personal taxes

12.50   This example shows how trading at arm's-length prices to pre-empt the need to make transfer pricing adjustments can have unforeseen tax consequences. Suppose that an airline business operates through three companies: one company (A) deals with engineering and maintenance, one (B) owns aircraft, and the third (C) operates scheduled flights. Each company employs staff, and they are able to take advantage of discounted prices for otherwise vacant seats on scheduled flights. The price paid by staff is equal to the marginal cost of them being on the aircraft (additional fuel consumption, in-flight meal, etc) and so the price paid is significantly less than the cost of a scheduled seat sold to the public for the same journey.

12.51 Transfer pricing analysis of the facts above will show that company C, which operates flights, is making provision by means of a transaction, or series of transactions to both company A and B that employ workers who take advantage of flight offers. (See *Waterloo plc & Ors v IR Commrs* (2001) SpC 301, which illustrates that the transaction truly provides value to the employer.) The value of the provision is the difference between the scheduled price of the seat and the amount paid by the employee, as this is not reimbursed to company C. Therefore the taxable profits shown in the tax return of company C must be increased to comply with UK transfer pricing legislation. Thereafter, both companies A and B might apply for a compensating adjustment to reduce their taxable profits to eliminate double taxation and, if the qualifying conditions are met, this will be allowed. Suppose also that both companies A and B transfer funds to company C either to pay the additional tax due or to pay the additional price of the flights in full. Does the transfer pricing adjustment imposed on company C, or the compensating adjustments claimed by companies A and B, or the balancing payments made by companies A and B to company C amount to an additional cost that should be taken into account in looking to the personal tax position of the employees and the obligations both companies A and B as employer to operate wage tax withholding?

12.52 Based on the original facts (before any transfer pricing actions) the additional value provided to employees is not taxable on them and not subject to wage tax withholding by the employer. This follows the case of *Pepper v Hart* (1992) 65 TC 421 which provides that, where the employee has met the marginal cost of the benefit, there is no additional taxable value to be assessed for personal tax purposes. However, what is the impact on this position of transfer pricing adjustments, compensating allowances and balancing payments? Fortunately, the answer is 'no impact'. Making an intra-group transfer pricing adjustment in respect of the provision of employee benefits does not, in itself, affect the valuation of that benefit for the purposes of taxing benefits in kind or related National Insurance liabilities. The same goes for any adjustment or balancing payment following a transfer pricing adjustment. Experience has shown that HMRC agrees with this analysis.

12.53 So far, the conclusion is that any actions that might be taken to comply with UK transfer pricing legislation and thereafter, to address any cash or accounting problems that arise, will not change the personal tax analysis. Yet the common reaction to the facts given in this example is to suggest that the companies should transact with each other using arm's-length prices in order to pre-empt transfer pricing adjustments to the tax return of company C and any resulting claims for compensating adjustment and balancing payments, as this will reduce compliance costs. If that approach is taken, then the additional payment made by companies A and B will not be a 'balancing payment' and the marginal cost to the employer of providing that benefit will rise. This in turn means that the employee will be subject to taxation on the additional value. So the transfer pricing approach – to trade at arm's-length prices – will increase (albeit inadvertently) the tax bill for employees.

Interaction with VAT

12.54 For many UK businesses VAT is not a direct cost as they charge appropriate VAT on all of their sales and recover all of the VAT that they incur. Some businesses, such as those in financial services, do not charge VAT on (at least some) of their sales and, as a result, they cannot recover all of the VAT that they pay. These 'partly exempt' businesses therefore incur VAT as an actual cost. Regardless of whether a business reclaims all of its VAT, the VAT returns that it submits must be accurate and penalties can be imposed if they are not.

12.55 VAT is charged on the value of transactions where consideration is given. If the price paid between related parties is less than market value, then VAT may be charged on the value of the transaction, not the price, if and when HMRC issues a direction to that effect. Any transfer pricing adjustment agreed for direct tax purposes might also have implications for the VAT-able value of transactions declared on the VAT returns submitted. The potential to impact indirect taxes (including customs duty and other indirect taxes) should be kept in mind when agreeing a transfer pricing adjustment for direct tax purposes.

12.56 Where a transaction takes place without any consideration (eg if a free service is provided) then in theory there will be no VAT value, even between related parties. That is because the market value rule applies only if there is consideration given. In practice, it may be that consideration is given in a non-cash form (such as reciprocal services) and HMRC will certainly look at all circumstances closely where VAT is at stake. However, a transfer pricing adjustment in a tax return, and a claim to compensating adjustment, will not, of themselves, alter the fact that consideration has not been given, so there is no change required to the VAT returns submitted just because such an adjustment is agreed. However, if a balancing payment is made, then this is 'consideration' in respect of the transaction, so the VAT accounting must also be adjusted. In some circumstances, the making of a balancing payment might enable HMRC to issue a 'market value' direction, requiring the parties to account for VAT on the basis of the market value of the transaction, rather than the amount of the balancing payment.

Partnerships and subsidiary companies

12.57 One final example of the consequences of making a transfer pricing adjustment and claiming a compensating adjustment can be seen in relation to partnerships that, as is found commonly, make use of subsidiary companies to carry on some of their business. The partnership, composed of individuals (subject to income tax) controls the subsidiary company (subject to corporation tax). The UK's transfer pricing rules require that taxable profits are calculated using arm's-length prices if a UK tax advantage would otherwise accrue to that taxpayer. There are two options available to achieve compliance with UK transfer pricing rules: either actually charging the arm's-length price, or by making an adjustment to the tax return of the potentially advantaged party and claiming a compensating adjustment in the tax return of the counter-party.

SMALL AND MEDIUM-SIZED ENTERPRISES

12.58   Transfer pricing is a resource-intensive compliance process and it is unreasonable to expect smaller businesses that represent an inherently smaller risk to the UK tax base, to commit the resources necessary for transfer pricing monitoring and compliance. It is similarly unreasonable to expect HMRC to commit its limited resources to policing transfer pricing compliance where little tax can be at risk. UK legislation recognises this by providing an exemption from transfer pricing rules for most transactions of a 'small or medium sized enterprise' (SME). This applies to profits earned on, or after, 1 April 2004 (see *TIOPA 2010, s 166*).

12.59   What constitutes a small or medium-sized enterprise is based on a modification of the European Union recommendation (see EC 2003/361). However, before looking to that definition, it is important to recognise that there are exclusions from the exemption:

- for transactions with connected parties in non-qualifying territories – those territories with which the UK does not have a double tax treaty with an appropriate non-discrimination article (see *TIOPA 2010, s 167(3)*);

- when notice has been given by HMRC to a medium-sized enterprise that transfer pricing rules should apply (see *TIOPA 2010, s 168*). Such notice would not be given lightly and, as of December 2012, no such notice has been issued;

- where the enterprise (be it small or medium-sized) elects to remain within the scope of transfer pricing legislation (see *TIOPA 2010, s 167*). This election is made for a single accounting period and, if made, applies to all transactions of the company and it is irrevocable; and

- for both a small and for a medium-sized enterprise, for transactions related to Patent Box income HMRC may issue a notice to require the computation of profits in accordance with transfer pricing rules in respect of that provision only.

12.60   The modifications required from the EC definition are:

- rights of a liquidator or administrator (acting in that capacity) are left out of account in determining whether the enterprise, or any other enterprise meets the numerical tests;

- whether the enterprise is an SME will be determined solely by reference to the period for which a return is being made;

- the declaration as an autonomous enterprise in Article 3, paragraph 5 is omitted;

- the numerical tests are by reference to annualised figures for the chargeable period; and

- the estimate for a newly established enterprise is omitted.

12.61   The European Commission published a revised recommendation on 6 May 2003 concerning the definition of micro, small and medium-sized enterprises and a User Guide (see EC 2003/361). The definition applies to any entity engaged in an economic activity, irrespective of its legal form and includes entities subject to income tax as well as corporation tax; hence it applies to both companies and partnerships subject to UK transfer pricing legislation. Qualification as a small or medium-sized enterprise is based on meeting two criteria. First, staff headcount must be less than 50 (small) or 250 (medium). Secondly, the enterprise must meet one (though it can meet both) of the financial limits; small requires either annual turnover or balance sheet total value (ie assets, not reduced by liabilities) to be less than €10 million, whilst medium requires annual turnover of less than €50 million or balance sheet value of less than €43 million. If the entity is a member of a group, or has an associated entity, these limits apply to the whole group and not the specific entity.

12.62 Staff includes employees, persons seconded to work for a business, owner managers and partners, though part-time staff count only for an appropriate fraction. The turnover and balance sheet values are net of VAT and are based on ordinary accounting principles.

12.63 The European Commission recommendation recognises that in the case either of 'linked enterprises' or partner enterprises the staff and financial data of associated enterprises must be included in the test.

12.64 Linked enterprises are those with the right to control (directly or indirectly) the affairs of the enterprise. 'Linked enterprises' are enterprises which have any of the following relationships with each other:

- an enterprise has a majority of the shareholders' or members' voting rights in another enterprise;

- an enterprise has the right to appoint or remove a majority of the members of the administrative, management or supervisory body of another enterprise;

- an enterprise has the right to exercise a dominant influence over another enterprise pursuant to a contract entered into with that enterprise or to a provision in its memorandum or articles of association; and

- an enterprise, which is a shareholder in, or member of another enterprise, controls alone, pursuant to an agreement with other shareholders in or members of that enterprise, a majority of shareholders' or members' voting rights in that enterprise.

For the purposes of calculating the data for an enterprise, all data for any linked enterprise must be aggregated, together with data for any other enterprise that is linked or partnered with them. All the staff, turnover and balance sheet entries must be taken into account regardless of the extent of control (ie 51% control is no different to 99% control in this matter).

12.65 Enterprises are 'partner enterprises' where one holds at least 25% of the capital or voting rights of the other but they are not linked enterprises (more than 50% control relationship). However, rights of linked enterprises are aggregated to see if they meet the 25% threshold. Unlike linked enterprises, only a proportion of the data from partner enterprises is aggregated, based on the percentage control interest. Where partner enterprises have their own linked or partner enterprises, the data from those enterprises must be aggregated first before applying the percentage holding.

12.66 Certain categories of investor provide a positive role in business creation. The European Commission (EC) recognises limited circumstances in which an interest should not result in the loss of its small or medium status:

- public investment corporations and venture capital companies;

- individuals or groups of individuals with a regular venture capital investment activity who invest equity capital in unquoted businesses ('business angels'), provided the total investment of those business angels in the same enterprise is less than €1,250,000;

- universities or non-profit research centres;

- institutional investors, including regional development funds; and

- autonomous local authorities with an annual budget of less than €10 million and fewer than 5,000 inhabitants.

The EC identifies groups that are excluded from data to be augmented. (Excluding here cases where the investment enterprise is linked to the enterprises in which it had invested under the other tests detailed earlier.) Additionally they cannot be linked enterprises solely by reason of being able to exercise a dominant influence by virtue of the terms of their investment, provided that they are not involved directly or indirectly in the management of the enterprise.

Chapter 13

The attribution of profits to permanent establishments

INTRODUCTION

13.1 Whilst the concept of the permanent establishment has a long history reaching back into the nineteenth century, the question of how to attribute profits to a permanent establishment has always been somewhat fraught. It is seen as an arcane and tricky area subject to differing interpretations of the basic principles by tax authorities with a consequently high risk of double taxation. The perceived difficulty and risk of double taxation has often driven behaviour with multinational groups preferring to establish local subsidiaries rather than setting up permanent establishments.

13.2 The difficulties lie in the very nature of a permanent establishment (PE). A subsidiary company has its own legal identity, audited financial statements and board of directors. In contrast, a permanent establishment is part of the same person as the 'head office' and so it has no separate legal identity other than for tax purposes. It is part of a larger whole – a legal entity resident for tax purposes in another state. The permanent establishment concept requires the profits of this larger whole to be divided in some way between the head office and the permanent establishment because the host country has primary taxing rights over the profits attributable to the permanent establishment – a requirement that is fraught with difficulty. This difficulty is often compounded by the fact that in many countries there is no legal requirement or commercial need to produce local branch accounts – other than for tax purposes. As a result, there is not the solid foundation of a set of audited financial statements to form the basis of calculating taxable profits. Rather, the starting point is often local management accounts or accounts that are produced solely for tax purposes.

13.3 In order to address the above uncertainties, states have developed their own rules in domestic law in order to provide a legal framework setting out how the profits of a permanent establishment located in their particular country should be calculated. Many also have rules on how to attribute profits to outbound permanent establishments of companies resident in their country. However, whilst giving a degree of clarity from a domestic law perspective, these domestic laws have in some ways compounded the problem. Again, the reason for this a basic one – attributing profits to a permanent establishment in its very nature requires the division of the profits of one legal entity between two jurisdictions. If the domestic rules of both jurisdictions are not wholly aligned on how to calculate those profits, then double taxation is likely to result. In practice, domestic law in the area of PE profit attribution has tended to be more diverse across countries than in the area of transfer pricing between related parties. In the area of transfer pricing most countries have domestic rules that are based upon the arm's-length principle. Whilst most jurisdictions start with the 'separate enterprise principle' (discussed further below) to attribute profits to permanent establishments, domestic laws often include interpretations of that principle which are not universally followed or have additional accretions – for example formulaic rules on attribution of interest expense to a permanent establishment or artificial caps on the amount of head office expenses that can be attributed to a permanent establishment that result in significant differences between the 'measure' of profit to be attributed to a permanent establishment under the domestic laws of the host and head office countries. Double taxation (or indeed in rare cases less than single taxation) is the result.

13.4   These difficulties have been recognised by the OECD which over several decades has attempted to address and resolve these problems through detailed work with the various Member States of the OECD in order to try to reach a consensus position on an agreed conceptual framework on how to attribute profits to permanent establishments. At first this work took the form of the production of the Model Treaty and in particular a standard wording for Article 7 of the OECD Model Tax Convention on Income and on Capital (the Convention) (which is the article dealing with the attribution of profits to permanent establishments) and its associated commentary. However, this work did not fully resolve the issue so the OECD undertook a major project in the late 1990s which culminated in the 2008 Report on the Attribution of Profits to Permanent Establishments. This report was subsequently issued in a revised form in 2010 (the Report). This revised report in essence contained the same conclusions but was designed to align its wording with the new version of Article 7 of the Model Treaty that was released in the same year. The Report encapsulates the OECD's current thinking on how profits should be attributed to permanent establishments.

TECHNICAL REFERENCE MATERIAL

13.5   The analysis in this chapter focuses on the approaches to attributing profits to permanent establishments as set out in the relevant OECD material. It does not examine the rules set out in the domestic legislation of various Member States of the OECD (or indeed of non OECD countries) nor does it look at other potential approaches such as that included in the UN Model Double Taxation Convention between Developed and Developing Countries.

13.6   As mentioned above, the most authoritative statement of the current OECD position is set out in the Report. The Report itself is designed to provide detailed guidance on how to interpret Article 7 of the Convention and indeed the most recent version of Article 7 reflects the conclusion of the Report. As stated in the Commentary on that Article: 'The current version of the

Article therefore reflects the approach developed in the Report and must be interpreted in the light of guidance contained in it'.[1]

The Report is divided in four parts. This acknowledges the fact that special considerations apply to enterprises within the financial sector which warranted separate examination and guidance. Part I deals with permanent establishments in general. Part II deals with permanent establishments of banks, Part III with enterprises carrying on global trading of financial instruments and Part IV with insurance enterprises[2].

13.7   It is important to remember that the Report should be read in conjunction with the Commentary on Article 7 itself and a subsequent publication from the OECD in March 2018: *Additional Guidance on the Attribution of Profits to Permanent Establishments* (the Additional Guidance). This latter document was the response by the OECD to the recommendation in the OECD Report on *Preventing Artificial Avoidance of Permanent Establishment Status* that further guidance was needed on how the existing rules would apply (particularly to permanent establishments outside the financial sector) given the changes to the PE threshold recommended by that Report[3].

13.8   Finally, it should be noted that care should be taken in applying the guidance set out in the OECD documents in practice. Aside from the normal caveat that the wording of individual bi-lateral tax treaties may deviate from the standard wording of the Convention, it is important to bear in mind that some states may not recognise that the Report has any legal status or bearing when interpreting the PE profit attribution article of a particular treaty. This could be the case where, for example, domestic law principles of treaty interpretation do not permit material produced after the treaty was signed to be used as aides in interpreting that treaty. In these situations, the guidance set out in the Report should be seen as an authoritative rendition of modern thinking in the area but excessive reliance on the detailed wording of the Report (and indeed the overall approach set out in the Report) would be unwise. Moreover, given that the current version of the Report was finalised in 2010 it is likely that it will take many years for countries where such an approach prevails to modernise their treaties to include the new Article 7 and thus bring the guidance in the Report into play. More confusingly still it is quite possible that a particular state has some treaties that are still in force that include older versions of Article 7 whose interpretation is governed by earlier guidance and other more recent treaties which include the most recent wording linked to the Report. It is entirely possible, therefore, that a company resident in that state with multiple permanent establishments in other states could be obliged to apply different approaches to attributing profits to its permanent establishments resulting from having different versions of Article 7 in its respective tax treaties.

---

1 Commentary on Art 7 of the Convention, para 9.
2 It should be noted that the 2008 version of the Report is potentially more relevant to interpreting treaties which include the old as opposed to the 2010 version of Art 7 of the Convention.
3 *The Additional Guidance* – p7.

INTERACTION BETWEEN PE PROFIT ATTRIBUTION AND TRANSFER PRICING RULES

13.9   Whilst the Report mandates the application of the arm's-length principle by analogy to attribute profits to permanent establishments, it is critical to note that Articles 7 and 9 (Associated Enterprises) are separate sets of rules and do not have to be mutually compatible. Indeed, as the Additional Guidance notes: 'The Model Tax Convention and its Commentary do not explicitly state whether a profit adjustment under Article 9 should precede the attribution of profits under Article 7'.[4]

Moreover, given that the Report was completed in 2010 its approach and wording cannot possibly reflect the revisions to the OECD *Transfer Pricing Guidelines for Multinational Enterprises and Tax Administrations* (the Guidelines) that resulted from the BEPS project. In particular, the revised approach on how to reward risk in the Guidelines does potentially conflict with the approach set out in the Report on attributing profits to permanent establishments. This is particularly relevant in the case of dependent agent permanent establishments and in particular where personnel of the dependent agent are managing risk on behalf of PE enterprise. The principles of the Report would suggest that the reward to risk would remain with that enterprise as the legal bearer of that risk but would be attributed to the dependent agent permanent establishment whilst the current Guidelines might suggest that the reward to risk under the modern interpretation of the arm's-length principle should be reallocated to the dependent agent entity itself. The Additional Guidance touches upon this but does not entirely eliminate the uncertainty arising from the different approaches by setting out clear guidance as to what is the preferred approach in these circumstances.

THE SEPARATE ENTERPRISE PRINCIPLE AND THE AUTHORISED OECD APPROACH (THE AOA)

13.10   As noted in Paragraph 15 of the Commentary:

"'Paragraph 2 of the Convention sets out the basic rule for the determination of the profits that are attributable to a permanent establishment. According to the paragraph, these profits are the profits that the permanent establishment might be expected to make if it were a separate and independent enterprise engaged in the same or similar activities under the same or similar conditions taking into account the functions performed, assets used and risk assumed through the permanent establishment and through other parts of the enterprise". This rule is known as the "Separate Enterprise Principle"'.

---

4   Additional Guidance, p14, para35.

258

As noted above, the Report gives detailed guidance on how to apply this basic rule in practice. The approach set out in the report is known as the Authorised OECD Approach (AOA).[5]

Key features of the Separate Enterprise Principle and the AOA are as follows:

(1)   Under the AOA references in the guidance to attributing profits should also be taken as applying equally to losses.[6]

(2)   The AOA sets a ceiling on the amount of profit that may be taxed in the host country of the PE.[7]

(3)   There is no 'force of attraction principle' – in other words 'the right to tax does not extend to profits that the enterprise may derive from that state otherwise that through a permanent establishment'.[8]

(4)   Profits may be attributed to the permanent establishment for tax purposes even if the enterprise as a whole has made losses.[9]

(5)   Under the AOA a two-step analysis is required:

–   first, a functional analysis needs to be undertaken to identify the economically significant activities undertaken by the PE; and

–   second, any dealings between the PE and other parts of enterprise are remunerated by applying the principles set out in the Guidelines by analogy.[10]

(6)   'The AOA attributes to the PE those risks for which the significant functions relevant to the assumption and/or management … of risks are performed by people in the PE and also attributes to the PE economic ownership of assets for which the significant functions relevant to the economic ownership of assets are performed by people in the PE'.[11]

(7)   The aim of the AOA is 'not to achieve equality of outcome between a PE and a subsidiary in terms of profit but rather to apply to dealings among separate parts of a single enterprise the same transfer pricing principles that apply to transactions between associated enterprises'.[12]

THE TWO-STEP ANALYSIS

13.11   Paragraph 44 of the Report summarises conveniently the two-step analysis (and the sub-steps).

---

5   The Report, Pt I, parag 3.
6   Ibid.
7   Ibid, para 9.
8   Ibid, paras 8 and 12 of the Commentary.
9   The Report, para 8.
10   Ibid, para 10.
11   Ibid, para 15.
12   Ibid, para 55.

Step One

- A functional and factual analysis leading to:
  - the attribution to the PE as appropriate of the rights and obligations arising out of transactions between the enterprise of which the PE is part and separate enterprises;
  - the identification of significant people functions relevant to the attribution of economic ownership of assets and the attribution of economic ownership of assets to the PE;
  - the identification of significant people functions relevant to the attribution of risks and the attribution of risks to the PE;
  - the identification of other functions of the PE;
  - the recognition and determination of the nature of those dealings between the PE and other parts of the same enterprise that can appropriately by recognised having passed the threshold test; and
  - the attribution of capital based on the assets and risks attributed to the PE.

Step Two

The pricing on an arm's-length basis of recognised dealings through:

- the determination of comparability between the dealings and uncontrolled transactions established by applying the Guidelines' comparability factors directly ... or by analogy ... in light of the particular factual circumstances of the PE; and
- selecting and applying by analogy to the guidance in the Guidelines the most appropriate method to the circumstances of the case to arrive at an arm's length compensation for the dealings between the PE and the rest of the enterprise, taking into account the functions performed by and the assets and risks attributed to the PE."

The summary above introduces some key concepts involved in the application of the AOA. These are examined in more detail below.

SIGNIFICANT PEOPLE FUNCTIONS OR SPFS (AND KEY ENTREPRENEURIAL RISK TAKING FUNCTIONS OR KERTS)

13.12 The SPF concept is a key one in the application of the AOA as it determines the attribution of risk (and hence the reward associated with assumption of risk) between the constituent parts of the enterprise as well as the economic ownership of intangible assets. There is no specific definition of SPFs. A key point in reaching this determination is that it is critical to get a full understanding of the activities performed by the enterprise as a whole (not just the permanent establishment) and the value drivers of the business it performs as a determination of the SPFs of a particular enterprise can only be properly made in that context rather than looking at the PE in isolation[13]. Despite there being no set definition of an SPF, the Report does provide guidance on what are the SPFs as opposed to more routine people functions. Very broadly SPFs can be defined as the personnel that make active day to day decisions with respect to critical aspects of the business. An important distinction is drawn between day to day decision making and more strategic functions – such as giving a 'Yes' or 'No' answer to a proposal. With respect to the determination of where risk is assumed paragraph 68 states:

'... The PE should be considered as assuming any risks for which the significant people functions relevant to the assumption of risk are performed by the personnel of the PE at the PE's location. For example, the PE should, generally, be treated as assuming the risks arising from negligence of employees engaged in functions performed by the PE'.

Similarly, paragraph 85 states:

'The significant people functions relevant to the determination of the economic ownership of internally created intangibles are those which require active decision-making with regard to the taking on and management of individual risk and portfolios of risks associated with the development of intangible property'.

Whilst paragraph 87 goes on to say: '... the focus for determining the significant people functions relevant to the determination of economic ownership is on the active decision-making and management rather than simply saying yes or no to a proposal. This suggests that, just as for financial assets, economic ownership may often be determined by functions performed below the level of senior management'.

It should be noted that Parts II to IV of the Report do not use the term SPFs. Rather they use the term Key Entrepreneurial Risk Taking Functions (KERTs). In practice it is difficult to draw a distinction between the two concepts other than the sectors in which the relevant enterprises operate. Parts II to IV are, however, more forthcoming as to indicating what are the typically the KERT functions in their respective industries with the sales/trading function being seen as the presumed KERT in traditional banking, the trading function being the KERT with respect to global trading activity and the underwriting function typically being seen as the KERT in the insurance sector.

DEALINGS

13.13   As the PE is legally simply a constituent part of the overall enterprise it cannot as a matter of fact enter into transactions with other parts of the enterprise that have legal consequences. As a result, a key feature of the Report is the development of the concept of 'dealings'. Dealings are defined

---

13   The Report, paras 62 and 65.

as 'the intra-enterprise equivalents of separate enterprise transactions between the hypothetically separate PE and other parts of the enterprise of which the PE is part'.[14]

In other words, under the AOA, provided it is supported by the functional analysis, it is possible (and indeed a requirement) to postulate a hypothetical transaction (or 'dealing') between a PE and other parts of the same enterprise in order to arrive the correct amount of profit to attribute to the PE for tax purposes.

13.14   However, as the Report points out, since a dealing has no legal consequences for the enterprise as a whole a higher degree of scrutiny is needed before a dealing is accepted as having taken place than for transactions between separate legal entities[15] and 'a threshold needs to be passed before a dealing is accepted as equivalent to a transaction that would have taken place between independent enterprises acting at arm's length'.[16]

13.15   Thus, preparation of documentation or internal agreements showing a dealing has taken place are a useful starting point. However, they are not necessarily sufficient in themselves to lead to a dealing being recognised for tax purposes. Dealings will only be recognised for tax purposes if the functional analysis is supportive of this result. For example, a dealing that purports to transfer risk from one part of the enterprise to another without any transfer of functional activity and responsibility from managing that risk would not be recognised as that would violate one of the key pillars of the AOA which aligns allocation of risk with the function managing that risk[17].

13.16   Assessing whether or not a dealing has taken place is therefore a critical aspect of the application of the AOA in practice and requires detailed functional analysis in order to arrive at a conclusion one way or the other. This will involve a detailed understanding of both the business and the particular facts and circumstances of the particular matter in question. Of especial importance is an understanding of the relevant people functions involved in order to arrive at a conclusion as to what are the SPFs in this particular case and whether or not the SPF has changed from one part of the entity to another.

13.17   It is of course possible to have a 'dealing' without a transfer of SPFs. For example, the PE could employ personnel carrying out a particular function which, as shown by the functional analysis, should not be considered an SPF. However, a dealing would still be seen as taking place if those personnel provide services to another part of the enterprise (for example where the SPFs are located) and the dealing would still need to be compensated appropriately by applying the principles set out in the Guidelines by extension – for example on a cost plus basis if it was similar to the supply of routine services in a legal entity to legal entity situation.

---

14   The Report, Pt I, para 14.
15   Ibid, para 34.
16   Ibid, para 35.
17   Ibid, para 36.

ATTRIBUTION OF RISK

13.18 Attribution of risk and reward to risk is critical when seeking to calculate the profits attributable to a PE. The AOA addresses this by aligning the attribution of risk (and thus reward associated with risk) to the location of the SPFs: 'The functional ... analysis will ... attribute to the PE any risk inherent in, or created by the PE's own significant people functions relevant to the assumption of risks...'.[18]

However, it is possible that that risks initially assumed by the PE (or another part of the enterprise) can be treated as having been transferred to another part of the enterprise by means of a dealing. Assessing whether or not such a dealing has taken place is a necessary step as the recognition or non-recognition of the purported dealing will have a material impact on the amount of profit (or losses if the risk materialises) attributable to the PE. As the Report notes:

> 'A dealing within a single legal entity is not something which is self-evident but is a construct, the existence of which is inferred solely for the purposes of determining an arm's length attribution of profit. Consequently, intra-entity dealings are perhaps more susceptible to being disregarded or restructured than transactions between associated enterprises'.[19]

13.19 The starting point for evaluation of a potential dealing which may transfer risk will normally be internal documentation and/or accounting records showing the 'purported existence of such a dealing'.[20] However, such records are of themselves not sufficient. There has to be 'a real and identifiable event' for the dealing to be recognised. This is determined by the functional analysis rather than documentation or accounting records: '... ultimately it is the functional and factual analysis which determine whether a dealing has taken place, not the accounting records or other documentation provided by the enterprise.'[21]

13.20 Moreover, when assessing whether there has been a transfer of risk within the enterprise it is necessary not only to determine whether the test of dealing recognition has been met but also whether the dealing is one that transfers risk from one part of the enterprise to another. For this to happen there would need to be 'economically significant transfer of risk, responsibilities and benefits as a result of the dealing'.[22] This requires an event which would normally be that the SPFs in relation to that risk have ceased to be performed by one part of the enterprise (eg the PE) and are now performed by another part of enterprise (eg head office).

13.21 Whether or not an event has occurred which meets this criteria is not always clear cut and is an area of inherent difficulty when applying the AOA in practice. Part I of the Report does not give specific guidance in this area other

---

18   The Report, Pt I, para 21.
19   Ibid, para 176.
20   Ibid, para 177.
21   Ibid, para 177.
22   The Report, Pt I, para 178.

than indicating that the location of the SPFs in relation to that particular risk are the critical factor but the fine judgments involved can be illustrated by Part II of the Report which discusses this in more detail in relation to banking assets. Part II draws a distinction between 'risk monitoring' and 'risk management'. Risk monitoring whilst being a dealing (a supply of risk monitoring services) would not normally give rise to the assumption of the risks being monitored. In this case, if another part of the enterprise performs a risk monitoring function to an asset attributed to a PE, then it should be regarded as performing a service which would be priced appropriately but there would be no dealing transferring the asset (and the reward to risk associated with the asset) from the PE to the other part of the enterprise. Conversely, if the risk management function began to be performed by another part of the enterprise that would be seen as a dealing leading to the transfer of the banking asset (and the risk/reward associated with that banking asset) from the PE to the other part of the enterprise.[23] The distinction between risk monitoring and risk management is a fine one (and the Report also suggests distinctions between different levels of risk management function with some being akin to risk monitoring!)[24] but ultimately risk monitoring is seen as a more passive activity such as monitoring the credit status of a borrower compared to risk management as being a more active function[25] which would involve amongst other things activities such as hedging and taking decisions around what to do if the borrower became distressed such as calling in security or selling the loan to specialist distressed debt operator.

Finally, it should be noted that there as two special categories of potential dealing that are explicitly rejected by the Report. First, there is no scope for internal guarantees under the AOA.[26] Second, in the case of insurance entities a dealing akin to reinsurance should not be recognised for tax purposes except in exceptional circumstances.[27]

TANGIBLE ASSETS

13.22 The attribution of physical assets under the AOA is straightforward. Economic ownership of tangible assets for the purposes of attributing profits within an enterprise are attributed to the place of use[28].

INTANGIBLES

13.23 Under the AOA, it is necessary to identify intangibles which play an important role in generating profits of the enterprise and through the functional

---

23 The Report, Pt II paras 179–181.
24 See paras 173–186 of the Report, Pt II for the detailed discussion of this point.
25 The Report, Pt II, para 180.
26 The Report, Pt I, para 19.
27 The Report, Pt IV, para 177–179.
28 The Report, Pt I, paragraphs 75–76.

analysis assess what intangible property the PE uses and under what conditions. For example, should the PE be treated as the economic owner of the intangible or that the intangible is used by the PE but economically owned by another part of the enterprise.[29] It follows from this that it is necessary to develop a principled approach to decide how to determine economic ownership of IP between different parts of the enterprise.[30] The approach adopted by the Report is to use the functional analysis to identify the SPFs in relation to the intangibles and attribute economic ownership (and hence taxable profits in relation to those intangibles) to the part of the enterprise where the SPFs are located.[31] The Report also concludes that these principles apply broadly to internally developed trade intangibles, acquired trade intangibles and marketing intangibles.

13.24   With respect to intangibles the Report does seek to give more guidance as to how to identify the SPFs than in relation to SPFs more generally. As noted above in the discussion on SPFs, the focus is on active day to day decision making rather than simply approving proposals with the suggestion that the SPFs are likely to be at a level below senior management.[32] The Report suggests that:

> 'Although not a definitive or prescriptive list, functions which may be relevant include designing the testing specifications and processes within which the research is conducted, reviewing and evaluating the data produced by tests, setting the stage posts at which decisions are taken and actually taking the decisions on whether to commit further resources to the project...'.[33]

It should be noted that the Report was finalised before the DEMPE concept in relation to intangibles was articulated in the latest version of the Guidelines. However, given that the basic tenet behind the AOA is to apply the Guidelines by extension it would not appear unreasonable for either taxpayers or tax administrations to apply the DEMPE concept in the PE profit attribution context in order to arrive at a conclusion as to where the SPFs in relation to a particular intangible are located.

If the functional analysis determines that the SPFs in relation to a particular intangible are performed by head office but that PE uses that intangible in the course of its business to generate profit then this is a dealing between head office and the PE and needs to be taken into account in calculating the profits attributable to the PE. As noted above, Step 2 of the application of the AOA requires the Guidelines to be applied by analogy in order to price the dealing. One potential approach would be to characterise the dealing as a notional license from head office to the PE on which an appropriate arm's length notional royalty charge would be due and which would be a notional deduction

---

29   Ibid, para 8.3
30   Ibid, para 80.
31   The Report, Pt I, para 80.
32   Ibid, paras 85 and 87.
33   Ibid, para 88.

when arriving at the calculation of the PE's taxable profits.[34] It should be noted that such an approach whilst mandated by the AOA is contrary to previous historical guidance in the Commentary and may well not be accepted by tax authorities which do not accept the validity of the AOA in their domestic law or in a particular tax treaty.

ATTRIBUTION OF 'FREE' CAPITAL TO A PE

13.25 The concept of 'free capital' has been applied for many years by some jurisdictions to measure the appropriate level of taxable profits of banking PEs. 'Free capital' is very broadly the non-interest bearing capital of the enterprise such as shareholder equity and accumulated reserves. This concept is developed in the Report and is now an element in step 1 of the two-step process outlined above. Indeed, the Report states that 'The attribution of "free capital" among parts of the enterprise is a pivotal step in the process of attributing profits to the PE.'[35]

Unfortunately, however, it proved impossible during the course of the OECD's work on PE profit attribution that lead to the production of the Report for governments to arrive at a consensus position on how to allocate capital. As a result several approaches are set out in the Report all of which are "authorised approaches" which, as discussed in the Report, have their individual strengths and weaknesses.[36] The two primary methods are:

- The capital allocation approach; and

- The thin capitalisation approach.

It should be noted that the 'Safe harbour approach/quasi thin capitalisation/ regulatory minimum capital approach'[37] is explicitly described as a non-authorised OEC approach.[38]

13.26 The capital allocation approach is essentially a 'top down' approach in that it allocates 'free capital' across the enterprise on a proportionate basis so if a PE has 10% of the total assets and risks of the enterprise it will be attributed 10% of the enterprise's total capital.[39] This approach has the advantage of simplicity. However, it may prove difficult to apply in practice – for example it raises the question as to how to put a value on assets and risks a question which is not necessarily easily answered. Any valuation adopted is vulnerable to challenge and could easily be disputed between different tax authorities and the taxpayer and tax authorities. It is also problematic in certain circumstances. For example, where the enterprise has amassed a 'war chest' of surplus capital

---

34 Ibid, paras 206 and 209.
35 Ibid, para 146.
36 See the Report, Pt I, paras 115 to 149.
37 Ibid, paras 135 to 138.
38 Ibid, para 135.
39 Ibid, para 121.

for acquisitions it is not immediately obvious why it is appropriate that a share of that surplus should be allocated to the PE.[40]

13.27   The thin capitalisation approach by contrast is 'bottom-up' and arguably more in line with the separate enterprise concept and the overall approach under the AOA. Under the thin capitalisation approach a PE is required to have:

'... the same amount of "free" capital as would an independent enterprise carrying on the same or similar activities under the same or similar conditions in the host country of the PE by undertaking a comparability exercise of such independent enterprises'.[41]

In order to apply the thin capitalisation approach it is necessary to identify the amount of funding needed to support the functions, risks and assets of the PE and then use comparables to determine what part of that funding need should be made up of free capital. However, a concern with this approach is that identifying an appropriate amount of 'free capital' from external comparables may in practice prove difficult given the diverse range of debt-to-equity ratios observable from comparables.[42] A further weakness of this approach identified by the Report is that the sum of the capital allocated to individual PEs may exceed the amount of free capital of the enterprise as a whole[43]. This latter weakness is arguably a function of the separate enterprise concept itself and it is slightly odd that it is flagged by the Report as a problem given that in other situations it does not see a problem with the PE being out of line with the enterprise as a whole – for example it finds it perfectly acceptable for the PE to be profit making even if the enterprise as a whole is loss making.

13.28   The fact that there is more than one authorised approach for calculating the free capital (and indeed funding costs of a PE – see below) clearly risks double taxation as the host tax authority could adopt one authorised approach in its domestic rules and the head office authority another. The OECD acknowledges this risk and has attempted to address it through the new version of Article 7 of the Convention and its Commentary together with the wording of the Report itself. First, the Commentary includes an injunction that where a taxpayer has used an authorised OECD approach consistently when calculating the profits attributable to a PE for the purposes of its tax return in both the head office and PE jurisdiction, tax authorities should not seek to adjust onto another authorised OECD approach[44]. Second, Article 7(3) of the Convention is designed to include a mechanism to ensure that where adjustments have been made by a tax authority a reciprocal adjustment is made by the other tax authority albeit it may be necessary to resort to the mutual agreement procedure in some cases.[45]

---

40   Ibid, para 126.
41   Ibid, para 129.
42   Ibid, para 132.
43   Ibid, para 134.
44   The Commentary in relation to Art 7, para 46.
45   See the Convention, Art 7(3), paras 44–70 of the Commentary and paras 149 and 156 of the Report.

ATTRIBUTION OF FUNDING COSTS TO PES

13.29   As with the attribution of capital, it was not possible to arrive at a single agreed approach to allocating funding costs to a PE. Accordingly, the Report sets out three alternative authorised approaches. These are:

(1)   The treasury dealing approach.

(2)   The tracing approach.

(3)   The fungibility approach.

The Report acknowledges that both the tracing and fungibility approach in their purest form have weaknesses.[46] However, it stresses that the overall goal under any of the approaches is the same: namely to ensure that '... the amount on interest expense claimed by the PE does not exceed an arm's length amount and that any treasury functions are appropriately rewarded'.[47]

As noted above, the Report introduced the concept of a 'treasury dealing' and recognises that in certain circumstances it is appropriate to recognise an internal interest dealing.[48] This is seen as being potentially appropriate where the functional analysis identifies one part of the enterprise 'as undertaking in substance the significant people functions relevant to determining the economic ownership of the cash or financial asset in order to be treated as the "owner" of the cash ... and therefore entitled to an arm's length return from the cash ... under an internal "treasury dealing"'.[49] It should be noted that the concept of an internal interest dealing is a divergence from the approach adopted in earlier versions of the Commentary on Article 7 which specifically prohibited internal interest charges except in the case of financial enterprises such as banks. If internal interest charges are used with respect to internal dealings (hypothetical loans) from one part of the enterprise to another it is possible that a tax authority will not respect this approach when calculating the profits of a PE in its jurisdiction if it does not accept the use of the AOA as the correct approach to attributing profits to PEs.

13.30   Under the tracing approach any internal movements of funds are traced back to the original provision of funds by third parties. The interest expense paid to third parties would be allocated to the PE.[50] The obvious problem with such an approach is the difficulty of accurately tracing such funding through to its original source particularly given that the funding may in practice come from a fungible pool made up from various sources of funding with the funding not necessarily being raised originally to provide funding to the PE.

13.31   The fungibility approach involves allocating a proportion of the enterprise's actual interest expense paid to third parties using a formula or

---

46   The Report, Pt I, para 155.
47   Ibid, para 156.
48   Ibid, para 151.
49   Ibid, para 153.
50   Ibid, para 154.

allocation key. Actual flows of funds within the enterprise are ignored under this approach.[51] The obvious problem with this approach is that there is scope for disagreement between tax authorities as to the appropriate allocation key leading to potential double taxation.

INTERACTION BETWEEN 'FREE CAPITAL' AND INTEREST EXPENSE ALLOCATION

13.32 Finally, the interaction between the allocation of free capital and the allocation of interest expense needs to be considered. This is addressed in paragraphs 162 to 171 of the Report, Part I. In summary, 'where interest bearing debt attributed to the PE ... covers some part of the arm's length amount of "free capital" properly attributable to the PE, any interest on the amount so covered would not be deductible in arriving at the PE's taxable profits'.[52]

POTENTIALLY PROBLEMATIC AREAS ARISING FROM CONFLICTING HISTORIC GUIDANCE AND THE GUIDANCE IN RELATION TO THE AOA

13.33 As noted above, some countries have not accepted that the AOA is fully compatible with the pre 2010 version of the Convention and earlier versions of the Commentary. Where treaties are modelled on pre 2010 versions of the Convention, some countries do not accept that the AOA can be used as an approach to attributing profits to permanent establishments. Other countries accept that the AOA can be used as a helpful guide to the modern approach to attributing profits to PEs but that there are certain situations where it cannot be applied in practice to overrule domestic law where the relevant treaty is based on the historic rather than the current wording of Article 7 of the Convention. There are three circumstances in particular where the application of the AOA is seen as being problematic as follows:

(1) Charging internal royalties in relation to IP regarded as economically owned by one part of the enterprise under the AOA.

(2) Charging internal interest on 'lending' within the enterprise for non-financial concerns.

(3) Applying the AOA to permit charges at other than cost where one part of the enterprise has provided services to another part of the enterprise.

The first two circumstances have been discussed in the relevant paragraphs above dealing with these matters. In relation to the third point, certain countries are of the view that the old wording of the Convention (and thus treaties modelled on it) did not permit anything other than an allocation at cost

---

51 The Report, Pt I, para 154.
52 Ibid, para 164.

of an appropriate share of expenses incurred by another part of the enterprise to the permanent establishment. Of particular concern was the wording of paragraph 7(3) which ran: '... there shall be allowed as deductions expenses which are incurred for the permanent establishment including executive and administrative expenses so incurred ...'.[53]

This is seen as being particular relevant when the services being performed are more of a supportive nature rather than directly linked to the business of the enterprise itself. In these cases, host countries who follow this approach are likely to resist any attempt to claim a deduction in the PE based on the arm's-length price for the provision of such services (often calculated on a cost plus a mark-up basis) and only permit a deduction on a cost basis.

CONCLUSION

13.34 In theory, by establishing a conceptual framework and providing detailed guidance on how that framework should be applied in practice, the Report (and the introduction of the AOA) should have marked a great step forward in providing more clarity in the previously fraught area of attributing profits to permanent establishments. In practice much uncertainty remains. This uncertainty is not primarily driven by problems with the AOA itself but rather by the fact that the adoption of the AOA in countries' domestic laws and in their treaties has been patchy. Whilst this is changing, the pace of change is slow and it is likely to be decades rather than years before all treaties reflect the revised wording of Article 7 on which the Report is based. This means, unfortunately, that the area of PE profit attribution will remain a problem area with a relatively high risk of double taxation for many years to come.

---

53   See the Annex to the Commentary on Art 7 and in particular paras 35–37.

Appendix A
United Kingdom Transfer Pricing Summary

Transfer pricing in the UK remains an issue of political and public importance. This is reflected in the UK government's support for the G20/OECD Base Erosion and Profit Shifting (BEPS) recommendations.

With effect from 1 April 2015, the UK government introduced the new 'diverted profits tax' in advance of some of the BEPS changes. This tax applies to situations in which a UK permanent establishment has been avoided, or to transactions or entities that lack sufficient economic substance.

Advance pricing agreements with the UK now require that consideration be given to whether diverted profits tax applies.

Legislation and regulations were passed to implement the G20/OECD country-by-country reporting requirement for large UK multinationals. The country-by-country requirement takes effect for accounting periods beginning on or after 1 January 2016.

I GENERAL INFORMATION

Tax authority & law

HM Revenue and Customs (HMRC); following the UK's Tax Law Rewrite project, effective from 1 April 2010, for accounting periods ending on or after 1 April 2010, the UK transfer pricing legislation is found in *Part 4* of the *Taxation (International and Other Provisions) Act 2010* (*TIOPA 2010*) (*s 146 et seq*).

The mutual agreement procedure is set out in *Part 2* of *TIOPA 2010* (*ss 124–125*). APAs are in *Part 5* of *TIOPA 2010* (*s 218 et seq*).

Permanent establishment rules are in *CTA 2010* (*ss 1141–1144*). Rules about attribution of profit to permanent establishments are in *CTA 2009* (*Chapter 4, s 20*).

A diverted profits tax of 25 per cent was introduced in *Finance Act 2015*, effective 1 April 2015, and applies to arrangements designed to divert profit from the UK. These include arrangements that avoid the creation of a permanent establishment in the UK and those that involve transactions or entities that lack economic substance.

Regulations, rulings, guidelines

UK legislation on transfer pricing incorporates the OECD Model Treaty, including the arm's length principle as set out in Article 9 of the OECD Model Tax Convention, and the OECD's Transfer Pricing Guidelines for Multinational Enterprises and Tax Administrations. With effect for accounting periods beginning on or after 1 April 2018, this is the 2017 version of the Transfer Pricing Guidelines. The version mainly reflects a consolidation of the changes resulting from the joint OECD/G20 BEPS project.

In addition to the legislation and reliance on the OECD Model Treaty, HMRC publish guidance on their interpretation of transfer pricing legislation, OECD principles, and UK case law. This guidance is currently found in the International Manual at INTM410000 *et seq*, and includes guidance on thin capitalisation.

Guidance on advance rulings is available in Statement of Practice SP2/10, which provides details on advance pricing agreements, and Statement of Practice SP1/12 provides details on advance thin capitalisation agreements. These statements of practice provide details of the processes to enter into such agreements in the UK.

Statement of Practice SP1/11 provides guidance on mutual agreement procedures and arbitration in relation to transfer pricing matters.

Nature/extent of relationship between parties to a transaction required for transfer pricing rules to apply?

Parties are related when one party directly or indirectly participates in the management, control, or capital of the other, or when the same person or persons directly or indirectly participate in the management, control, or capital of both parties. Generally, there is a 51 per cent test of control, but this can be reduced to 40 per cent in joint venture situations. Persons 'acting together' to exert control in relation to financing arrangements are also treated as being related.

Do the local transfer pricing rules or tax authorities allow the use of transfer pricing analyses to calculate profits attributable to a permanent establishment or branch?

UK chargeable profits of a permanent establishment/branch are calculated as though the UK operations were conducted on arm's length terms with any connected parties and the remainder of the entity of which the permanent establishment/branch is part (the 'separate enterprise principle'). The profit attribution approach is consistent with the commentary on Article 7 of the OECD Model Treaty and the OECD's guidelines for attribution of profits to permanent establishments.

Accordingly, the arm's length principle and OECD transfer pricing methods are used for the attribution exercise.

II METHODS AND COMPARABLES

Acceptable methods

The comparable uncontrolled price (CUP) method, the resale price method, the cost plus method, the profit split method (residual analysis, contribution analysis), the transactional net margin method (TNMM), and unspecified methods (provided the derived result satisfies the arm's length principle).

Priority of methods

The 2017 OECD transfer pricing guidelines, which were incorporated into UK law for accounting periods beginning on or after 1 April 2018, do not impose a distinct hierarchy of methods, because the choice of one method over another is based 'on the most appropriate method to the circumstances of the case'. Nevertheless, certain comparisons must be undertaken, in particular with regard to the availability and reliability of the data. Moreover, the OECD transfer pricing guidelines state that taxpayers retain the freedom to apply other unspecified methods, provided the derived result satisfies the arm's length principle.

Availability of benchmarking/comparative data

Detailed financial information on UK registered companies is available.

Are foreign comparables acceptable to local tax authorities?

HMRC's general preference is for UK comparables. However, foreign (in particular European Union) comparables are acceptable in practice if appropriately comparable UK data cannot be identified, or if foreign data sufficiently meet comparability criteria.

III SERVICES ISSUES

Are management fees deductible?

Yes.

Are management fees subject to withholding?

No.

May stock option costs be included in the cost base for intercompany services charges?

Historically, UK transfer pricing legislation did not include specific guidance on the treatment of stock options as part of a cost-plus arrangement. The UK tax authorities have published guidance that indicates they would like to see the cost of stock options added to a company's cost base and recharged with a mark-up. In September 2010, HMRC released updated guidance in their International Manual (currently INTM440210) that confirms HMRC will accept the spread on vesting or spread on exercise as pricing methods for share options at the relevant time. This development provides greater flexibility to multinational enterprises in deriving arm's length share option charges. However, HMRC have explicitly stated the importance of applying the chosen method consistently over the full length of the arrangement, and for all employees to achieve a result that equates to what might be expected in an arm's length situation.

IV   COMMISSIONAIRE ARRANGEMENTS

Are commissionaire arrangements allowed?

Yes, but such arrangements should be expected to be subject to HMRC challenge. In the UK, the equivalent of a 'commissionaire' is an 'undisclosed agent', and the UK's common law status must be taken into account in considering the treatment of a UK commissionaire. It will also be necessary to consider diverted profits tax with reference to the facts.

V   COST SHARING AGREEMENTS

Are cost contribution arrangements or cost sharing agreements accepted?

Yes. The UK follows Chapter VIII of the OECD transfer pricing guidelines, which incorporates the changes resulting from the G20/OECD BEPS reports.

Are cost contribution or cost sharing payments deductible?

Yes, although taxpayers may be required to recognise the underlying character of the costs shared and treat them accordingly.

Are cost contribution or cost sharing payments subject to withholding tax?

No.

What is the payer's tax treatment of payments to a contributor of pre-existing intangibles to a CCA or CSA?

Tax depreciation may be available on a buy-in payment for qualifying intangibles. A buy-in may also take the form of declining royalties. In such a case, the royalties may be deducted.

VI DOCUMENTATION AND TAX RETURN DISCLOSURES

Tax return disclosures

No separate disclosure is required (by signing the tax return, the taxpayer will be implicitly confirming compliance with the arm's length standard).

Country-by-country reporting

The UK government has introduced a new statutory instrument for UK-headed multinational enterprises, or UK subsidiary groups of multinational enterprises, with turnover in excess of EUR 750 million to file an annual country-by-country report to HMRC. Where the MNE Group draws up, or would draw up, its consolidated financial statements in a currency other than Euro, the reference to EUR 750 million has effect as if it referred to the equivalent in that currency at the average exchange rate for the accounting period.

Documentation requirements

Taxpayers should keep records to support details in the tax return. However, note the comments in the 'Deadline to prepare documentation' section below. Records should be retained for the later of (a) six years from the end of the relevant accounting period; (b) the date when the enquiry into the return is completed; or (c) the date on which HMRC are no longer able to open an enquiry (*TIOPA 2010, Part 4*).

UK legislation provides for penalties of up to £3,000 per tax return for failure to compile and retain transfer pricing documentation (*FA 1998, Sch 18, para 23(1)*).

Are the documentation requirements annual requirements? If so, what do they involve each year (for example, a complete report, a memo identifying any changes and the updated transaction values)? Must comparables be refreshed or a new search performed?

There is no obligation for a taxpayer to submit its transfer pricing documentation with its annual tax return. However, the tax authorities can request that evidence of compliance with the arm's length principle be made available as per the record-keeping requirements detailed in INTM483030. HMRC expect the taxpayer to prepare and retain documentation that demonstrates the taxpayer's compliance, in accordance with the UK Corporation Tax Self-Assessment regime. This means that contemporaneous transfer pricing documentation must be prepared in support of every tax return annually. This documentation must be made available at the request of the tax authorities within the time specified.

Deadline to prepare documentation

HMRC has issued guidance on documentation requirements in INTM483030. There is no prescribed mandatory format for such documentation, but the guidance stipulates that the taxpayer must have the following documentation available to HMRC to demonstrate that the results of transactions with related parties are determined for tax purposes according to transfer pricing rules (and, in particular, the application of the arm's length principle):

- Primary accounting records – these are the records of transactions occurring in the course of carrying on a business, and entered into a taxpayer's accounting system. These records are needed to produce a balance sheet and a statement of profit or loss, and must be retained for any audit of the accounts; as described above, there are legal requirements concerning the time for which such records must be retained. The requirements would still be necessary in the absence of any tax rules. These records include the results (in terms of value) of the relevant transactions.

- Tax adjustment records – these are the records that identify adjustments made by a taxpayer on account of tax rules to move from profits in account to taxable profits, including the value of those adjustments, when a tax return is made for the period in question. These adjustments might include the adjustment of actual results to arm's length results on account of transfer pricing rules.

- Records of transactions with associated parties – these are the records in which a taxpayer identifies transactions to which the transfer pricing rules apply.

- Evidence to demonstrate an arm's length result – this is the evidence in which a taxpayer demonstrates that a result is arm's length for purposes of the transfer pricing rules.

Because UK transfer pricing legislation states that the rules related to an arm's length result should be construed in a manner that ensures consistency with the OECD transfer pricing guidelines, documentation to demonstrate an arm's length result should therefore follow the guidance provided in the guidelines.

Records of transactions with associated parties and of any tax adjustments must be prepared by the filing date of the annual tax return. Evidence to demonstrate compliance with the arm's length principle in relation to each tax return may be requested by the tax authorities.

Deadline to submit documentation

Documentation should be contemporaneous (that is, prepared annually consistent with tax return dates), and must be made available upon request by the tax authorities within the time specified in the request. It is generally expected that documentation should be provided within 30 days of the documentation request.

Deadline to file income tax return

The UK imposes no requirement to file transfer pricing documentation with tax returns.

The annual corporation tax return is required to be submitted within 12 months after the end of the period of account (if the period of account is less than 18 months).

Acceptable languages for documentation

Documentation must be in English.

VII   TRANSFER PRICING ADJUSTMENTS

Must the transfer prices reflected on an income tax return be the same as those reflected in financial statements? In other words, are book/tax differences allowed?

UK taxpayers are obligated to self-assess their taxable results, which therefore requires upwards adjustments in the tax return if the results in the financial statements do not reflect an arm's length position, so that UK taxable profits are not understated or losses not overstated.

Self-initiated adjustments

The UK imposes a requirement to adjust to arm's length prices only when this increases UK taxable profit or reduces UK losses; there is no provision for downward profit or upward loss adjustments. There is an exception for intra-UK transactions, when an upward profit adjustment in the return of one party to a transaction can be compensated by a downward adjustment in the other party's tax return in certain situations on the making of a claim.

Statute of limitations on assessment for transfer pricing adjustments

Four years from the accounting period end. The period for HMRC to launch an enquiry into a return is extended to six years only when a company has acted 'carelessly'.

The period may be extended up to 20 years in case of 'deliberate misstatement'.

Taxpayer set-offs for other related-party transactions

The UK follows the OECD transfer pricing guidelines on separate consideration of transactions and when aggregation is permitted.

VIII   INTEREST AND PENALTIES

Additional assessment payment deadline

Generally 30 days from the date of receipt of the assessment notice. An extension may be requested.

Penalty on transfer pricing assessment

For returns due after 1 April 2009, penalties are linked to the behaviour that gives rise to the error: if reasonable care was taken – no penalty; careless behaviour – minimum 0 per cent and maximum 30 per cent; deliberate careless behaviour – minimum 20 per cent and maximum 70 per cent; and deliberate and concealed error – minimum 30 per cent and maximum 100 per cent. If there is no additional tax liability due to losses or availability of UK group relief, a penalty charged at a discounted rate of the gross adjustment may still apply.

Is interest charged on penalties?

No.

Reduction in transfer pricing penalties

HMRC will not charge a penalty if the taxpayer took 'reasonable care' but still made an error. Penalties may be avoided by: taking reasonable care to provide correct returns and documents; keeping adequate records to enable the taxpayer to provide complete and accurate returns and documents (that is, effectively reasonably supporting documentation/economic analysis); requesting a tax advisor's advice; and disclosure on submission of the return or document.

Is interest payable when a refund is due to the taxpayer?

Yes. Interest is paid by HMRC on both early payments and overpayments at a commercial rate. Credit interest runs from the date on which the overpayment arose to the earlier of the date when the overpayment is repaid and the date on which tax was originally due (*FA 2009, Sch 54*).

IX   ADVANCE PRICING AGREEMENTS

Are APAs available?

Yes, as per *TIOPA 2010, Part 5*.

HMRC has published a Statement of Practice, SP 2/10, that sets out best practices on APAs.

APA filing fee

No fee.

APA term of agreement

Generally three to five years forward; either the taxpayer or HMRC may seek rollback. APAs now include a clause giving HMRC the right to terminate the agreement in the event of changes to UK legislation or the OECD transfer pricing guidelines arising from the BEPS actions.

X   COMPETENT AUTHORITY

When may taxpayer submit tax adjustment to competent authority (CA)?

When an action giving rise to, or likely to give rise to, double taxation not in accordance with an income tax treaty has occurred, or when equivalent provisions in the European Union Arbitration Convention are satisfied.

May CA develop new settlement positions?

Yes.

May taxpayer go to CA before paying tax?

The taxpayer must agree that the amount is due and payable, but may be able to stand over actual payment pending the outcome of the mutual agreement procedure.

XI OECD BEPS RECOMMENDATIONS

Is the UK committed to following the recommendations of the OECD's October 2015 final report on Actions 8–10 of the BEPS Action Plan? If so, are there any material differences between the final report and your country's measures? What is the effective date of those measures?

Yes, the UK is committed to following the G20/OECD work on Actions 8–10. For accounting periods beginning after 1 April 2018, the 2017 version of the OECD Guidelines is now explicitly referred to in UK law. The UK law therefore already applies the principles in ongoing transfer pricing inquiries.

Has the UK enacted legislation implementing the country-by-country reporting requirement, or is it considering enacting such legislation? If so, does the legislation adopt the master file/local file requirement? Are there any material differences between the final report and your country's measures? What is the effective date of those measures?

The UK government has introduced a new statutory instrument for UK-headed multinational enterprises, or UK subsidiary groups of multinational enterprises, with turnover in excess of EUR 750 million to file an annual country-by-country report to HMRC. Where the MNE Group draws up, or would draw up, its consolidated financial statements in a currency other than Euro, the reference to EUR 750 million has effect as if it referred to the equivalent in that currency at the average exchange rate for the accounting period.

Has the UK signed-up to participate in the multilateral instrument developed under Action 15 of the BEPS Action Plan?

Yes.

Index